THE LANGUAGE OF
AMERICAN
POPULAR ENTERTAINMENT

THE LANGUAGE OF AMERICAN POPULAR ENTERTAINMENT

A Glossary of Argot, Slang, and Terminology

DON B. WILMETH

Greenwood Press
WESTPORT, CONNECTICUT ● LONDON, ENGLAND

Library of Congress Cataloging in Publication Data

Wilmeth, Don B
    The language of American popular entertainment.

    Bibliography: p.
    1. Performing arts—United States—Dictionaries.
2. United States—Popular culture—Dictionaries.
3. English language—Slang—Dictionaries. I. Title.
PN1579.W5   790.2′03   80-14795
ISBN 0-313-22497-8 (lib. bdg.)

Library of Congress Catalog Card Number: 80-14795
ISBN: 0-313-22497-8

First published in 1981

Greenwood Press
A division of Congressional Information Service, Inc.
88 Post Road West, Westport, Connecticut 06881

Printed in the United States of America

10 9 8 7 6 5 4 3 2 1

Contents

Preface

This preface was written the day after my first visit to the Circus Hall of Fame and the Ringling Museum of the Circus in Sarasota, Florida. Although I can trace my fascination with the circus to the 1940s and a visit to "The Greatest Show on Earth" under canvas, with Gargantua still in the menagerie, featuring in the big top such attractions as Damoo Dhotre's "Black and Spotted Leopards, Pumas, and Black Jaguars," Natal ("Man or Monkey?"), the Italian Zavattas ("First Time in America"), and Lou Jacobs in "His Midget Auto," this recent tour through the circus's past made its lure and fascination even more apparent to me. The most casual fan of the circus leaves these living museums with a vivid sense of the very special world of this institution, which, despite its European forebears, has become as American as apple pie. Other American popular entertainment forms have proven less durable than the circus and have either disappeared altogether or have been transformed into other forms. Still, each had its day. Minstrelsy, vaudeville, burlesque, the tent show, stage magic, and other forms reflected by the entries in this glossary were, at one time or another, the most popular entertainment forms in America.

With the growing interest in popular culture and the legitimization of popular entertainment as an acceptable area of scholarly inquiry—one well worth the time and effort—it is extremely satisfying to note that a previously limited and somewhat stodgy view of theatrical history has been altered to include popular forms alongside the more legitimate forms of theatre. Now, vaudeville, fairs, carnivals, and other popular amusements are being recognized as forces that have permeated and profoundly affected our society throughout history. As Ray B. Browne, a pioneer in the study of American popular culture, recently has noted, "Nearly all Americans have been active participants or 'closet' appreciators of popular entertainment." Since it no longer seems necessary to remain in the closet, one anticipates more meaningful contributions in this significant and enjoyable area of inquiry. The recording of the special language of American popular entertainment found in this glossary is intended as one small step in that direction.

Much of the work involved in compiling this glossary was accomplished for me by numerous authorities and fans who have dealt with forms of popular entertainment in a variety of ways—historical surveys, fictional accounts, dictionaries, biographies and autobiographies, and so forth. My indebtedness to these individuals is immense and has been specifically indicated in the select bibilography at the conclusion of the glossary. I have found the work of the following especially valuable: Bill Ballantine, Walter Bowman and Robert Ball, Bert Chipman, Larry Clark, Gladys Cook, William Gresham, Henry Hay, Marvin Kaye, Rhina Kirk, Maurice Kusell and M. S. Merritt, Edo McCullough, Brooks McNamara, David Maurer, H. L. Mencken, Jere Mickel, Ruth Mulvey, Esse O'Brien, Brett Page, Sherman Sergel, John Towsen, Marcello Truzzi, Harold Wentworth and Stuart Flexner, and especially Joe McKennon.

Despite the great contributions the above-mentioned individuals and others have made in recording the language of popular entertainment, no one source has adequately compiled the argot and terminology of all major American popular entertainment forms in one volume. This has been my prime objective. To accomplish this end in as exhaustive a fashion as I had initially desired proved impossible. Each day another possible entry seems to pop into view, and even after a stopping point was decided upon and that time had arrived, another batch of words and phrases were discovered and inserted in their proper places. Consequently, I can only claim that this glossary represents a reasonable cross section of the slang, argot, and terminology of major American popular entertainment forms. I am eager to learn of any notable exclusions and welcome such information from users of the glossary.

The arduous task of assembling this glossary has been made far more pleasant by the encouragement of my wife, Judy, and my son, Michael. Indeed, Mike's curiosity about words is without limit, and thus it is a special joy to dedicate this effort to him. I should be remiss if I did not give special thanks to Elizabeth Coogan of Brown University's interlibrary loan department. I gratefully acknowledge the resources of the Circus World Museum Library in Baraboo, Wisconsin, the marvelous collection of magic books in the private library of H. Adrian Smith, and the contributions of my students in my popular entertainment courses at Brown University. Although their contributions cannot be explained here, I wish to mention my dear friend Stephen

Archer, my former roommate Robert Palmer, the great stage magician Harry Blackstone, the very special people at Coney Island's dime museum in 1951, and a mélange of preeminent performing perfectionists from the present and past. Without the encouragement of Marilyn Brownstein of Greenwood Press and her faith in this project when it was no more than the kernel of an idea, this glossary would have been impossible. Patricia S. Carda, my production editor, was extremely helpful in making sense out of an often-confusing jumble. Finally, a special word of appreciation to Pamela Enos for her careful typing of a very difficult manuscript.

Introduction

Purpose

The serious study of American popular entertainment forms has begun to take its place alongside other so-called legitimate inquiries into theatrical history. This glossary attempts to collect in one source the special language of the principal forms of American popular entertainment: circus, carnival, vaudeville, burlesque, tent shows, popular theatre, magic shows, medicine shows, early optical entertainments, and fairs. Some attempt has been made to include general entries of less prominent forms, such as puppetry, pantomime, and the musical revue. In collecting entries for this glossary, my effort has been of the historian attempting to record words and phrases that have been (and in some cases still are) part of a special vocabulary of a substrata of American popular culture, that of the popular entertainer or showman. As such, the focus is on those forms produced by professional showmen for profit and aimed at relatively broad-based, unsophisticated audiences. The emphasis, therefore, is on forms that, with few exceptions, have passed into oblivion. This is not a dictionary; few words listed here offer pronunciation problems. Nor is my approach that of the etymologist, grammarian, lexicographer, or philologist.

The major forms[1]

Strolling, itinerant showmen were part of the American scene before the American Revolution. They brought to the colonists crude, disorganized entertainments of all sorts. By the beginning of the nineteenth century, organization of exhibits into "museums" or "cabinets of curiosities" replaced this early chaos. By mid-century the dime museum became a major center of entertainment, exploited to its fullest by America's first great Showman, Phineas T. Barnum, entrepreneur of the American Museum in New York, beginning in 1841. Barnum, and his successors and imitators, established a format and approach that spread to the majority of the forms of popular entertainment: cheap and comprehensible entertainment, acceptable on moral and religious grounds, and appealing to unsophisticated Americans and the growing number of immigrants.

Another branch of the roving performer moved into the realm of the quack doctor, selling tonics and elixirs combined with entertainment. With the phenomenal growth of the American patent medicine industry in the nineteenth century, the medicine show became a major business and entertainment form, moving throughout the country, often on established circuits, and employing the showman's and pitchman's tricks equally.

Competition from legitimate museums and theatres ultimately eliminated the dime museum, although vestiges can still be found. Legislation and the growing sophistication of the audience made the medicine showman little more than a crook, although his practices were still common in the 1950s (the selling of "hadacol," a late spectacular medicine show remedy developed by a Louisiana state senator named Dudley J. LeBlanca, is a prime example).

The American minstrel show was the first uniquely American form of entertainment, beginning in the 1840s, peaking in 1870, and dying out almost completely by the turn of the century. During its heyday, black-faced minstrelsy literally swept the nation, committing itself to the new, commonman audience. Whatever negative connotations the minstrel show might have today, its impact and entertainment value are unassailable. Its use of music and comedy, especially, was carried into subsequent forms—vaudeville, burlesque and even radio, motion pictures, and television.

The so-called golden age of the American circus began in 1871 when W. C. Coup persuaded P. T. Barnum to become a partner in a circus enterprise, and ended about 1917 with the rise of the Ringling brothers and the merger of several large circuses to become "Ringling Brothers and Barnum & Bailey Combined Shows." As the circus became big business, competitors were helpless in their attempt to challenge the supremacy of this conglomerate. Between 1910 and 1918, circuses had decreased in number and in extravagance—the parade became obsolete, the menagerie virtually vanished, and the canvas tent would, in time, practically disappear. Mechanization and the lack of individual incentive and initiative were the final blows for the majority of circus operations.

With the demise of the overland circus, the big top, the circus parade, and the many extra attractions offered by the bigger and better

American circuses, much of the circus's appeal had vanished, despite the fact that circus today is still a big entertainment business in this country. The hawker of souvenirs, the seller of chameleons (the bug-man), the menagerie, the sideshow, the smell of sawdust, elephant dung, and old canvas, and all the many components of the circus during its golden age have been replaced in major circuses by a care-fully rehearsed production equipped to play any local exhibition hall, civic center, or coliseum in the major cities of this country. There are less than a dozen circuses in the United States playing under canvas, and most are small operations, mud shows for the most part, with little of the appeal "The Greatest Show on Earth" once possessed.

The Wild West show, a form of outdoor amusement that initially attempted to present an exhibition illustrating scenes and events char-acteristic of the American Far West, began when William "Buffalo Bill" Cody consolidated and popularized this form of show business in the 1880s. During its heyday, there were over a hundred Wild West shows. By 1918, however, there were no major Wild West shows left. Its contemporary interest began to fade after the turn of the century; its focus moved from the reality to a romanticized, legendary version of its original inspiration and created its own illusion; and, ultimately, the increasing popularity of the motion picture, far more capable of presenting realistic portrayals of the cowboy, eclipsed its uniqueness.

The outdoor amusement industry, including the amusement park and the carnival, inspired by European traditions, as was the Ameri-can circus, began its phenomenal growth at the end of the nineteenth century as a result of improved transportation and technology. With the stimulus of the 1893 World's Columbian Exposition in Chicago, American showmen sensed the lucrative potential of outdoor amuse-ments. The great period of the traditional amusement park began with Coney Island's spectacular growth at the turn of the century and lasted until about World War II, although its decline, like that of all outdoor entertainment, began around World War I.

Though several large operations still thrive, the traditional amuse-ment park, with its showmanship, gaming operations, pitchmen, and somewhat seedy and worn attractions, has been replaced by the slick, homogenized, and almost hygienic "theme park," such as Disney World, Circus World, Busch Gardens, or Six Flags Over Texas. Since pitchmen are rarely found in these parks (replaced by very young personnel who work for minimal pay and have no commitment to the "business") or on carnival lots or in the circus, one of the more fasci-nating aspects of the entertainment is virtually lost forever.

The traveling carnival and its unique attractions, although closer to the original than the amusement park's transformation into the theme park, has undergone similar changes. Although there are approximately 580 carnivals on the road today and at least 75 traditional amusement parks, most are shabby suggestions of what the great shows once were. The sideshow, once a major attraction of the carnival, can no longer be populated with attractions and is virtually a phenomenon of the past. In the 1930s and 1940s there were several hundred such shows traveling with carnivals; today that number has shrunk to about nine.

The contemporary version of the amusement park in the form of the theme park is certainly a vivid example of Madison Avenue advertising packaging at its most persuasive best and an amazing example of organization know-how (especially the Disney operations). Yet, such concerns are no longer the products of professional showmen but the brainstorms of large corporations and businessmen. The entertainment values of these new amusement centers are not to be denied, and for a generation who never experienced the traditional amusement park, they are wonders to behold. Still, the old operations had a show appeal not to be found in today's harmless equivalents. Despite the illegality that permeated many old-time carnivals and amusement parks, their attraction was as much the knowledge of being taken, of seeing the bizarre and deformed in the sideshow or special shows under canvas, as it was the thrill of riding dangerous rides or seeing exhibitions billed as scientific or technological.

Like the minstrel show, American vaudeville was largely indigenous, growing out of early, more risqué variety, and becoming a symbol of Americanism. Its heyday lasted a scant fifty years or so, from the 1880s to the early 1930s, but during its time Americans of all classes were amused and found relief from the relatively new industrial complex through vaudeville's collection of "turns," which helped to dictate morals and attitudes.

Burlesque, rooted in native sources and complex in its origin, experienced its golden age from 1905 with the organization of the Columbia circuit or wheel, and began to change in the 1920s when greater permissiveness was added and the comic soul of burlesque was tainted by greater stress on erotic stimulation. The rise of the stripper and the striptease in the 1930s changed the structure and uniqueness of American burlesque completely. Although burlesque is clearly dead, the recreated burlesque show, *Sugar Babies*, running successfully on Broadway in 1979-80, sans strippers, suggests what the form once was and why its appeal was broad and its impact relatively harmless to one's moral fiber.

Popular native theatre fare has endured on the American scene since the creation of the stage Yankee, Jonathan, in Royall Tyler's *The Con-*

trast (1787). As more common people found their way into theatres, the popularization of drama became a necessity, providing audiences momentary escapes into a world of fantasy and freedom. After the Civil War, previously inaccessible towns became important and profitable stops for touring companies. In time, small towns on the road were invaded by too many of these touring companies, each doing the same or similar fare. During 1900, 340 theatrical companies were touring; by 1920 the number had decreased to less than 50. Much of this peak period is marked by the addition of tent-show repertoire, part of the trend of the time toward outdoor entertainment. Remote areas were able to support one-night-stand companies that could not subsist in larger towns. Relative obscurity also eliminated the possibility of comparison with stronger companies and served as protection against tightened copyright enforcement. This movement was encouraged, ironically, by cultural and religious organizations, the most popular of which was the chautauqua. Between 1900 and 1910 there were well over a hundred repertoire companies under canvas. Emerging from this tradition was one of the last native stock characters, Toby, a rustic country boy who became a fixture of many tent-repertoire companies. By the summer of 1921, faced with a recession, the golden years of tent repertoire ended. Popular theatre in general, although forms such as melodrama and farce continue to dominate the popular market, was generally taken over by films, which could be brought into America's heartland inexpensively and with little effort.

It is clear from these brief summaries that all the major forms of American entertainment were eclipsed by the times and changes in communications media by the end of the first quarter of this century. With their passing (or, in the case of the circus, carnival, and amusement park, their evolutions brought about by shifting tastes, sophistication, and loss of a large mass audience), their special milieu and large cultural substrata of American culture passed with them, including their own special language.

The Special Language

There is no language like show language, to paraphrase the well-known anthem of American show business. Like all contained and identifiable social groups or specialized occupations, and perhaps moreso than most, show people over the years have developed their own unique slang and argot, a vocabulary devised for both private communication and special transference of information, frequently designed as a secondary function to confuse and block out outsiders. Although in the strictest sense of the word, few examples of true cant belong in this vocabulary, the words and phrases do produce an individualized language or jargon when combined with one another. This is especially true of the examples from the carnival and the circus. The traveling tent circus was, in reality, a moving city with all the necessities of life within its boundaries and populated by people with similar backgrounds and interests, although there were clear-cut social structures within the circus world, each developing its own vocabulary. Carnival people's special language, as Jack Dadswell explains, seems to have no counterpart anywhere. Furthermore, according to Dadswell, carnival talk cannot be confused "with any other brogue, dialect, or jargon on this earth; nor do I believe it can be traced to an ancient foundation as some lexicographers have tried to do. It is purely and simply a 'convenience language' and its sole purpose is for communication within the clan."[2] A similar situation seems to prevail in each definable form of American entertainment, although the carnival remains the prime example.

It is not surprising, therefore, that the words and phrases in this glossary are dominated by examples from the circus and the carnival. Although vaudeville and burlesque, in particular, were fairly closed communities of entertainers, it was far more common for artists to pass from one entertainment form to another, very much as today's actors might perform in film, television, and on the stage. Likewise, however, circus people and carnies sometimes did move into other forms, carrying some of their specialized terminology or jargon with them. Harry Houdini, for example, made the transition from the dime museum to the circus and ultimately to variety and vaudeville. Although certain words clearly belong to one particular form, the hodgepodge of transference and subsequent subtle changes complicate any attempt to pinpoint origin. Mixed in with carnival jargon, for example, are slang words from the world of the pitchman, gangland underworld, Gypsy cant, English slang, and so forth. The same is true of circus language and, to a lesser extent, the other forms represented in this compilation. The important point is that the words found in this glossary were for the most part coined for use in private communication. In truth, many of the words identified by some scholars as having been transferred from the world of the gangster or the pitchman to the carnival, for example, might have just as well passed from the carnie to other subcultures instead. Many of the entries, in fact, are now found in general usage. I make no apologies for words or phrases that have crept into this glossary that the purist would otherwise identify or whose meaning is not as precise as one might wish. Exact explanations are frequently impossible. And, as H. L. Mencken wrote over thirty

years ago, "Running back the history of such words is a harsh enterprise, and usually unrewarding."[3]

Unlike the language of the circus, popular theatre, vaudeville, or
burlesque, the language of the carnival is made more complex by what
is called by Dadswell *Z-Latin* or as *Carnie* (see entries). The addition of
Z-Latin to carnival slang further obscures the comprehension of carnival language. As Dadswell explains it: "It is quite an easy matter . . . for
'carnies' to carry on a conversation in the thick of a crowd without
dropping the slightest hint as to what is said."[4]

Marcello Truzzi and Patrick Easto have divided carnival argot into
two major categories, which, in many respects, can be applied to all
forms included in this glossary: 1) "words designating unique carnival
features for which no simple other words exist," and 2) "words used in
the carnival which have roughly equivalent terms in everyday language."[5] Such a division clearly is applicable to the language of the
circus, vaudeville, minstrelsy, and burlesque as well. To a lesser extent, it can be applied to tent theatre and the vocabulary of the magician or puppeteer.

Much of this glossary is dominated by pitchmen's slang, a special
group that was once clearly on the fringes of society and heavily
involved with various entertainment forms, in particular the circus,
carnival, medicine show, and amusement park. Their language was
easily and naturally adopted by many showmen, especially those who
depended on the pitch for the attraction of an audience or for the
selling of wares. Of all the slang words and expressions in this glossary, theirs are undoubtedly the most picturesque and fascinating.

Popular theatre forms have experienced the greatest changes over
the years and, unlike the majority of forms represented in this glossary, have been the least static. As theatre technology, stage practices,
and approaches to production change, so does the vocabulary used by
theatre practitioners. Of all the eras of American theatre, however,
none produced as special and colorful a language as did the period
covered by this glossary, especially the dramatic tent tradition. Troupers of seventy-five to a hundred years ago were far more insulated
from the outside world as a result of their profession than the theatre
artist of today. As a consequence, their special jargon remained more
obscure to the outsider than today's theatre language.

One major conclusion emerges from my study and the subsequent
compilation of words and phrases. Whatever the form or the special
context and circumstances of the form, each group included in this
glossary evolved an argot of its own which is both picturesque and
largely unintelligible to anyone not a member of that profession. The

words and phrases included here are marvelous reflectors of the vigor and vitality of American entertainment. As Bill Ballantine explains about circus talk: "Though circus jargon is ancient, it stays a lively, roaring language because it means every word it says. Every syllable has been rained on, and splattered, baked by summer suns, smoked over kerosene torches, coated with dust kicked up by long-gone elephants."[6] Like all language, however, the words and their meanings retain their fascination, even though they pass out of usage.

This glossary makes no attempt to answer all the many questions involved in word study, although such explorations would be welcomed. Little to date has been accomplished in this regard, and, as Truzzi and Easto have suggested, studies of variations in carnival language (and, by extension, other specialized languages of show-business forms), would be most rewarding. Likewise, studies of etymology and history of the various languages would be most useful in understanding more completely America's special contributions in popular entertainment as unique segments of American popular culture.

Finally, a comment included in David W. Maurer's listing of carnival terms (1931) provides perspective for the rationale behind this glossary:

As might be expected, the high birth-rate in show-lingo is equalled by a death-rate sufficient to insure the survival of none but the fittest. Words appear today and sink into oblivion tomorrow. When a word is singularly apt, it may stick for a year or five years or twenty years, accordingly as it fulfills the demands of varying conditions and circumstances.[7]

The very special language recorded in this glossary should not be allowed to sink into total oblivion. Although far from the definitive collection, this colorful and expressive listing aims to lessen this possibility.

Design and Strategies

The organizational scheme used in this glossary is straightforward and designed to be accessible to the general user as well as the specialist. Most of the strategies are self-explanatory. In general, the arrangement follows Eric Partridge's suggestion of a "something before nothing" scheme rather than a strictly alphabetical listing. As Partridge indicates in his *Dictionary of Slang and Unconventional English*, "No arrangement is, for no arrangement can be perfect."[8] This is especially true because of the inclusion of phrases in addition to single words. Since the length of the glossary, numbering approximately 3,200 entries, is not so great as to be unwieldy, some reasonable exploration will be enough to locate most entries. The following points should be noted:

1. Within the definitions, the major form or forms that utilize the words or phrases are included. Frequently, the same word is used in various forms or in a general category of forms, such as outdoor amusements. Instead of being rigid in classifying words, it seemed preferable to remain flexible in assigning forms to words. When several definitions of the same word or phrase are included, each definition indicates the context in which that meaning occurs.

2. Variant definitions are included when available, not only completely different meanings of the same word or phrase (as explained above). In compiling this list, corroborative sources have been consulted as often as possible. This has meant either the inclusion of as many shades of meaning as available or the construction of as definitive an explanation as could be accomplished from the assimilation of many sources.

3. Some cross-listing of words is included, especially if words or phrases have virtually identical or similar meanings, or if other entries within the glossary are useful in understanding any one specific entry. Some non-American terms are included, in particular those common in England, if American equivalents are provided in the glossary or if it seemed useful. Such entries have been highly selective and kept to a minimum. Some words of foreign origin have assimilated into American slang and argot and thus are rightfully included in the glossary as major entries.

4. Since the etymology of entries has not been my principal purpose in compiling this list, only selective entries attempt to provide origins and then only if such origins help to illuminate meanings. The origin of a large number of entries can be found in the illustrative or descriptive nature of the word or phrase itself, once the definition is known. Many of the entries are clouded in obscurity and thus, rather than postpone the completion of the glossary almost indefinitely, the decision was made to proceed as outlined above. Historians have had similar problems in dating the majority of these entries; dates of usage, therefore, are indicated only rarely and then only if made with some assurance of accuracy. Generally speaking, it can be assumed that the majority of the terms and phrases passed into obsolescence with the demise of the form or forms with which they were associated. A few have been assimilated into general usage. Terms and slang related to extant forms, such as the circus and the carnival, are exceptionally resilient and long-lasting. Therefore, obsolescence has not been indicated in every case, even though a word or phrase may no longer be in universal use. Some words, such as those associated with the smaller traveling circuses, are quickly passing out of usage as transportation methods and circus operations change. It should be noted that speculative origins of some of the more intriguing terms, such as *doniker* or *nut*, are included, as are those terms based on proper names, such as *Brodie* or *Joe Miller*.

5. Terms used in definitions found elsewhere in the glossary are marked with an asterisk if of some relevancy in the explanation of the major entry. These and major similar terms are listed at the end of the definition. Not all

related terms are cross-listed or indicated for each term, although there has been a careful effort to supply as many cross-listings as seemed most useful.

6. My aim throughout has been to collect only popular entertainment usages, although it is important to note than many of the slang words included belong to other argots in addition to those indicated in the definition. More general dictionaries of slang should be consulted for their meanings and identifications. Of particular value in this regard are Eric Partridge and Flexner and Wentworth (see bibliography).

Scope and Exclusions

Most legitimate theatre terms have been omitted unless they are associated inseparably with popular forms such as vaudeville or burlesque. Sources for more general theatrical terminology can be found in the select bibliography. A definitive dictionary of theatre terminology is currently in preparation under the general editorship of Joel Trapido, Professor Emeritus, University of Hawaii. Major technical terms for most of the popular forms are included, especially those associated with tent shows, circuses, and the carnival. Principal stage terms closely related to vaudeville and burlesque have been included as well. Because of the close relationship between the English and American circuses, some terms of common usage have been included. Exclusively English forms, such as the music hall and British pantomime or panto, are excluded, except as general entries. Terms associated with forms since the advent of mass media and the film, other than those with continuous histories such as the circus and carnival, or those contemporaneous with the rise of the movies, such as vaudeville, burlesque, and the traveling tent show, have been omitted. Some entries, however, cover early optical forms such as panoramas, dioramas, peep shows, and the like. In all cases, the forms included fit the definition of live performance and shows, or exhibitions and amusements, performed or supervised by professional showmen for profit and aimed at relatively unsophisticated patrons or participants. Although the striptease altered the audience of burlesque to a predominantly male audience, it is included because of its close association with earlier burlesque. A number of entries now would be totally unacceptable because of their racially derogatory connotations. Because of their once-common usage, however, these must be included in a historically accurate compilation.

Further Study

The select bibliography at the conclusion of the glossary lists major sources consulted in the compilation of the words and phrases found in this collection. A more detailed listing of sources on the major forms of American popular entertainment can be found in my *American and English Popular Entertainment* and in my forthcoming volume, tentatively titled "Stage and Outdoor Entertainment: A Reference Guide," part of the Greenwood "American Popular Culture" reference series. My essay, "American Popular Entertainment: A Historical Perspective Bibliography," included in *American Popular Entertainment*, edited by Myron Matlaw, provides a brief listing of sources with some evaluative commentary. For succinct historical surveys of the major American forms, along with a checklist of sources and evaluation of the literature, the reader can turn to my two essays in volumes 1 and 2 of *Handbook of American Popular Culture*, edited by M. Thomas Inge. Volume 1 contains "Stage Entertainment" and volume 2 covers "The Circus and Outdoor Entertainment." For more detailed studies of various forms the bibliography in this volume can serve as a starting point. Specific entries in this glossary provide some historical data for such forms as circus, minstrelsy, burlesque, the revue, and so forth, but such explanations are not meant to be exhaustive.

Notes

1. Portions of this section appeared originally as "Stage Entertainment," in *Handbook of American Popular Culture*, ed., M. Thomas Inge, 2 vols. (Westport, Conn.: Greenwood Press, 1978), 1: 294-322, and as "Circus and Outdoor Entertainment," in *Handbook of American Popuar Culture*, ed., M. Thomas Inge (Westport, Conn.: Greenwood Press, 1980), 2: 51-77.

2. Jack Dadswell, *Hey There Sucker* (Boston: Bruce Humphries, 1946), p. 84.

3. H. L. Mencken, "Mencken on the Idiom of the Ham," *Theatre Arts* 32 (Summer 1948):20.

4. Dadswell, *Hey There Sucker*, p. 85.

5. Marcello Truzzi and Patrick Easto, "Carnivals, Road Shows and Freaks," *Society* 9 (March 1972):33.

6. Bill Ballantine, "Circus Talk," *American Mercury* 76 (June 1953):21.

7. David W. Maurer, "Carnival Cant: Glossary of Circus and Carnival Slang," *American Speech* 6 (June 1931):327.

GLOSSARY

A

Aba-daba: In the circus and some traveling carnivals, any dessert served in the cookhouse.* *see also* COOKHOUSE.

Ace: 1. In theatrical jargon, a one-night stand* or, sometimes, a split week.* 2. A well-liked member of a theatrical company; now in general usage. 3. In the circus, anyone who performs any particular act* exceptionally well. 4. The outdoor amusement business, especially carnivals and circuses, adopted the underworld meaning of *ace*, that is, a dollar, either paper or silver. *see also* ACT, ONE-NIGHT STAND, and SPLIT WEEK.

Ace in the hole: A person hired by the circus owner or manager as a standby or replacement for one of the bosses or heads of a department in danger of dismissal. If the person to be replaced found out about this possibility, he usually left the show before he was dismissed. *see* BOSS BUTCHER, BOSS CANVAS MAN, BOSS ELEPHANT MAN, BOSS HOSTLER, BOSS OF PROPS, and BOSS OF RING STOCK.

Ace Svengali deck purveyor: Pitchmen's term for a card manipulator. The notion is that the manipulator (the Svengali) keeps his opponent so "hypnotized" that he will not be aware of the manipulator's trickery.

Acquitment: In magic, a series of manipulations involved in a sleight or sleight-of-hand* to make an object, such as a ball, coin, or thimble vanish or be concealed. Generally, the magician, in executing an acquitment, is able to show both hands empty while something is actually being concealed. Of the various acquitments, the changeover palm* is the most useful. *see also* SLEIGHT OR SLEIGHT-OF-HAND and CHANGEOVER PALM.

Acrobatic-equestrian clown: Originally, a branch of British circus clowns involving stunts on horseback borrowed by the American circus. This type of clown performs stunts demanding great skill and eliciting laughter from the audience. An infrequent specialist in the contemporary American circus. *see* CASCADEUR.

Act: 1. In vaudeville, one segment of a performance or a bill.* On occasion, a skit was called an act. The British call an act a turn,* a term which was sometimes used in the United States. *see also* BILL, SKIT, and TURN. 2. In magic, the complete rehearsed program* as presented. *see also* PROGRAM. 3. *see* ACT-TUNE.

Act-beautiful: *see* PICTURE ACT.

Act in one: An act* in vaudeville playing in one.* *see also* ACT and IN ONE.

Act-tune: Music played between the acts of a theatrical performance. The shortened form of this term was the "act."

Actor's Bible: Originally, this was the New York *Clipper* but in 1905 was replaced by *Variety*.

Ad curtain: A front curtain immediately behind the stage opening, once common in most theatres, especially small-town opera houses and playhouses, which was raised just before the performance and bore advertisements, usually of local concerns.

Ad lib: Abbreviation for ad libitum. In vaudeville, ad lib had the meaning of talking extemporaneously so as to pad or lengthen a scene or act* or to heighten laughter. *see also* ACT.

Adagio: A musical and ballet term that has been borrowed by the circus and alludes to a two-person acrobatic (dance) act with deliberate balletic movement, lifts, and carrying.

Add-A-No: In magician's parlance, an important piece of equipment used in a mentalist's act: a common writing pad with an attached pencil, constructed so that it switches information written by spectators for that written by the magician.

Add-up-joint: *see* COUNT STORE.

Adjuster: Circus term for one who adjusts claims or liabilities. *see* BAG MAN, ICEMAN, MENDER, PATCH, and VULCANIZER.

Admish: Slang coined by *Variety* for admission price.

Advance: 1. In carnival terms, everything pertaining to the carnival show on its route* before it arrives in a town or at a new location. *see also* ROUTE. 2. In the circus, advance applies to contracting and billing agents who go ahead, some weeks in advance of the circus, to handle contracts and advertising. *see* ADVANCE AGENT OR ADVANCE MAN and ADVERTISING CARS.

Advance agent or advance man: Frequently referred to as simply the "agent." The man who travels ahead of a show for the purpose of locating lots, procuring licenses, and putting up heralds and posters publicizing the arrival of the circus or carnival. The job frequently involved the "fixing" of local officials (this once was especially true of carnival agents). The job, similar to that of a theatrical press agent, is principally concerned with stirring up interest in the show. According to McKennon, there are three distinctive kinds of agents used by circuses and carnivals: 1) the contracting agent* who takes care of all necessary contracts for a show's exhibition date; 2) the general agent* who lays out the route of a show and negotiates for the exhibit date; and 3) the special agent* who precedes the attraction in order to make final arrangements. In carnivals, this agent usually sold advertising banners* to local merchants; in circuses, one person sold the banners and a twenty-four-hour man handled the preexhibition details. Carnivals usually combined the functions of the contracting and general agents into one job. Also called a biller. *see also* ADVERTISING CARS, BANNER, CONTRACTING AGENT, GENERAL AGENT, SPECIAL AGENT, and TWENTY-FOUR-HOUR MAN.

Advanced or refined vaudeville: A type of vaudeville that featured major stars, either created in vaudeville or brought in from legitimate theatre. Sarah Bernhardt, who appeared at the Palace in 1913, is a prime example. Her appearance to open the Palace helped establish this trend. *see* TOP-LINE VAUDEVILLE.

Advertise: Carnival slang for attracting undesirable attention by causing a scene in a public place.

Advertising cars: Special train cars used by the circus in advance work for a circus's appearance. There were four principal cars, each with special functions. Car No. 2 traveled the route* thirty days ahead of the circus in order to place posters at prearranged locations. Car No. 3 arrived fourteen days ahead of the circus with lithographs* to be placed in storekeeper windows and over or next to the posters previously posted by Car No. 2. Car No. 4 arrived a week in advance and covered the same locations again. Car No. 1, the skirmishing car, had no regular route but carried troubleshooters who handled last-minute problems and possible rerouting. *see* ADVANCE AGENT, LAYERS OUT, LITHOGRAPH, OUTRIDERS, and RAILWAY CONTRACTOR.

Aerial ballet: A circus performance of rhythmic gymnastics performed by circus chorus girls usually on webs* and frequently including iron-jaws,* trapeze,* or other similar performers, as well as a center-ring star. *see also* BALLET BROADS, IRON-JAWS, and TRAPEZE.

Aerial perch: A vertical circus apparatus suspended high above the performing arena on which acrobats do tricks, frequently quite dangerous.

Aeronauts: A rather high-blown term used around the turn of the century for balloon ascensionists, popular attractions at fairs and amusement parks.

Aetheroscope: *see* PEPPER'S GHOST.

Afghan bands: The name given to a basic magic trick, in which a band or loop of some material about four inches wide and three feet long is torn lengthwise, producing two loops. One of these two is torn again, thus producing two more loops, but these loops are interlinked. The other loop is torn into a single ring twice the length of the original.

After show: An added circus attraction, at extra cost, after the main performance. Originally the after show was a musical concert; later it became more varied, e.g., a Wild West exhibition, wrestling match, and the like. *see* CONCERT.

Afterpiece: In the eighteenth and nineteenth centuries, this was a term for a short play, musical, or other entertainment at the end of the bill,* preceded by a full-length entertainment. In early American variety, an afterpiece referred to a short sketch* that followed the olio.* *see also* BILL, OLIO, and SKETCH.

Agent: 1. In vaudeville, the business agent for an act.* 2. In the carnival, one of the terms for a carnival game operator. *see also* CONCESSIONAIRES. 3. *see* ADVANCE AGENT OR ADVANCE MAN.

Aginner: In the outdoor amusement business, one opposed to amusement.

Ahead: In carnivals and some circuses, to be in advance of the show.

Airdome: Popular name for a special type of open air theatre during the early part of this century. It consisted of an area surrounded by a temporary wall of canvas, metal, or wood without any kind of covering, the ground as the floor, and seats placed on a flat. The stage was placed at one end and was covered, along with offstage spaces and dressing rooms masked from the audience, usually with canvas.

(In the) Aisles: A performance that is so funny or entertaining that the audience falls (figuratively) out of their seats with laughter.

Aisle-sitter: A critic who is given an aisle seat so that it is possible to escape quickly in order to make a deadline.

Al-a-ga-zam: The hailing sign of pitchmen. *see also* PITCHMAN.

Alderman: A circus and carnival term; an office stooge or stoolie. *see* OFFICE.

Alfalfa: Circus slang for paper money.

Alibi agent: A carny* who stands behind a counter and explains why the mark* lost a game of chance or missed a target, and such, or if apparently the mark won the game, why he won't be paid off because of fouling or breaking a rule. *see also* ALIBI STORE, CARNY, and MARK.

Alibi store: A carnival game which pretends to be a skill or science game* but which gives the players little or no chance to win. In an alibi store, the operator always had an alibi to explain the player's loss. *see also* ALIBI AGENT and SKILL OR SCIENCE GAME.

All out and over: Circus phrase to indicate that the entire performance has been concluded.

All right on the night: *see* IT WILL BE ALL RIGHT ON THE NIGHT.

All the tea in China: A circus phrase meaning a great deal of cash money.

All wet: In vaudeville, a bad performance or performer.

Allez-hup: From the French *"allez"* (go) and English "hup" (up), this literally means "go up," and in the circus means "ready—go" to alert acrobats to a synchronized routine.

Alligators: Circus performers' wives. Term probably comes from the alligator bags that were popular among the ladies on the lot;* nonperformers' wives were once called excess baggage,* although this term has broader meanings. *see also* LOT and EXCESS BAGGAGE.

Alvin: A rustic or unsophisticated, inexperienced individual. When used in the carnival or circus, its meaning is that of one who is easily hoaxed or taken in. *see* RUBE.

Am: An amateur performer or actor; a ham.* *see also* HAM ACTOR.

Ambish: Short for ambition and meaning; in theatrical use, a performer's aggressiveness.

America's Greatest Hit: A phrase most often associated with *Uncle Tom's Cabin* because of its unprecedented position as a show business institution and its phenomenal popularity. *see* TOM SHOW, TOMMERS and UTC or U.T.C. COMPANY.

Amusement Business: *see* CHUMP EDUCATOR.

And cakes: Although rare today, an actor once found these words in a contract to indicate that the manager would supply board or money for board. *see* CAKES.

Angel: Since the early part of this century (according to Horton), an outsider who backs a show; a show-backer. Used today in the general sense of financing an enterprise.

Angle-proof: A magical effect or device that can be used with spectators on all sides of the performer.

Ankle a show: Voting with your feet* or leaving a show prematurely; to walk out.

Annex: A circus and carnival term for a sideshow.* Most frequently refers to an additional attraction of a sideshow or a girlie show.* *see also* GIRLIE SHOW, KID SHOW, SIDESHOW, TEN-IN-ONE.

Annie Oakley: A complimentary ticket or free pass named after Anne Oakley Mozee Butler (1860-1926), better known as Annie Oakley, Buffalo Bill's famous woman rifle-shot in his Wild West exhibition. Oakley would throw into the air a playing card or a card with a picture of her about five inches by two inches, make it look like a punched meal ticket, and then throw them to the audience as souvenirs. Free tickets were similarly punched (and frequently still are), as if by bullets, to show they had been properly purchased by or provided to the customer. The term probably originated in the circus world but spread to most areas of entertainment, including the theatre. *see* BROADS, DUCAT OR DUCKET, FAKE, GRABBER OR SNATCHER, PAPER, and SKULL.

Announcer: A position in the circus differing from either the equestrian director* or the ringmaster* although it has been frequently confused with both. During the golden age of the circus, this was the man who announced the acts in the main show, using nothing but his voice without special amplification or a whistle. On some circuses he also managed the sideshow, making first openings* and then went into the big top where he announced the acts. *see also* EQUESTRIAN DIRECTOR, RINGMASTER, and OPENING.

Anticipation: In magician's parlance, a way of misleading the audience into thinking that a secret move or piece of trickery has not yet taken place when, in fact, it has. *see* MISDIRECTION.

Antipodist: An upside-down performer who juggles with his feet while lying in a cradle called a trinka.* *see also* RISLEY ACT and TRINKA.

Ape: 1. In the theatre, especially vaudeville, a performer who filches material, lines, or business* from others. *see also* BUSINESS. 2. In the carnival, sometimes used in reference to outsiders or towners.* *see also* TOWNERS.

Apple knocker: 1. Circus term for a rustic. 2. In the tent-show business, it referred to an unruly or misbehaved tent-show customer.

Apple-sauce: A general term in the sphere of the medicine show* for a song-and-dance routine, a spiel,* or a pitch.* *see also* MEDICINE SHOW, PITCH, and SPIEL.

Aquatic drama: A spectacular form of popular entertainment during the first half of the nineteenth century in which mimic sea battles or other aquatic events were staged on stages equipped with water tanks. Also called nautical drama or tank spectacle.

Arch: The front gate of a carnival, used extensively before the thirties by carnies* to mean the midway* entrance. *see also* CARNY and MID-WAY.

Arrow the route: Circus phrase meaning to mark a route from town to town with arrows placed along the road. *see* RAIL-THE-ROUTE and TELEGRAPH WAGON.

Artiste: Circus word for a performer; more common in the English circus.

(The) asbestos is down: Burlesque phrase indicating that the comics could not get laughs. Asbestos refers to the fireproof curtain which, when lowered, separated the audience from the stage.

Aside: Theatre and vaudeville term for a brief speech or monologue directed by the performer at the audience while in the presence of other characters, some or all of whom are supposed not to overhear the words.

Assembly: A card trick in which several cards of a kind are made to come together, such as four kings or all the cards of a suit.

Assistant: A person who appears with a magician as part of the act and aids the magician during the performance. *see* CONFEDERATE, STOOGE, and VOLUNTEER.

Astral projection: Term used by magicians or mentalists to describe the so-called mystical ability to send the spirit out of the body to distant places during sleep or while in a trance. Also called OBs or obies, for out-of-body experiences. *see also* MENTALISM.

At liberty: In most areas of entertainment, this means unemployed or out of work. In the circus, it can also mean out of an act.* Theatrical people prefer to apply to this term the notion of not having a current acting engagement or of being available for casting, thus between engagements.* The British use the term "resting." *see also* ACT, BE-TWEEN ENGAGEMENTS, and LAY OFF.

At show: A carnival midway* attraction featuring athletic contests between boxers or wrestlers who belong to the show, and local opponents or contenders. *see also* MIDWAY.

Attention control: The ability, especially of a magician, to control the audience's interest and direct their attention to the sights and sounds necessary in order to enjoy a magical routine or any other entertainment. In other words, all the action that takes place in a performance.

Attractions: Word used in the circus for freaks, a word rarely if ever used by circuses. *see* HUMAN ODDITIES.

Auction store: *see* JAM STORE.

(The) audience in his palm: Ability of a performer to capture and manipulate the attention and mood of an audience.

Auguste or August: A slapstick circus clown who appears stupid and clumsy and performs in flamboyant makeup including a red rubber nose and white paint round the eyes and mouth. He is usually at the receiving end when pies or water are flying from the hand of the more elegant and clever white-face clown.* Some authorities claim that the Auguste is of French origin, although Towsen points out that this type of clown was apparently introduced by Tom Belling in Berlin in 1869 and originally wore little makeup. Towsen says that, in the Berlin dialect from which it is derived, the word is august (or Aujust) and means "silly" or "stupid." Today the Auguste is usually seen in a baggy suit. The early American version of the Auguste apparently wore ill-fitting, formal wear to mock the refinements of gentlemen or the pretensions of upstarts, depending on the patrons' point of view. *see also* WHITE-FACE or WHITEFACE.

B

B. & O.: 1. Form of shorthand used in traveling repertoire advertising, especially for the Toby show,* meaning that actors were expected to double in the band and orchestra. Larger companies advertised a "military band" concert in front of the theatre or tent before performances, and all had orchestras of at least two or three pieces. Some had as many as twenty or more musicians and actor-musicians in their bands. Thus, such doubling was important. *see also* TOBY SHOW. 2. In the circus, this meant brass, or the band, and implied that the musicians were also expected to help out with the heavy work. 3. In vaudeville, B. & O. referred to the band and orchestra. *see also* DOUBLING IN BRASS and B. &.S.

B. & S.: Meaning that musicians in repertoire shows were expected to act, and actors were expected to play instruments as well, since few of these shows could afford to carry both musicians and actors. *see* B. & O.

Babies: The name given to pumas in the circus.

Baby ballet: A corp of children featured in spectacular extravaganzas in the nineteenth century. *see* SPECTACULAR EXTRAVAGANZA.

Back: In the circus, short for a back somersault; usually qualified as a triple back or a layout back. *see also* SOMERSAULT.

Back door: The performer's entrance to the big top* in the circus. Usually a large opening in the main tent connecting with the back yard.* *see also* BACK YARD and BIG TOP.

Back-end: Generally speaking, that portion of a carnival midway* consisting of rides and shows. In actuality, not a literal description of the geographical arrangement or patterning of the carnival, but the portion of a carnival that consists of the larger shows and the taller rides, which are sometimes placed in the rear center of the standard horseshoe configuration of a carnival. The back end more specifically alludes to the shows. The distinction between front and back is also a distinction between those who hawk wares and those who are performers in some sense, according to Easto and Truzzi. *see also* FRONT-END and MIDWAY.

Back-end people: Those who work in the back-end.* *see also* BACK-END and FRONT-END PEOPLE.

Back-end run: A term used almost exclusively for an English fair that occurs toward the end of the season in September or October.

Back of the door: Predominantly an English fair term for short-changing* or "tapping." *see also* SHORT-CHANGE ARTIST.

Back palm: In magic, to conceal an object at the back of the hand.

Back-piece: The name of a special wig worn only on the back of the head.

Back room: In repertoire companies, especially the Toby show,* a back room usually meant a set representing a farm kitchen. *see also* TOBY SHOW.

Back track: The circus hippodrome track* section located in front of the bandstand and the back door.* *see also* BACK DOOR and HIPPODROME TRACK.

Back yard: 1. In general terms, any area behind the scenes at the circus. 2. Specifically, the space between the entrance to the main tent and dressing rooms, where properties used during performance, wardrobes, and wagons were kept. 3. Collectively, the corps of performers, clowns, musicians, and other similar personnel, as opposed to the administrative staff of the circus.

Bad actor: Circus term for a mean, vicious, or badly trained animal.

Bad score: In a carnival, a poor showing for an exhibit.

Bag guy: A circus balloon vender.

Bag man: 1. A carnival term for a local official, or anyone acting for him, to whom protection money is paid. Also called a fixer or an iceman. *see* ICEMAN. 2. In the circus, a bag man was a ticket seller (and frequently a short-change artist) who worked on the circus grounds, making change from a bag strapped around the waist or hanging from a shoulder strap. *see also* SHORT-CHANGE ARTIST.

Baggage: In the circus, virtually anything carried by a show, including freight, equipment, and other assorted paraphernalia.

Baggage horse and stock: Heavy circus draft or work horse or horses used to pull heavy spectacle* floats or heavy parade* wagons, plus all wagons to and from the runs* where they were loaded on railroad flatcars. Used extensively before caterpillar-tractor days. *see also* PARADE, RUNS, and SPEC OR SPECTACLE.

Baggage section: The portion of a circus train that carried the big top,* seating, and heavy properties. *see also* BIG TOP, HEAVY SECTION, and LIGHT SECTION.

Baldheaded row: The front row of seats in the orchestra of a theatre, in particular at a burlesque* or girlie show,* where elderly playboys, usually with some wealth, sat to have the best view. Figuratively, the term was used to describe these older men or a group of such men who stared at women. *see also* BURLESQUE, CROTCH ROW, and GIRLIE SHOW.

Bale of straw: Description of a large and sturdy blonde woman in both the circus and carnival world. Apparently, such women were preferred by the men involved with outdoor amusements.

Bale ring: A solid, round, heavy steel ring put around every circus center pole* to which was hooked or laced the open sections of canvas before being pulled up. Since few circuses today travel with tents, such practices are quickly disappearing. *see also* CENTER POLE.

Bale-ring tent: A tent constructed for use by circuses, in particular when a pushpole tent* construction would not carry the heavy spread of canvas. A few large tent shows also utilized the bale-ring tent. In this system the center poles* are erected first with the iron bale ring* at the bottom or butt end of the pole. From the top of the center pole is a pulley system and a bale ring is at the bottom of each center pole. After quarter poles* and side poles* are in place and the separate canvas parts of the tent have been laced together and tied to the bale ring, the bale rings, attached to the tent by ropes, are hoisted. Any tent over fifty feet wide would necessitate a bale-ring tent. *see also* BALE RING, CENTER POLE, DRAMATIC END TENT, PUSHPOLE TENT, QUARTER POLES, ROUNDTOP, and SIDE POLES.

Bale ring to stakes: A circus phrase used to encompass the whole range of circus property.

Balled up: Circus term describing the usual position of an acrobat executing a somersault,* that is, with the arms hugging the knees to the chest. *see also* LAY OUT and SOMERSAULT.

Ballerina act: Term most frequently associated with the English circus that erroneously has been applied to bareback riding when it more correctly refers to an act involving high-school horses* in which a ballerina dances alongside the horse.*see also* HIGH-SCHOOL HORSE.

Ballet broads: Female supers* in the circus who perform in the specs* but not in specialty* acts. Also known as bally broads or bally girls. *see also* SPEC OR SPECTACLE, SPECIALTY, and SUPER.

Balloon: 1. In theatrical terms, to forget lines or business; to go up in one's lines. *see* GO UP IN THE AIR. 2. In the circus, especially the English circus, a paper hoop through which a rider, usually a girl, jumps from horseback.

Bally or ballyhoo: One of the most common terms in all of popular entertainment jargon. Used as part of pitchmen's slang in virtually all forms of outdoor and environmental entertainments, especially the medicine show,* carnival and circus. A bally, ballyhoo, or, sometimes bally act, is simply an attraction used to draw a crowd. The platform on which the sample performance is given is also called a bally, as are the people in the free show. The spiel* given by the talker* can also be called bally. Bally is used by sideshows, girlie shows, and the like to give the tip* an idea of the show to be seen inside (the bally is located immediately outside the structure or tent). The pitchman used bally to urge wares on a crowd attracted by a spiel. Its origin is unclear. Ballantine in *Wild Tiger* suggests that it is an abbreviation of "Bally-hooly truth," an English music-hall tag from the early 1880s, which in turn possibly was derived from "whole bloody truth" or "holy bloody truth." H. L. Mencken in *The American Language: Supplement II* (p. 684) offers two conflicting theories. One notion is that it might have come from a sea term meaning a small West Indian craft or odd rig, apparently a loan from the Carib through the Spanish, although the connection here is not clear. The second theory is that in the 1840s and

1850s many traveling tent shows were conducted by roving Irishmen who spoke both Gaelic and English. Their job was to talk up the show and to pass the hat. The Gaelic word for collect is bailinghadh, pronounced ballyoo (dissyllable) by Munster speakers and bállyoo by Connacht speakers. At intervals in the show the cry of *Bailinghadh anois* (Collection now) would be heard. See also the terms below related to bally. *see also* BALLY STAND, MEDICINE SHOW, PITCHMAN, SPIEL, and TALKER.

Bally act: *see* BALLY OR BALLYHOO.

Bally broads or girls: *see* BALLET BROADS.

Ballyhooers: In the circus and carnival, girls who bally* or ballyhoo* in front of shows to draw attention and a crowd. *see also* BALLY OR BALLYHOO.

Ballyhooing: The act of making a bally.* *see also* BALLY.

Ballys: Plural of bally;* also small gifts of merchandise placed in boxes of candy, Cracker Jacks, or the like at carnivals and other forms of amusements. *see also* BALLY and COPS.

Bally show: A show with continuous or regularly scheduled performances, about once an hour, with repeat performances. Used in both circus and carnival, but more prevalent in the latter.

Bally stand or box: A more specific term than bally* for the platform in front of a sideshow tent where the talker* stands and on which the free show is exhibited in order to lure spectators inside. Also called bally platform or stand. *see also* BALLY and TALKER.

Balonie or baloney: Show-business jargon for nonsense or spurious.

Balto: Abbreviation for Baltimore.

Banana: A burlesque* comic. The most important, and usually the best or senior comedian, is the top banana,* the next is second banana,* and so forth. Name possibly came from the soft (banana-shaped) bladder club carried as a standard item by burlesque comics and usually used to hit other comics over the head, as in the judge bit. *see also* BIT, BLADDER, BURLESQUE, SECOND BANANA, THIRD BANANA, and TOP BANANA.

Band call: In the circus, and to some extent in the carnival, a rehearsal with the band to assure that all is well—parts are correct and distributed, the conductor understands the cues, and so forth.

Banner: The canvas paintings or pictorials hung in front of a sideshow* or midway* show depicting the attractions within. Also called a valentine. In the early traveling circus and carnival, banners were also cloth signs of advertisements of local merchants used by advance men displayed on riding devices and rolling stock of shows, or tacked on buildings or sign boards. In the English fair, banners are informative notices or slogans, hung from rafters and other supports, sometimes stating the price of the rides and sometimes giving warnings on how not to ride. *see also* BANNER LINE, MIDWAY, and SIDESHOW.

Banner line: Specifically, a series of canvas or paper pictures stretched in front of an attraction. The most common banner line was that for a sideshow* with displays lined up on either side of the entrance, sometimes on individually framed metal plates, but most frequently on separate sections of canvas or a banner.* *see also* BANNER and SIDE-SHOW.

Banner man: A salesman of banner advertising. *see also* BANNER.

Banner puller: A circus employee who removed banners and tacks. This person usually traveled with the show. *see* BANNER, BANNER SQUARER, and BANNER TACKER.

Banner squarer: A circus employee responsible for arranging for permission to attach banners to brick buildings (with tacks instead of paste) with the understanding that they would be removed after the show's date was completed. *see* BANNER, BANNER PULLER, and BANNER TACKER.

Banner tacker: The circus employee responsible for tacking banners to walls. Also known as the tack spitter.* *see also* BANNER, BANNER PULLER, BANNER SQUARER, and TACK SPITTER.

Banners: In the circus, especially in the English circus, broad strips of cloth over which a bareback rider jumps. Not to be confused with banner. *see* RIBBON.

Bar act: An acrobatic performance on horizontal bars set about eight feet apart. It is considered one of the more strenuous acts in the circus.

Bar-to-bar: A term applied to a trapeze artist who dispenses with a catcher* and flies from one bar to another. *see also* CATCHER.

Bar-to-catcher: An aerial act in which the flyer* leaves the bar of his own trapeze* and is caught by his partner. *see also* CATCHER, FLYER, and TRAPEZE.

Barber shop: A theatrical term in vogue around the turn of the century that meant a discordant note.

Bare stage: In vaudeville, a stage without scenery.

Barker: A term used by nonoutdoor show people to describe the man who, at the entrance to a show, talks the people into buying tickets for a sideshow* or other extra-admission attraction. Used by writers and some First-of-May* showmen who don't know better. In a short con* game the spieler* or talker* is sometimes called a barker. *see also* BALLY, BALLYHOO, FIRST OF MAY, LECTURER, OPENER, SHORT-CON GAME, SPIELER, and TALKER.

Barn: Theatrical term for an over-large theatre, usually found in cities with all-purpose auditoriums. A fairly recent use of the word.

Barn burner: Describes a performance so good and so startling that it is like a barn full of hay catching fire and burning at night, capturing everyone's attention because of its uniqueness and "brightness."

Barnstorm: To tour, making short or one-night stands* in barns or other such simple structures in rural towns, frequently without advance arrangements. *see also* ONE-NIGHT STAND.

Barnaby: Theatrical term used around the turn of the century to describe those who submit to the rule of their wives. *see* (TO) JUMP THROUGH.

Barnstormer: One who barnstorms. Originally, the reference was to an actor; now, it often refers to a traveling carnival act or stunt man. In British terminology, a barnstormer once meant one who hammed or ranted; hence, barnstormer sometimes connoted an inferior actor or performer. *see* PRAIRIE COMEDIAN.

Barnum: *see* HE HAS GONE WITH BARNUM.

Barny or barney: In the English circus, a fight. The closest American equivalent is clem.* *see also* CLEM.

Barrelhouse: Originally, a combination cheap saloon, rooming house, and brothel.

Batoude: A plank sloping steeply down and ending in another shorter, springy board sloping up, which gives more lift when an acrobat is leaping obstacles. This term is more common in the English circus than in the American circus.

Batte: *see* SLAPSTICK.

Battery-whip: Rarely seen today, this was a whip with an electric lash used in handling circus animals.

(To) be had: In medicine-show* jargon, this meant to be dealt with. *see also* MEDICINE SHOW.

(To) be on the earie: In carnival slang, to keep one's ears alert. *see* BEING ON THE ERIE.

Bead-als: In the carnival, a woman who wears beads.

Bearer: In the English circus, the supporter of an acrobatic act, roughly equivalent to the American bottom man* or understander.* *see also* BOTTOM MAN and UNDERSTANDER.

Beat it: Circus and carnival for depart hastily. *see* DUCK and SCRAM.

Beat my chops: Show-business slang for talking to no avail or "spinning one's wheels."

Beat the clock: An English fair stall (or booth) game; a precursor of bingo.

Beddy: A winter hangout or quarters for an individual connected with the circus or carnival.

Bee or B: *see* PUT ON THE BEE OR B.

Beef: Circus and carnival slang meaning to bellow or complain over a real or an imagined wrong. As DeBelle explains it, "Cookhouse beef isn't meat." The phrase "beef and squawk" has the same meaning. *see* BELCH.

Beef trust: In early burlesque, a chorus of stout, large, or fat girls or women, preferred by many male audiences. The name is a reference to Billy Watson's famous "Beef Trust" company, the billing of which announced that it offered "two tons of women." Today, beef trust, if used, refers to any group of stout or fat people. *see* BIG HORSE and HILL HORSES.

Beetle: Circus slang for a female. *see* FRAIL.

Behind the cork: Pitchmen's* phrase for when the bottle is empty and the contents are in the imbiber, thus the bottle is no longer behind the cork but the drinker is. *see also* PITCHMAN.

Behind the parade: In the circus, this meant to be considered old hat or passé.

Behind-the-tent show: In the 1890s, this referred to a carnival-type show with a kind of dirty burlesque presentation. *see* TURKEY SHOW.

Being on the erie: Circus slang for eavesdropping. *see* (TO) BE ON THE EARIE.

Belch: In the circus, a complaint or a beef; also, to complain, to beef, to squeal, or to inform. *see* BEEF.

Bell-ringer: In vaudeville, a tobacco chewer. Derived from the common vaudeville joke of causing a bell to ring at the instant a chewer scores a bull's-eye on a cuspidor.

Belly joint or store: A gaff wheel* of chance with a hidden control or brake on the counter that can stop the wheel by having the operator lean on or against the counter. *see also* GAFF WHEEL, JOINT, and STORE.

Belly laff: A large comic reaction.

Belly platform or belly stand: *see* BALLY STAND OR BOX.

Belly stick: A person who works outside a carnival game of chance and entices players for the game. He "bellys up" to the counter and acts as if he is playing the game. *see* STICK.

Belly wow: In vaudeville, this meant particularly riotous laughter in response to an act.* *see also* ACT and WOW.

Belvedere: Circus and carnival term for the belly of a railroad car which was used as a storage space. *see* POSSUM BELLY.

Bench act: A type of song-and-dance team in vaudeville in which the team went into their act* by sitting on a park bench on stage at the beginning of the number. There were numerous standard ways to initiate an act, this being one of the most popular. *see also* ACT.

Bender: Circus contortionist who specializes in bending backward. *see* FROG and LIMBER JIM.

Bending: A circus acrobatic movement.

Benny (also Ben): Carnival slang, borrowed from the underworld, for an overcoat.

Between-acts: Specialty variety routines between the acts of a dramatic piece; principally used among vaudevillians.

Between engagements: Actor or performer out of work. *see* AT LIBERTY.

Bible: Circus program or souvenir magazine.

Bible-backs: The floorboards for the grandstand section in a circus tent.

Bicycle operas: Carnivals that travel by trucks and trailers. *see* MUD SHOW.

Big Bertha: *see* (THE) BIG ONE.

Big Cage: The barred or steel-mesh collapsible arena used for exhibiting wild animal acts in the circus ring.* *see also* CAT DEN and RING.

Big dance in Newark: One of numerous show-business phrases (and excuses) for bad business. When the weather, the time of the year, or some other excuse does not suffice, then only a big dance in Newark will serve as a fitting excuse.

Big horse: Name given to a very hefty chorus girl* during burlesque's early days. *see* BEEF TRUST, CHORUS GIRL, and HILL-HORSES.

Big killing: Medicine showmen's and pitchmen's* phrase for a financial coup. *see also* PITCHMAN.

(The) Big Lot: Where a circus performer goes after death. *see* LOT.

Big-money performance: In tent-show jargon, the first performance after a company has met its overhead expenses during one stand. *see* (TO) CRACK THE NUT.

(The) Big One (also Big Bertha): The Ringling Bros. and Barnum & Bailey Circus, in contrast to all other smaller circuses.

Big rag: The main tent of a circus. *see* BIG TOP.

Big rubber: The slang name for large balloons, airships, animals, or other inflatable objects sold on a circus midway.

Big-time: Vaudeville theatres or circuits that played straight vaudeville with no movies, twice a day. By extension, big-time* has come to mean big league or the higher strata or most successful entertainment. *see* TWO-A-DAY.

Big-time single turn: In medicine-show parlance, this meant a capable assistant.

Big tom: A stuffed cat in a carnival ball-throwing game placed usually in the center of the cat rack* and heavier and larger than the rest to make a deceptive target. The size makes him easy to hit and the weight hard to knock down. *see also* CAT RACK, MODUC, and SIX-CAT.

Big top: The main performance tent of a circus (never a carnival and never the circus as a whole). Common since circa 1890. Also called the big rag*, old rag* and, occasionally, Big Bertha* (although more commonly this is the same as the big one*). *see also* (THE) BIG ONE.

Big-top gang: Circus canvas men* and utility men who work on the main tent equipment. *see also* CANVAS MEN.

Big turk: Circus jargon for an ostrich.

Bight: Magic term for a loop of rope, string, or the like, contained in a knot.

Bill: 1. A single play in the repertoire of a Toby show* company. *see also* TOBY SHOW. 2. A series of acts in a variety show; the entire show. 3. Circus paper advertising. *see* HANDBILL, HERALD, PAPER, and PLAY-BILL.

Bill board: A board on which a theatrical advertisement might be posted and the advertisement itself.

Bill car: A circus advertising car.* *see also* ADVERTISING CARS.

Bill-Show: A Wild West show* or exhibition, such as Buffalo Bill's or Pawnee Bill's. By extension, A Bill-Show cowboy is a show-off cowboy of the Buffalo Bill variety. *see also* WILD WEST SHOW.

Bill-sticker: In the English circus, one who posts or puts up printed handbills.

Bill tube: A common piece of magical apparatus; a sealed tube in which paper money is made to appear.

Billboard: Well-known theatrical weekly that began publication in 1894 but has been replaced in the outdoor amusement business by *Amusement Business*. *see* CHUMP EDUCATOR.

Billboard pass or bill pass: A free admission pass given to people who donate space to advertise a show or let the space out at lower than customary rates.

Billboard wedding: DeBelle explains this midway* rite this way: carnival boys and gals are united in Holy Matrimony by both placing their hands on the Showmen's Bible, *Billboard** (today this would be *Amusement Business*), and saying "I do." *see also* BILLBOARD and CARNY WEDDING.

Biller: *see* ADVANCE AGENT and PAPER BOY OR MAN.

Billet: A small piece of paper used in mind-reading effects on which something is usually written or drawn. *see* MENTALISM.

Billet switch: A simple sleight* used by a magician for substituting the performer's own billet* for one written or drawn on by the spectator. *see also* BILLET and SLEIGHT OR SLEIGHT-OF-HAND.

Billing: 1. The ranking or mention of a performer's name in a show's ads or notices, which are displayed inside or outside a theatre or other place of entertainment, or distributed by hand. Top billing is a hold-over from vaudeville* in which the main attraction would be listed at the top of a bill of a program of a number of acts, eight being the usual number. After top billing, an act, especially a new attraction, would prefer bottom billing, which was considered by many the first indication of success or recognition for virtual unknowns. *see also* VAUDE-VILLE. 2. Also the name for the notice or advertisement for a production or show.

Billing in a box: The placement of an attraction or performer's name in a box in the advertisement or notices of a show. Also called a coffin.**see* BILLING.

Billing star: A performer who achieves recognition or prominence over the name of the attraction, sometimes by underhanded or shady means, such as payoffs. Not to be confused with box-office star.* The billing star does not necessarily guarantee success for the attraction, as does the box-office star. *see also* BOX-OFFICE STAR.

Bimbos: Carnival slang for women, other than those in girlie shows or girlesk* attractions. *see also* GIRLESK and GLITTERGALS.

Biograph: The intensest competitor to Thomas A. Edison's early motion-picture operations. Formed in 1896 by William Kennedy, Laurie Dickson, and a group of men as the American Mutoscope and Biography Company. Shortened to Biograph.

Bioscope: Not to be confused with Biograph. This is the early name for a motion-picture projector used in shows before World War I in England. The English fair used the term to refer to traveling booths for the display of motion pictures.

Bird: *see* FISH.

Bird dog: In the circus, a local person who does the leg work for an advance agent or advance man. *see also* ADVANCE AGENT OR ADVANCE MAN.

Birdlime: English circus argot for the time.

Biseauté: International magic term to describe cards that are narrower at one end than the other. *see* STRIPPER PACK.

Bit: 1. In burlesque, a brief scene or skit.* Some authorities would use bit only in the context of burlesque. *see also* SKIT. 2. In vaudeville, a successful little stage scene complete in itself or a small part in an act.* *see also* ACT. 3. A small part in a play or entertainment. 4. In the carnival, a bit refers to a percentage of monies due or expected. *see* BIT PART and SKETCH.

Bit part: Actor with only a few lines. *see* BIT.

Biz: Show-people's term for "business." *see* BUSINESS.

Black and tan: A black-face* act in vaudeville. *see also* BLACK-FACE.

Black art: In magic, the technical name for an optical principle and the tricks done by its aid. *see* BLACK-ART PRINCIPLE.

Black-art principle: The principle that black upon black appears invisible, especially if bright lights are directed toward the audience. With all shadows obliterated, the eye cannot distinguish the outline of objects masked in black. *see* BLACK ART.

Black-art table: A magician's table, invented by Robert Heller and Professor DeVere, that facilitates the black-art principle.* *see also* BLACK-ART PRINCIPLE.

Black-face or blackface: The covering of the face by black makeup, such as the burnt cork* used by most nineteenth-century minstrel companies. Also refers to the material used and the performer wearing it. *see also* BURNT CORK, MINSTREL BLACK, and MINSTREL SHOW.

Black light: A modern addition to the magician's apparatus: fluorescent lighting that is invisible until it shines on specially treated surfaces and makes them visible even though in complete darkness.

Black tober: English circus term for a site where there is no grass, such as slag or wasteland. *see* TOBER.

(To) Black Up: To put on black-face makeup, especially for a minstrel show.* *see also* BURNT CORK, MINSTREL BLACK, and MINSTREL SHOW.

Blackout: In vaudeville and revues, a very short sketch or comic bit* that builds up to the end in a blackout* on the punch or curtain line. Also called a blackout skit.* It can also mean a surprising ending to a scene or act with the lights going out quickly or a fast curtain. *see also* BIT, LIGHT UP, and SKIT.

Blackout skit: *see* BLACKOUT.

Bladder: 1. A toy balloon sold in the circus. 2. An animal bladder or some synthetic substance inflated like a balloon and used as a comic weapon by circus and burlesque clowns. The animal bladder variety dates back to the medieval court fool. 3. An obsolete theatrical term for a dissipated female trouper. *see* BLISTER.

Blank out: In the carnival, a small-time concessionaire who does not make expenses during a stand.* *see also* STAND.

Blanket: In the circus, a word used to describe any elephant covering, no matter how extravagantly decorated. *see* WARDROBE.

Blanket game: The name given to a gambling game played by circus show people on a blanket outside show cars or on the show grounds.

Blind or blind shuffle: Magician's term for a shuffle, riffle,* cut,* or cull,* designed to appear regular but actually retains the cards in their original order or arranges them into some preconceived order. *see also* CULL, CUT, and RIFFLE.

Blind pig or tiger: Mid-nineteenth-century name for a speakeasy, or an English "sly-grog shop."

Blister: Outdoor amusement-business slang for a woman of loose morals. *see* BLADDER.

Block: Circus and medicine-show slang for a watch. Also called a turnip.

Block and tackle: Carnival and pitchmen's slang for a watch and chain. *see* SLANG.

Block booked: In vaudeville, an entire group of acts (usually eight) having the same agent and engaged for a series of theatres in succession. This provided the performers with a certain amount of security and gave the mediocre acts an audience resulting from the box-office appeal of the better acts.

Block boys, block watch, or blocks: Circus terms for square pine blocks, six inches by six inches and one inch thick, placed on the ground for footing legs of seat jacks to keep them solid and prevent slipping. The boys who handle the blocks and retrieve them after the circus are also sometimes called block boys.

Blocking: Common theatrical term also used in magic to describe the patterns of movement the performer uses during a presentation.

Blood and thunder: A spine-tingling type of melodrama* of the popular theatre, probably first applied to the melodramas presented at New York's Bowery Theatre during the nineteenth century. *see also* MELODRAMA.

Bloodstopping: A bogus hypnotic stunt used by magicians as a method for making the pulse in the wrist apparently register no pulse beat. Also known as Pulse control.

Bloomer: 1. Theatrical and general show-business term, now obsolete, for a town or stand* that failed to respond to various forms of entertainment, or one in which small profits were made. 2. Also, a theatrical flop. 3. In the medicine show, a bloomer was a faux pas as well as poor business. *see also* PLAY A BLANK and STAND.

Blow: 1. In the theater, to forget or blunder one's lines or business.* 2. The circus has several meanings for blow: to depart; a big wind; or to eliminate. 3. In the world of the carnival, blow can mean to lose money or to give a big prize by mistake or through failure of a mechanical device in a game of chance. Similar to the circus's "to depart," blow can also mean to leave a hotel without paying the bill. *see* (TO) GO WRONG.

(To) blow between moons: Similar to the carnival meaning of blow* (to leave), this phrase meant to disappear without notice. *see also* BLOW.

Blow down or blowdown: Term associated with both the circus and traveling tent shows, meaning: 1. A heavy storm that levels tents and portable equipment. 2. The general chaos caused when the tents are blown down. 3. The leveling of the tents and equipment.

Blow off: 1. In the circus, the grand finale of the show, its climax, or the point when the concessionaires come out. 2. Patrons leaving the midway* or grandstand of a circus. *see also* MIDWAY. 3. A behind-the-curtain show at a carnival that "caters mostly to morons." 4. The large photographs used on the fronts of carnival tent theatre shows. 5. In a burlesque show, the belly dancer or other exotic dancer who comes on just before the finale and does a suggestive grind* and bump* number. *see also* BUMP and GRIND. 6. Pitchmen's usage includes two variations: high-pressure selling used to liquidate stock before moving on or the first sale or sales on which no profit is made but business is stimulated. 7. Traveling tent shows used blow off to mean to close a show suddenly without paying salaries. 8. In sideshows, dime museums, and the like, an extra attraction seen for an additional charge. *see* CONCERT.

Blow the stand or blow the show: Circus phrase meaning to cancel a town already selected, routed, or billed. Blow the show meant to leave the show. *see* BLOW and STAND.

Blower: A carnival concession in which celluloid balls or Ping-Pong balls float in an airstream and are picked for prizes by the customers.

Blowers: The name given to sideshow* front talkers* during the 1860s and 1870s. *see also* SIDESHOW and TALKER.

Blue: In vaudeville, used to indicate material (lines or business*) that bordered on the obscene or had questionable overtones. *see also* BUSINESS.

Blue bird: Part of circus and carnival lore. When the well-known symbol of happiness was first heard in the spring, circus troupers* knew it was time to start forth on their annual pilgrimage. In general, a symbol of optimism. *see also* TROUPER.

Blue comedy: Repertoire company* expression for dirty jokes. *see* REPERTOIRE OR REPERTORY COMPANY.

Blue gags: Jokes in questionable taste. *see* BLUE.

Blue one: Pitchmen's term for poor business or a poor location for a business or a store.* *see also* LARRY SPOT, RED ONE, and STORE.

Blue shirt lead: In the Toby show,* a leading man who plays a country bumpkin or some other rural role, occasionally a two-fisted he-man, whose working shirt is blue instead of white. *see also* TOBY and TOBY SHOW.

Blue stuff: Dirty comedy or risqué stage business. *see* BLUE and BLUE GAGS.

Blues: Circus and tent-show terminology for general admission seats. In the circus, these were plain board or cheap seats usually painted blue and situated generally around the ends of the big top.* In traveling tent shows the blues were situated at the back of the tent and comprised a small portion of the total seating capacity. *see also* BIG TOP, HARD TICKETS, and OLD STAR BUCKS.

Blunt: Circus and general lot* term for coin. *see also* LOT.

B. O.: Theatre, carnival, and circus abbreviation for box office.

Boa: The long, thin stole of feathers or fur draped over a stripper's shoulders that is subsequently wrapped around the body and through the legs in the course of the performance. *see* STRIPTEASE.

Boards: Show-business term for tickets to an entertainment.

Boat: Minstrelsy* term for a train. *see also* MINSTRELSY.

Boat-show: 1. A showboat.* 2. A dramatic show on a showboat. During the early history of the showboat, a boat-show meant a circus, variety show, or some other form of entertainment on a showboat in contrast to a dramatic show on a showboat.

Body: A term for a man as used in the nomenclature of show girls.* *see also* SHOW GIRL.

Body pole: A light hickory pole that connected six- and eight-horse teams to the pole of a circus wagon in one unit. Such poles were fitted between the "body horses." A six-horse team required one body pole; an eight-horse team needed two.

Body take: *see* TAKE.

Boff: Its basic meaning is a hit show. It also can mean a laugh from an audience or the joke causing the response. Used most frequently to refer to a popular play or musical comedy. *see* BOFFO.

Boffo: A loud laugh, a joke, or a very successful performer or entertainment, usually with the connotation of being extremely funny. *see* BOFF.

(To) Boil up: Circus slang for washing clothes.

Boilermakers' convention: Vaudeville slang for an audience.

Bomb: An obvious failure of either an entertainment or a performer.

Bona: English circus slang for good. Also cushy. Bona seems to be one of the few circus terms derived from Italian origin.

Bones: One of the end men* in a black-face* minstrel show,* so called because of the rhythm clacker bones such an entertainer often played. By extension, any black-face comedian. *see also* BLACK-FACE, END MAN, MINSTREL SHOW, and TAMBO.

Bonehead: Medicine-show slang for one of strong character.

Boob: Medicine-show slang for a hick or yokel. Such a role portrayed in the Toby show* was called a boob character. *see also* TOBY SHOW.

(To) book an act: In vaudeville, to place on a manager's books for playing contacts; to secure a route.* *see also* BOOKED INTO and ROUTE.

Book test: In magician's jargon, a word selected at random from a dictionary or some other book in such a way as to preclude all possibility of collusion. The magician then discovers the word and reveals his knowledge of it in some dramatic way.

Booked into: When a vaudeville act definitely had an engagement and was sure of survival for the length of the contract. *see* (TO) BOOK AN ACT and BOOKED INTO WITH TOP BILLING.

Booked into with top billing: An even more desirable situation than simply being booked into.* *see also* BOOKED INTO.

Booking manager: In vaudeville, one who booked acts for theatres.

Booners: Talent scouts, so named after the frontier scout Daniel Boone.

Booster: 1. In pitchmen's terms, a confederate or assistant who pretends to buy in order to start real buying, or is hired to win. Also called a lumper and sure-thing man. *See* CAPPER, COME-ON, SHILL, and STICK. 2. *see* PLUGGER. 3. A circus booster was a thief who stole merchandise from stores.

Booster-handler: Although few in number today, a booster-handler would stand behind the mark* and relieve him of money as quickly as he picked it up. *see also* BOOSTER and MARK.

Booth stage or theatre: Early term for a temporary outdoor stage erected in a street, marketplace, or other open area. Rarely used in the United States.

Boother: An actor in a booth theatre.* *see also* BOOTH THEATRE.

Born in a trunk: Theatrical adage meaning to be born into a show-business family. Also, "born in a dressing room." The English use the phrase "born in a property basket."

Borscht circuit or belt: The summer vacation hotels in the Catskill Mountains (New York), which formed a circuit beginning around 1935 where many entertainers, both well known and beginners, perform. Many of these hotels have a predominantly Jewish clientele and the name comes from a Russian soup of beets and potato, a favorite of the Jewish patrons.

Boss: A carnival term for one who estimates the value of stolen articles for thieves; the boss is normally not a legitimate pawn broker.

Boss butcher or candy boss: In the circus, the head of refreshment stands and their workers.

Boss canvas man: The person whose job it is to determine where and how the circus tents should be put up at a new lot.* *see also* LOT.

Boss elephant man: The head of the elephant department in a circus and generally the trainer.

Boss hostler: Originally, the person in charge of all the horses used in a circus. It came to mean the one who traveled ahead of the mud show* in order to mark the way for the circus caravan. *see also* MUD SHOW.

Boss of props: Person responsible for properties (or props*) used in the rigging and staging of a circus, including all articles used by performers in acts. *see also* PROPS.

Boss of ringstock: Man who is responsible for the horses and ponies used in circus performances. *see* RINGSTOCK.

Boss tenter: *see* BOSS CANVAS MAN.

Boston version: Ostensibly a burlesque and vaudeville term referring to a show that has been cleaned up and purged of its worst indecencies in order to avoid censorship by municipal authorities such as those in Boston, where "banned in Boston" has long been a catch-phrase to suggest prudery and censorship.

Bottler: In the early English Punch and Judy show,* the name given the collector of contributions following a street presentation. *see also* INTERPRETER, PARDNER, and PUNCH AND JUDY SHOW.

Bottom billing: *see* BILLING.

Bottom card: In magic, the card on the face of a deck or the card whose face can be seen when the deck is assembled.

Bottom deal: Gambling term used by magicians to denote the secret dealing of the bottom card of the deck instead of the top card.

Bottom man: In the circus, the bottom person in an acrobatic act whose major role is to push, pitch, or throw other acrobats or to support them on his or her hands, shoulders, head, or feet. The bottom man sometimes supports a perch* on which other acrobats perform. *see also* BEARER, UNDERSTANDER, and PERCH.

Bottom stock: In magic circles, that portion of a deck of cards which is on the bottom.

Bounce: In the circus, the roar or rush of a wild cat, or as a verb to make noise or a hullabaloo, such as the roaring and snarling of a cat act. In the English circus, a bounce, bunce, or bunch* is a profit. *see also* BUNCH.

Bouncer: Primarily, used in the English circus to mean a wild cat trained to bound about the cage.

Bounding rope act: A circus act in which the performer works on a thick slack rope attached to a spring that enables him or her to bounce the rope up and down.

Box: 1. General term for a theatre doorkeeper's receptacle for ticket-stubs; also the stubs themselves. 2. A magician's term meaning to cause cards to face each other in the deck.

Box-Office Star: A major name performer who can guarantee the success of an attraction.

Boxed: *see* OPEN SET.

Boxings: Metal bearings in the wooden steel-tired circus wagon wheels.

Bozo the Clown: The registered trademark for a commercial clown whose appearance is normally an exaggerated version of the Auguste* clown and whose behavior is that of stupidity. *see* AUGUSTE.

B. R.: Circus and carnival abbreviation for bankroll or a roll of currency.

Bradawl or ice pick: Appartus often used by magicians in conjunction with the "Funnell" or "the Chinese Wands" whereby the nose of a volunteer is apparently pierced.

Brady: Seat reserved for a friend of the management; so called after the American manager/impresario William A. Brady (1863-1950).

Brainwave deck: Magician's special deck of cards, which, in its simplest terms, can be used to show any card as reversed in the deck.

Brass: 1. Money (coin-sized pieces of brass) used by some old-time carnivals in lieu of standard currency. 2. Fake jewelry peddled by pitchmen.

Break: 1. General show-business term meaning the end of a performance. 2. Magic term for a space, gap, or division held in a deck of cards and maintained, normally by the tip of a finger. 3. *See* BLOW.

Break a leg: *see* I HOPE YOU BREAK A LEG.

Break in: In vaudeville, this was an out-of-the-way, small theatre where a new routine could be tried out.

Break the ice: For a pitchman,* the first sale of the day. *see also* PITCHMAN.

Breakaway: An object made to collapse easily at the pull of a string, the press of a concealed button, or by executing some similar device. A striptease* dancer might use a breakaway dress made to fall off at the pull of a string; an actor might use a breakaway knife with a blade made to recoil into the hilt at the push of a button; magicians use the term to describe numerous comedy properties, such as the breakaway fan and the breakaway wand, which seem to come to pieces in a spectator's hand. *see also* STRIPTEASE.

Breakdown: Originally a swift dance popular in minstrel shows and nineteenth-century English burlesque. In minstrelsy, it came also to mean sayings interjected into songs.

Breaking: The elementary training of a circus animal.

Breaking in an act: In vaudeville, the playing of an act until it runs smoothly. *see* BREAK IN.

Breen, Joseph I.: *see* JOEBREENED.

Breeze: Pitchmen's term for traveling from one place to another. Also fly, hop, jump or trot. *see* JUMP.

Bridge: In magicians' parlance, a gap or break in the deck of cards caused by bending some cards. *see* CRIMP.

Bring down the house: To elicit an enormous ovation from an audience.

British pantomime: *see* PANTOMIME.

Broad: In the carnival, a woman whose morals are doubtful, whether she works on the carnival, is just a spectator, or follows the carnival.

Broad mob: Carnival pitchman who works as a three-card monte* dealer and ultimately loses to broads.* *see also* BROADS and MONTE.

Broad tosser: A three-card monte* dealer on a circus lot,* rarely found with a carnival. Called broad after the queens in the deck frequently used by the operator. *see also* LOT, MONTE, and THREE-CARD MONTE MAN.

Broads: Circus term for tickets.

Brodie: General show-business word for a flop, failure, mistake, blunder, mixup. Literally, a show that takes a dive or a "bath," named after Steve Brodie, the man who is said to have dived or jumped from the Brooklyn Bridge on July 23, 1886. He was found in the water under the bridge, but his feat was never proved and thus without witnesses he jumped in vain. After the jump (or nonjump), he ran a very prosperous saloon on the Bowery.

Brother: Used by carnival women for a husband or steady. They say, ''I got a brother,'' meaning they are tied up or committed.

Brown top: The main tent at a chautauqua,* the equivalent of the circus's big top. The brown color of the chautauqua tent was to distinguish it from the white of the circus tent and thus symbolized its cultural inspiration. *see also* CHAUTAUQUA.

Brudder Bones: *see* BONES.

Brudder Tambo: *see* TAMBO.

Brush your teeth: Burlesque comic's retort to a Bronx cheer from the audience.

Brutal: Slang for a blow in vaudeville. *see* BLOW.

Brutal brothers: A vaudeville act in which the performers beat each other up to draw laughs.

Buck: Circus lingo for one dollar. *see* CASER.

Buck and wing: Originally, an American clog dance* popular in minstrel shows and marked by winglike steps. Later, popular in vaudeville. *see also* CLOG DANCE.

Bucket gunner: In the carnival and on most midways,* a hidden person who operates the gaff* on a bucket joint.* *see also* GAFF, JOINT, and MIDWAY.

Buckeye boy: Circus slang for a male native of Ohio, the Buckeye state.

Bucklebuster: In vaudeville and burlesque, a scream or a laugh line that would receive a large reaction from the audience.

Buffer: An English circus term for a dog. The English call performing dogs slanging buffers.

Buffoon: 1. A general term for a clown who is usually portrayed as a bumbling rustic and bases audience response on his supposed stupidity, broad humor, or burlesque of something serious. Early buffoons amused crowds at fairs and other gatherings with crude witticisms and obscene gestures or postures. 2. In opera, a male singer (usually a bass) who specializes in comic roles. 3. In the circus world, an Auguste* would be considered more a buffoon than a white-face clown.* *see also* AUGUSTE and WHITE-FACE CLOWN.

Bug: A flashlight carried by a circus or carnival night watchman. *see* CARRY THE BUG.

Bug board salesmen or bug-men: A circus vendor who sells live chameleons (and sometimes turtles) on the midway.* *see also* BUGS and MIDWAY.

Bugs: A term dating from the early nineteenth century. Most specifically, chameleons (and sometimes turtles) sold on the circus ground by vendors. Also used to describe any small, cheap item of merchandise sold by a novelty vendor or pitchman.

Build up or build-up: 1. Act performed by a pitchman* and his shills* to arouse the player's gambling spirit during a carnival game so that he will bet large sums. *see also* CON ACT, PITCH, PITCHMAN, and SHILL. 2. In the English fair, to assemble the rides, shows, and stalls or booths on the fairground. *see* FRAME.

Bull: Circus term for all elephants of either sex, although most elephants in American circuses are female. Also called pigs and rubber cows.

Bull act: A performing elephant act in the circus.

Bull-hand: A handler of circus elephants who helps to care for and sometimes to display and work elephants. Also called bull men.

Bull-hook: An elephant goad with a handle (usually wooden) and a metal hook, resembling a short boat hook (the ankus of India), used to help manage elephants in the circus. *see* HOOKING.

Bull-hooker: The trainer working with circus elephants. Also called bull-hands and bull men.

Bull line: Circus elephants on a picket line or in the menagerie.

Bull men: Men who handle elephants, or elephant keepers. Also called bull-hands and bull-hookers.

Bullswool: In the circus, slang for a sham or an untruth.

Bum: Pitchmen's term, especially in medicine shows,* for a mental defective, often a plant* or a shill.* *see also* MEDICINE SHOW, PLANT, and SHILL.

Bum rap: Pitchmen's slang for an indictment for a crime not committed by the person accused. Now in general usage.

Bum steer: Circus and carnival slang for sending one on a wild-goose chase or giving one the wrong information. It might also refer to cookhouse* meat. *see also* COOKHOUSE.

Bump: A movement by a striptease* performer or erotic dancer in which the pelvis is suddenly thrust forward. *see also* STRIPTEASE.

Bump reader: Circus term for a phrenologist.

Bumper cars: *see* DODGEMS.

Bun: Theatrical term from around the turn of the century describing what an intoxicated person had.

Bunch: 1. Theatrical term, now obsolete, for members of a chorus. 2. In the English circus, bunch means profits. *see* BOUNCE.

Burgess: Contemptuous pitchmen's term for a small-town justice or judge.

Burlesque: In its ultimate form, American burlesque combined elements of the revue* form with comedy acts and strip numbers. Its components included English and American literary burlesque and parody,* the circus, the knockabout farces of the medicine show* and dime museums,* popular farces, sketches of the minstrel show,* concert saloons and beer gardens, Western honky-tonks,* and even the stage Yankee.* The word comes from the Italian *"burla,"* a broad takeoff of some serious work, where laughter results from the contrasts between subject and treatment. American burlesque emphasized broad farcical treatments coupled with vaudeville-type entertainment. By its demise it had become a low comic show featuring girls underdressed and rough, bawdy humor in songs, acts, dances, and sketches.* When the word was outlawed in 1937 in New York City by Mayor Fiorello H. LaGuardia, the form had changed drastically, no longer emphasizing the humor and the comics, but placing more stress on the scantily clad females and, in time, the striptease.* Early in World War II, burlesque as a type of show was outlawed in New York, although today it is back in the form of strip clubs, strip theatres, or "burlesk." The comic is virtually gone, and even the strip has lost its artistry. *see also* BIT, DIME MUSEUM, MEDICINE SHOW, MINSTREL SHOW, PARODY, REVUE, SKETCH, STRIP, and STRIPTEASE.

Burlesque ingenue: Usually pronounced as "burlap ingenue," this is not a term of praise but suggests that the actress or performer is totally incompetent. Even if totally naked, a "burlap ingenue" would put the audience to sleep, turn them out of the theatre, or keep them from ever coming in.

Burlesque props: The basic necessities for a burlesque bit,* such as beds, hall trees, blank pistols, and bladders.* Most bladders used in burlesque were steer bladders bought from a slaughterhouse, dried, and then blown up. Although quite harmless, a loud noise was produced when one comic hit another. *see also* BIT, BLADDER, and THIRD BANANA.

Burley, burleycue, burlecue, burlicue: Alternate spellings and titles for a burlesque* show. *see also* BURLESQUE.

Burly show: This was the more specific name for a burlesque attraction at a carnival.

Burma circuit: Once a number-two theatrical circuit which played small towns. *see* KEROSENE CIRCUIT.

Burn: In the circus, to become irritated.

Burn the lot: *see* GILLY SHOW.

Burn up: To exploit, so as to make unprofitable through dishonest practice, a route, territory, or circus name. Pitchmen used the phrase "to burn up the territory" to indicate that an area or town did not have good business prospects because some of the more unscrupulous pitchmen had taken advantage of the people there and thus made the place "too hot" to work in. *see* LARRY SPOT.

Burnt cork: Makeup ingredient used by black-face* minstrels for darkening the skin. Also called smut. *see also* BLACK-FACE and MINSTREL BLACK.

Burr: Pitchmen's term for expenses. *see* NUT.

Burr-head: Minstrel term for a minstrel performer, so called after the furry wigs worn by most white performers in minstrel shows.* *see also* MINSTREL SHOW.

Bus: Theatrical shorthand for stage business. *see* BUSINESS.

Bus and truck: A theatrical company that plays off-the-track places, with the physical production traveling by truck and the company by bus. *see* MUD SHOW.

Business (Bus and Biz): 1. Any movement an actor makes on the stage when used to give extra meaning to the words or to get across a meaning without words. 2. Used in vaudeville and most other forms of popular entertainment to mean "the profession."

Busk: To show or give a performance on a street corner, vacant lot, or other location where passersby might stop, and then pass the hat for a collection of money. In England, the term, derived from "buskin," also means to journey about performing with simple theatrical equipment. *see* BUSKING.

Busker: A performer who entertains on the streets and then passes the hat after his show. Buskers may also be found in restaurants, taverns, or other public places. Today, several famous street entertainers appear nightly in front of several major New York theatres, and buskers in general are once more becoming common in most major cities here and abroad.

Busking: Performing for handouts. In the late-eighteenth century the word busking had the meaning of searching, and vagrants' slang of circa 1850, probably deriving from the standard English of the eighteenth century, gave it the meaning of going about probing for salvageable items, using a corset steel as a ragpicker might. This meaning also suggests a connection with the French "busc" or Italian "busco," or from the nautical term "busk," to cruise as a pirate.

Busking the crowd: Busker* performing his act in order to keep paying customers in a line until they get to the ticket window, or getting a crowd's attention so that they do not leave the immediate area. *see also* BUSKER.

(To) Bust or blow an arrow: When one-night stand* carnival operations followed arrows that could be seen in the middle of the night to their next stop and failed to see one or more, they were lost and thus "busting an arrow." *see also* ONE-NIGHT STAND.

Bust the lacing: *see* LACING.

Bust developer: A performer who croons offstage while a strip* number is being performed on stage. *see also* STRIP.

Buster: In the circus, an accidental or bad fall. Joseph "Buster" Keaton received his nickname from Harry Houdini after the young Keaton fell down a flight of stairs.

Butcher: A circus refreshment merchant or peddler. Also called a candy butcher. *see* BOSS BUTCHER.

Butter and egg man: Show-business slang for a naive or unsophisticated angel or backer of a show.

Butterfly: 1. In the English circus, an acrobatic movement. 2. In the American carnival, a term sometimes used to mean a woman.

Butterfly suspension act: *see* IRON-JAW.

Button: Circus word for an officer.

Button-buster: Circus slang for a braggart. *see* HANGING HIS OWN, PUTTING UP PAPER FOR YOURSELF, and THREE-SHEET OR THREE-SHEETING.

C

Cabaret: An intimate entertainment, often in a nightclub, restaurant, or some similar surrounding, performed while spectators eat or drink. The traditional, intimate nature of the cabaret as it developed in this century provides for more biting and outspoken humor than is normally possible in entertainment for larger audiences and halls, thus it has served as an important breeding ground for comic satirists. Today, some cabarets, such as those in Las Vegas, have grown into spectacular revues. *see also* REVUE.

Cabinet of curiosity: An early type of exhibit or museum, often displayed by strolling or traveling showmen, designed to entertain and amuse a largely uneducated and unsophisticated audience. Popular in the United States during its early history when there were few largely populated areas and legitimate or serious museums had yet to develop. An early form of the later dime museum.* *see also* DIME MUSEUM.

Cacky: Burlesque and striptease term for obscene or smutty.

Cage act: Any wild animal circus presentation requiring use of a steel cage in the circus ring.

Cage boy or cage-hand: In the circus, a wild-animal attendant, but not a handler, who feeds and waters the animals and cleans the cages. Sometimes this term refers to a trainer's assistant, who works outside the big cage.

Cain's: A storehouse for theatrical failures. *see* GO TO CAIN'S.

Cake: On the midway* of a carnival, and in some circuses, a short-con game.* *see also* CAKE CUTTER, MIDWAY, and SHORT-CON GAME.

Cake cutter or cut the strawberry cake: A short-change artist* or one who short-changes the public. Used primarily in the circus. Cake cutting is thus short-changing. *see also* SHORT-CHANGE ARTIST.

Cake eaters: In the carnival and circus, townies* or towners,* gawks, and rubes. In more general use, this refers to a ladies' man or a dude. *see also* GAWKS, RUBES, TOWNERS, and TOWNIES.

Cakes: Meals furnished in addition to pay in a Toby show* operation. *see also* AND CAKES and TOBY SHOW.

Cakewalk: 1. Originally, a competitive dance performed by American Negroes, for which the prize to the winning couple was a cake. The dance was noted for its lively music, high stepping, and proud carriage of the dancers. The couple with the most style would literally take the cake. 2. In terms of the fairground and amusement park, especially in England, it is an amusement device comprising oscillating bridges over which the public walks. Also called in England the Rock 'n' Roll.

Call: In the circus and the theatre, a notice to report or the specific time for rehearsal or performance; also, to be brought before the audience because of their extraordinary response.

Calliope: Popular circus musical instrument consisting of a series of steam whistles played like an organ. Circus people pronounce it "kally'-ope." Also called a *steam fiddle.*

Camel punk: In the circus, a boy who takes care of camels. *see* PUNKS.

Camp: As used in entertainment circles, camp had the meaning early in the century of outrageous behavior or bizarre or unusual-looking ladies with manners to match. It would be applied to such female impersonators as Julian Eltinge or to chorus boys. It has now become common usage in its meaning of consciously contriving a pretentious gesture, style, or form. *see* FEMALE IMPERSONATOR.

Canary: Circus and carnival term for an informer.

Candy boss: *see* BOSS BUTCHER.

Candy butcher: In burlesque, a hawker who peddled his wares during intermission in "raucous times and murderous English." *see* BOSS BUTCHER.

Candy top: Circus tent housing outside candy concessions.

Cane brakes: Pitchmen's slang for the people of Louisiana, especially those who lived in small towns and rural districts.

Canvas boss: Circus and tent-show supervisor of the tent put-up and tear-down.

Canvas men: Circus tent-show men who work on canvas tents. *see* ROUGHNECK and ROUSTABOUTS.

Caper: Outdoor entertainment term for a thieving or fraudulent exploit.

Capper: 1. In pitchmen's slang, an assistant, confederate, or shill* in a confidence game who is used to win. *see also* BOOSTER, COME-ON, SHILLS, and STICK. 2. Also used to describe a sideshow* worker who, when patrons are hesitant to buy tickets, rushes up and buys an entrance ticket in hopes a crowd will follow. Usually more than one capper is needed to make this move successful; thus cappers. *see also* SIDESHOW.

Captain, major, or colonel: O'Brien describes these as circus and midway* troupers who carry military titles bestowed upon them by their help. *see also* MIDWAY.

Caravan: A carnival troupe that travels overland with all their baggage and equipment. *see* MUD SHOW.

Cards: Carnival term for window cards used for advertising, known in the business by such names as dobs, dates, and snipes.* see DATE SHEETS and SNIPE.

Card box: In magic apparatus, a box rigged for vanishing, exchanging, or producing a playing card.

Card index: Piece of magical apparatus made of manila board fastened together at the bottom and sides in such a way as to hold twenty-six cards in the pockets formed by the manila board. The cards are then arranged in overlapping rows, each card projecting from its pocket. With the index, any card can be found by touch with the fingering of not more than four cards.

Card setups: Arranging all or some of the playing cards used by a magician in an order memorized by the performer.

Carnie: *see* CARNIFOLKS, CARNY, and Z-LATIN.

Carnifolks: In the professional outdoor amusement industry, a collective amusement organization consisting of shows, riding devices, and various types of gaming concessions. It is possible for a carnival to incorporate in its organization a circus as one of the shows on a carnival midway.* A circus may also include a carnival midway. *see also* BACK-END, FRONT-END, and MIDWAY.

(The) Carnival: Insiders' name for the Hagenbeck-Wallace Circus, a major circus operation during the first quarter of this century.

Carnival dice games: Popular percentage games found at carnivals and in other kinds of gambling joints, including "Beat the Dealer," "Hazard," "Chuck-a-Luck," and "Under and Over Seven." Similar are games like "Penny Pitch," "Skillo," and "Ring Toss." *see also* JOINT and PERCENTAGE OR P.C. STORE.

Carnival louse (lice): A hanger-on who follows a carnival but who has no official connection with it. Also called carnivalites. *see also* LOT LICE.

Carnival wheel: A traditional carnival game that comes in many variations but all still basically the same. They may be called "Big Six," "Money Wheel," or "Racehorse Wheel," but all adhere to the following pattern. The wheel, usually of wood, rotates around a steel or bronze bearing mounted on a steel axle that is set either horizontally or vertically. A circular area around the wheel's rim is divided into sections, usually painted in flashy colors or bearing numbers. A nail or pin projects from the wheel's surface between each section, and these projections brush against a leather, rubber, or plastic indicator or spring fixed to a wall or post of some kind. When the wheel stops, the indicator is between two nails or pins, and the section at which it points is the winning section. *see* FLASHER, FLAT JOINT OR STORES, and SPINDLE.

Carnivalites: *see* CARNIVAL LOUSE.

Carny (carney, or carnie): A corruption of carnival. Also refers to a carnival worker or one who is "with" a carnival (well-integrated into it), the carnival world, and the special idiom, language, or argot spoke by carnival workers. *see* Z—LATIN.

Carny's Christmas: Labor day on the midway* of a large fair, amusement park, or carnival. *see also* MIDWAYS.

Carny wedding: A common-law union between carnival men and women usually lasting one season, although some have been lifetime arrangements and have been made legal unions. *see* BILLBOARD WEDDING.

Carousel or carrousel: Originally, an equestrian sport practiced in Arabia and Turkey during the twelfth century, although the earliest visual record of such a device appears to be a Byzantine bas-relief of some 1,500 years ago. Later it became an elaborate spectacle involving tournaments and ultimately the carousel or "merry-go-round." The word carousel has been used most extensively in the United States and on the continent. The English equivalent is most usually called a roundabout,* galloper, or tilt. In the United States, it has been called many names, including flying horses, jenny, whirligig, flying Dutchmen, flying jenny or jinny, Kelly's goats, spinning jenny or jinny, hobby horses, steam circus, steam riding galleries, galloping-horse steam carousels, and carry-us-alls. *see also* ROUNDABOUTS.

Carpet: In the circus, the covering of the ring* area on which acts perform. *see also* CARPET ACT and RING.

Carpet act: An acrobatic act worked on the ground, usually on a carpet* spread over the sawdust or in the ring* area. *see also* CARPET and RING.

Carpet clown: In simplest terms, a clown who works either among the audience or on the arena floor, thus on the carpet.* Today such a clown is a fill-in performer used several times during a show, doing reprises between the acts. In English circus, called a run-in clown. Sometimes this clown is also known as a production clown, for if something unforeseen occurs behind the scenes the clown may be required to perform for an extended period of time. *see also* CARPET and CLOWN STOP.

Carps: Theatrical name for stage carpenters; rarely used today.

Carry lumber: Circus expression meaning to carry seat boards, Bible-backs* or seat stringers. *see also* BIBLE-BACKS.

Carry the banner: Phrase used in the circus and carnival and by most pitchmen to mean having to sleep in a park, stay up all night, or walk the streets because of not having a bed or being penniless.

Carry the bug: Circus and carnival phrase meaning to work as a night watchman with a flashlight. *see* BUG.

Cars: The name given by railroad traveling outdoor shows to sleeping cars.

Cascade: 1. In circus acrobatics, a series of tumbling tricks without pause, also known as tumbling pass. 2. In solo juggling, this is the most basic three-ball pattern, that is, the safe home ground which jugglers usually work from and return to. The balls follow patterns which cross, thus creating a lively bubbling effect. *see* SHOWER.

Cascadeur: An acrobatic clown or a tumbler who specializes in knock-about comedy and falls or cascades. *see* ACROBATIC-EQUESTRIAN CLOWN and CASCADE.

Case money: Early twentieth-century theatrical and vaudeville term implying to be down to the last penny.

Caser: Pitchmen's term for looking over the prospective customers so that the pitchman will be able to judge to some extent the amount of business he will be able to do.

Casting act: Principally, an English circus term for an aerial act in which the flyer* is thrown from one performer to another. *see also* FLYER.

Cat: 1. In traveling carnivals and midways, a Caterpillar or any other track-laying type of tractor. 2. In the circus, a member of the feline family, be it a lion, tiger, panther, leopard or the like.

Cat act: Any performance of a group of large performing cats or felines in the circus.

Cat den: A cage for circus cats. *see* BIG CAGE.

Cat rack: A midway* game in which the player tries to knock dummy cats made of canvas off a fence or platform with balls. *see also* BIG TOM, MIDWAY, MODUC, and SIX-CAT.

Cat rack queen: A female operator or agent* on a ball-throwing cat rack concession.*see also* AGENT.

Catch or grab a handful of boxcars: Circus phrase meaning to leave the show and ride a freight train out of town.

Catch all tricks: In vaudeville and burlesque, the ability of the drummer to provide sound effects through sight cues for pratfalls, bumps* and grinds, by striking various items in his trap case such as a cowbell, ratchet, or tom-tom. *see also* BUMPS, CATCH THE BUMPS, and GRIND.

Catch the bumps: Stripper's bumps effectively marked with the drummer's rim-shots. *see* BUMP.

Catch trap: One name for the trapeze used by a catcher* in an aerial act. *see also* CATCHER.

Catcher: In a circus aerial act or flying trapeze act,* the member of the team who catches the flyer* after he leaves the trapeze or hands of another catcher.* The catcher is roughly the equivalent of a bottom man* and is frequently not given the credit he deserves, although a good catcher, through expert timing, can often make a mediocre flyer look much better. *see also* BOTTOM MAN, CATCHER, FLYER, and FLYING TRAPEZE ACT.

Caterpiller: *see* SWITCHBACK.

Cattle guards: In the circus, low seats placed in front of the blues* or general admission seats in order to accommodate overflow audiences. *see also* BLUES.

Cats: In the circus and carnival, rebel-yelling, troublesome southern hillbillies.

Catwalk: *see* RUNWAY.

Caviar set: Theatrical term once used to describe a snobby circle.

Center: *see* SPLITS.

Center or centre door fancy: 1. In vaudeville, an interior set with an ornamental arch and dressed with fine draperies. 2. In the Toby show,* a set representing a wealthy man's drawing room with an arch up center (wall farthest from audience), doors right and left, and usually with a table and chairs right and a settee left. Also known as front room set. *see also* TOBY SHOW.

Center pole: A large perpendicular pole that holds up the circus tent at the peak and is the first pole of the tent to be raised. Also called the main mast. *see* KING POLE, MAINMAST, QUARTER POLE, and SIDE POLE.

Center tear: A magician's maneuver allowing the performer to ascertain the contents of a secretly written message.

Century: Circus, carnival, and other entertainment forms use this to mean a one-hundred-dollar bill or the same amount in smaller denominations.

Chain team: A circus term for a six- or eight-horse team rigged with an extra set of lead bars or double trees and an extra body pole,* while dragging a long heavy chain. Such a team was expecially useful in pulling wagons on muddy or sandy lots. Used correctly, as many as sixty-four horses could be hooked to one wagon. *see also* BODY POLE and HOOKROPES.

Chain to rails: This describes a circus that has been prevented from moving by legal interference, because it has been attached, declared bankrupt, or placed in receivership.

Chair seats: Seats with backs sold at an extra charge at tent repertoire shows. *see* INSIDE BOX.

Chalk-eater: A horserace gambler whose preference is to bet on the favorite, in particular an odds-on favorite.

Chalker: A circus worker who chalks or blocks wheels of wagons on trains. *see* CHOKERS.

Chambermaids' frolic: An all-female aerial ladder act in the circus.

Chandeliers: The name given in the circus to gasoline, kerosene, or gas lamps pulled in clusters around the circus poles to light the tents (before electricity). *see also* CENTER POLE.

Chandy: *see* SHANDY.

Changeover palm: A sleight in magic for transferring an object from one palm to another while in each instance showing the free hand empty. *see also* SLEIGHT or SLEIGHT-OF-HAND.

Chanteuse: In show business, this refers to a French female who can't sing and consequently talks the song. Extended to mean any continental "singer" who can't sing.

Character clown: Type of clown in the English circus who usually dresses in a tramp costume. *see* TRAMP CLOWN.

Character man or woman: In stock and repertory companies especially, an actor who plays certain character parts.

Characters: A circus and carnival tag for people not connected with the show.

Charivari, chivaree, or shivaree: In the circus, despite other meanings and a medieval or earlier origin, this is a noisy whirlwind entrance of clowns (and sometimes acrobats dressed as clowns) performing simultaneously with high energy and good-natured chaos. A charivari is often scheduled to begin or end a circus performance. Some sources trace its origin to the name for the ballooning pants worn by tenth-century or earlier Arab acrobats whose performance ended with a free-for-all period with the air filled with flowing "charivari." Others relate its character to the medieval custom of public ridicule.

Charley or Charlie: 1. A circus *tramp clown.** Such a clown originally was a black-face comic who wore a derby hat, tattered clothes, and worked through pathos. A Charley was also an English music-hall comedian dressed as a tramp or hobo. Charlie Chaplin, who began in the halls, supposedly adopted this character from a music-hall comic. Emmett Kelly was a type of Charley clown in the United States. *see also* TRAMP CLOWN. 2. In the English circus, especially, a wastepaper container in the car carrying the bills.* *see* BILL.

(To) Charley the hod: Circus phrase used by billposters to describe getting rid of some of the posters (the "hod") that are scheduled to be put up. *see* CHARLEY.

Charlier system: A method of marking cards originally by pricking minute holes in them at specified locations; named after the nine-teenth-century conjurer and magical inventer, Charlier, who originated the method.

Charter fair: An English fair established by royal charter or decree, as opposed to ancient fairs of Anglo-Saxon or earlier origin, which were established by prescription. *see* HIRING FAIR, MOP FAIR, and STATUTE FAIR.

Chase: 1. Carnival slang for being on the make. 2. Theatrical and circus meaning for an exit march or other music played as an audience leaves. 3. Also used to indicate the finale in an entertainment. *see* CHASER.

Chaser: A vaudeville act designed and placed in the final position of a bill* of acts to persuade the audience to leave the theatre, rather than stay to see the show a second time. Early movies were originally thought of as serving this function, especially the one-reel variety. For a time, ironically, they succeeded in this role before displacing vaude-ville. In continuous vaudeville,* a chaser might be placed in the open-ing position in order to clear patrons from the house who had already seen the show. *see also* BILL and CONTINUOUS OR CONTINUOUS VAUDE-VILLE.

Chat: English circus slang for anything or any object.

Chautauqua: A cultural and educational movement in the United States started in the summer of 1874 as a tent meeting on the shores of Lake Chautauqua in New York State. In a short time, there were chautauqua tents all over the country traveling established circuits, usually in the summer months. Show business crept in quite rapidly and a good chautauqua act, because of the extensive circuits, could sustain itself for several years. A typical chautauqua program would combine elements of vaudeville and dramatic sketches (plus the usual lectures and other "cultural" attractions). The advent of radio in the 1920s killed chautauqua, although the permanent home in New York State is still quite active.*see* LYCEUM.

Chavies: English circus term for children. Also called feeliers.

Cheaters: Pitchmen's term, borrowed from the criminal world, for spectacles or eyeglasses. *see* GLIMS and GOOGS.

Cheesecake: Photographs of female performers who display attractive areas of their anatomy for publicity purposes.

Cherry or chairy pie: Extra work done by circus personnel for extra pay (normally) necessitated by being shorthanded.

Chestnut: In the 1880s, this meant an old joke or a *Joe Miller.* * *see also* JOE MILLER.

Chesty: Early twentieth-century term for an actor who has a tendency to overrate his ability.

Chewing the scenery: Description of the zealous overacting common among third-rate performers on the kerosene circuit* or in the tents. Also called tearing a passion to tatters. *see also* KEROSENE CIRCUIT.

Chi: Show-business abbreviation for Chicago.

Chicago G-string: An especially revealing type of G-string* used by strippers which is sewn to an elastic waistband in a manner that allows "the bauble to fly" and reveal pudendum underneath. *see also* G-STRING.

Chicken: A circus clown who juggles; not commonly used in the American circus.

Chief: An executive title used in some circus operations.

Chill: Circus slang for halt.

Chiller: Show-business slang for melodrama; used rather indiscriminately.

China!: A circus exclamation used when the show moves into a new circus town.

(The) China circuit: The name given to a group of Pennsylvania towns (Pottstown, Pottsville, and Chambersburg) because of the china chamber pots made there; by extension, a circuit of small and relatively unsophisticated towns.

Chinee: Although not used very extensively in show business, this slang word for Chinese meant a complimentary ticket to an entertainment, usually a sporting event.

Chinese: Slang for doing heavy work around a circus lot, frequently without pay.

Chiseler: Underworld and outdoor amusement word for one who cheats, swindles, or uses some kind of petty connivance. Also called a chiz. *see* GYP.

Chiz: Show-business slang for a chiseler.* *see also* CHISELER.

Chokers: Circus workers who handle wagon-wheel blocks on the railroad flatcars. *see* CHALKER.

Chooser: A vaudevillian who stole some part of another performer's act for his or her own use.

Choosing day: A fairly uncommon practice among the older circus concerns of designating a day early in the season when unmarried personnel selected berth mates of the opposite sex for the season. No changes were to be made after that day.

Chopped grass: Pitchmen's slang for herb medicines. Used especially by medicine showmen. *see* MED MEN.

Chorine: Fairly contemporary American term for a chorus girl.* *see also* CHORUS GIRL.

Chorus girl: A female performer in the chorus of a musical, revue,* or the like. In burlesque, a chorus girl simply hoofed and sang in the ensemble. Frequently, however, chorus girls did not sing, and thus the phrase "dumb as a chorus girl" had literal as well as figurative connotations. An important stepping-stone for many subsequent stars, however. *see also* REVUE.

Chow: Medicine-show slang for incidental expenses.

Chowmeinery: Show-business slang for a Chinese restaurant.

Chuck: *see* GORGE and SCOFFINS.

Chump: Common term among most outdoor amusement workers and burlesque personnel meaning one who is easily duped or deluded. By extension, it is used to identify a paying customer or patron. *see* LUKEN, MARK, MOOCH, RUM or RUMMY, SAP, and SUCKER.

Chump educator: Originally this meant *Billboard,** the weekly publication devoted to the amusement business. Since 1960, *Billboard* has been a music magazine and has little of interest on outdoor shows. *Amusement Business* is the latest chump educator. The theatrical chump educator is *Variety*. Both publications "educate" chumps or outsiders. *see also* BILLBOARD.

Chump heister: A ferris wheel* on a carnival lot. Also called a hoister. *see also* FERRIS WHEEL.

Chump twister: A carousel* or merry-go-round at a carnival. *see also* CAROUSEL.

Chutes: Circus term for the inclined runs or chutes on which circus wagons are loaded on and unloaded from the flatcars. *see also* CROSSING and RUNS.

Chutzpah: Yiddish phrase, meaning colossal gall, adopted by outdoor amusement industry.

Cigar: From the carnival talker's* or spieler's* "give the man a big cigar," a prize for winning at a game, this has come to mean in the carnival a compliment. *see also* SPIELER and TALKER.

Cigarette fiend: A specialized sideshow freak attraction dating from the 1890s when cigarettes were an obnoxious novelty, linked with fantastic tales of what happened to unfortunates who smoked a pack a day. They turned yellow and stayed that way, living on a diet of nicotine, which sustained them instead of food, for their systems were saturated. A cigarette fiend then, was an artificial, man-made freak—a nicotine addict.

Cincy: Show-business abbreviation for Cincinnati.

Circle stock: Term used by traveling repertoire companies for playing the same play for a stated period, such as three days, first in one town and then in another. The same towns would be played in a cycle for the same length of time but with a change in play.

Circus: 1. An entertainment, as known in the United States, dating from the equestrian training circle of the eighteenth century, which has come to mean a traveling and organized display of animals, clowns, and skilled performances within one or more circular areas known as rings* before an audience encircling these activities. The American circus quickly moved toward mobility and size (as typified by the three rings), while most European circuses have remained permanent and follow the one-ring tradition. The American circus also exploited the menagerie, the sideshow of freaks, and other additional shows secondary to the main attractions. *see* EQUESTRIAN DRAMA and RING. 2. Used to describe an extravagant style of production or a theatre. 3. An obscene show, usually with a naked dance or nude dancing. 4. To reverse a scene or certain pieces of scenery so that the audience will see the other side—to circus a scene.

(To) circus a scene: *see* CIRCUS.

Circus bees: Body lice found, at one time, in great abundance about the smaller circuses and tent shows, especially when laborers were forced to sleep two in a berth and cleanliness was next to impossible. Also called circus squirrels, crumbs, and seam squirrels.

Circus job: An extravagant publicity effort in an attempt to promote a show, frequently one destined to fail.

Circus sideshow: Name used by carnival freak-show owners to designate their attraction.

Circus simple: The name given to someone obsessed with the circus, in particular anyone who ran away to join the circus.

Circus squirrels: *see* CIRCUS BEES.

City of Bang Bang: Pitchmen's slang for Chicago; reference is to the gangster wars for which Chicago was once known.

Civilian: Vaudeville's word for anyone not in show business.

Clairvoyance: *see* MENTALISM.

Classic dancer: An early cooch dancer* who specialized in interpretations of classical mythology. *see also* COOCH or COOTCH DANCING.

Claw: Show-business slang for one of a gang of pickpockets, used principally in the outdoor amusement world. *see* DIP, GUN, PRATTMAN, and (THE) SHOVE.

Clay, stick, and button: An illegal game played at English fairs in which a button, perched on a stick, had to be knocked onto a piece of clay to win a prize.

Clean: Circus term for devoid of anything of value.

Cleaner: An employee of a joint* who takes paid players aside and recovers the money or prizes they have won in order to make an impression on the crowd. *see also* JOINT.

Cleaning the stick: *see* STICK.

Cleffer: Show-business slang for a songwriter.

Clem: 1. In hobo cant, as a verb, clem means to starve. 2. In circus parlance, a local resident, any outsider, a rustic, or a small-town resident, one easily hoaxed or taken in. 3. Its most common meaning is that of a general fight or riot between town hoodlums who attack shows and the circus or carnival employees. Probably originated in the days of horse-drawn circuses when the townspeople and the show folk were at odds. 4. As an interjection, clem has replaced Hey rube!* as a battle cry for a forthcoming fight.

Click: In circus and theatre, especially vaudeville, a rousing success or accomplishment. *see* GET ACROSS WITH A BANG.

Clicker: A pass to an entertainment. *see* ANNIE OAKLEY, DUCAT, and SKULL.

Cliffhanger or cliffer: A melodramatic serial in which each chapter ends with the hero or heroine on the brink of disaster. Applied most specifically to film.

Climax: In vaudeville, the climax was the highest point of interest in a series of words or events and not used precisely as in the climax of a play in theatrical terms.

Clink: Circus slang for a jail.

Clip joint or clip-joint: General term for a place of public entertainment where one is likely to be cheated, swindled, robbed, or overcharged. *see* JOINT.

Clipped: Circus and some carnival use; to be without funds or deprived of possessions.

Clobber: English circus term for clothes.

Clog dance: A dance in which clogs or heavy shoes are worn for hammering out a lively rhythm. Popular in early variety and to a lesser extent in vaudeville. *see* LANCASHIRE CLOG.

Close the show: In vaudeville, the opposite of open the show.* The last act on a vaudeville bill. *see also* OPEN THE SHOW.

Closed town: Pitchmen's term for a town in which pitchmen are refused a license.

(To) close-in: In vaudeville, to drop a curtain.

Close-up magic: Magic using small apparatus and requiring the audience to be quite close to the magician. Most magicians popular in vaudeville used stage magic as opposed to close-up or parlor magic. *see* DRAWINGROOM MAGIC and PLATFORM TRICKS.

Closing woman: In burlesque, the featured woman in a show; the top banana* of the women. *see* BANANA and TOP BANANA.

Closs, Gravediggers, or Zekes: Circus slang for hyenas.

Clothes-horse: *see* SHOW GIRL.

Cloud swing: A midair circus performance on swinging ropes. *see* WEB.

Clown: According to John Towsen, clown is an English word that appeared first in the sixteenth century. Today, a clown is considered a comic performer who engages in eccentric or stupid behavior, frequently specializing in slapstick, physical humor. In the English circus, clown is used most frequently to describe the white-faced comic in a spangled costume (the Auguste* clown is called simply the Auguste).

Clown (capitalized) is also the name of the principal comic servant, popularized first by Joseph Grimaldi, in British or Christmas pantomime. *see also* AUGUSTE, JOEY, and WHITE-FACE CLOWN.

Clown alley: Originally, an aisle in the circus dressing tent occupied exclusively by clowns. When a man became a clown, he "went into clown alley." Today, if such a special area is part of a circus, it is the dressing tent or area where clowns put on their makeup and costumes and store their props. It also can be used to mean the corps of clowns and, infrequently, circus life in general.

Clown fiddler: A type of clown who carries a violin and uses it in various comic routines; e.g., to mime in mock seriousness a classical musician; to fill in a dramatic pause in the program with an off-key fiddle rendition; or to serenade in an absurd way some female member of the audience.

Clown stop: Brief appearance of circus clowns while props or equipment are changed or cleared from the circus arena. In English circus, called a run-in clown. *see* CARPET CLOWN.

Clown walk-around: *see* WALK-AROUND.

Clown white: Makeup material used by clowns and other performers to whiten the face. It was once made with a base of white lead, which was dangerous (some believed fatal) for the performer, although it now is made of zinc oxide. Some think white lead was responsible for American pantomime artist George L. Fox's derangement.

Clowning the come-in: *see* (TO) WORK THE COME-IN.

Club(s): The juggling implement used in most classic juggling acts. Once called Indian clubs, these clubs are often made by the juggler to suit individual needs and specialties.

Club passing: The routine of tossing clubs between two or more jugglers. *see* CLUB(S).

Coat-tail puller: A carnival term for one who attempts to pull a sucker away from a game or concession.

Cocktailery: A cocktail lounge.

Coconuts: Pitchmen's slang for money.

Coffee-and-cake time: Show-business phrase for small-time or bush league.

Coffee grinder: A type of classic act in striptease* involving a particularly strenous type of grind.* *see also* GRIND and STRIPTEASE.

Coffin: *see* BILLING IN A BOX.

Coils: 1. In pitchmen's slang, any kind of electrical gadget. 2. Magicians use this word to identify rolls of paper ribbons used in production, although they are given more specific names depending on their size and purpose (e.g., mouth, hat, or tambourine coils).

Coin happy: Show-business for being hungry for money or for making money.

Cold: Used in various forms of popular entertainment, such as the circus, vaudeville, and popular theatre, to mean a town or audience that does not respond readily, or a town in which small profits are made. It also is used to indicate an opening without rehearsal. *see* BLOOMER and RED.

Cold audience: A more specific term for an unresponsive audience. *see* COLD and COLD HOUSE.

Cold deck: Circus slang for one who cheats at anything.

Cold house: Like cold audience,* this refers to an audience that is unresponsive, although it does not suggest that the performance is weak or ineffective. *see also* COLD AUDIENCE.

Cold reading: A technical term in magic circles for fortune-telling or mind reading that relies on basic information that fits many persons, modified by the performer's careful psychological appraisal of the individual and additional data gleaned from the individual without the subject's being aware that such material is of value to the performer or that the performer is pumping the subject.

Colonel: One name given the manager of a circus. *see* GAFFER, GOVERNOR, and MAIN GUY.

Columbia wheel: The first major burlesque circuit, led by Sam Scribner, which began in 1905. *see* BURLESQUE, MUTUAL WHEEL, and WHEEL.

Combination: A type of touring company during the latter half of the nineteenth century that carried all that was necessary for a performance. *see* COMBINATION SYSTEM.

Combination house: A theatre that catered to a combination* company. *see also* COMBINATION.

Combination system: The name given to the practice of touring combinations. The combination system in time displaced the resident stock company,* since it was cheaper to book a traveling company and made it possible for theatres to feature fairly current New York productions. *see* COMBINATION.

Combo: Circus term for an act of versatility, or doubling in other acts.

Come-in: The interval of approximately thirty minutes between the gate opening of a circus and the grand entry or start of the show itself. *see* PARADE.

Come in to get warm: This was said of an audience that did not respond to the performers, especially in vaudeville.

Come-in worker: *see* TOBY CLOWN.

Come-on: In the circus and carnival, an employee who functions as an inducement to attract a crowd by buying the first ticket to an attraction, purchasing the first item from a huckster, or by gambling in order to entice real customers. *see* BOOSTER, CAPPER, LUGGER, SHILL and STICK.

Come-ons: The suckers or boobs that are easy marks* for the come-on.* *see also* COME-ON and MARK.

Comedy act: In vaudeville, a comic specialty* act. *see also* SPECIALTY.

Comedy team: A mainstay of burlesque and vaudeville. Two actors, like Weber and Fields or Smith and Dale, whose routines depended on the close rapport between them. The most successful teams worked with one as the comedian and the other as the straight man.* *see also* STRAIGHT MAN.

Comic opera or light opera: In the United States, a major early type of American musical with roots in the European-based operetta. Most American comic operas were little more than poor imitations of the imported originals and were plentiful from the late 1880s until their peak of popularity in the first decade of the twentieth century. Victor Herbert was the greatest composer to write for the American comic opera. It should be noted that, especially in the European form, comic opera was also used to describe dramatic shows, often romantic or even with tragic elements, with spoken dialogue and songs and dances, such as the work of Gilbert and Sullivan or Offenbach.

Comic up in all: A Toby-show* and tent-repertoire* phrase meaning a comic could dismantle the tent and help put it up (take-down and put-up). *see also* REPERTOIRE and TOBY SHOW. 2. It also was used to suggest that the actor's wife could play second lead characters, play an instrument, or assist the show in some other manner.

Comic's skull: The humorous facial expressions and takes of a burlesque comic. *see* SKULL and TAKE.

Comicer: A comedian in a comedy team.* *see also* COMEDY TEAM.

Commissary: A supply wagon for circus employees.

Committeeman: Circus and carnival term for the head of a concern or an organization, who can get a show anything it needs, but seldom does.

Commonwealth basis or show: Traveling repertoire-show (especially tent shows) system whereby the manager and the members of the company shared equally in the expenses and profits of a show. Although the system was rarely equitable for all concerned, during the latter period of the repertoire shows, when salaries were hard to guarantee, it was quite common. Some early circuses also used this system.

Comp: Abbreviation for a complimentary or free ticket and, by extension, a nonpaying guest or spectator. *see* FREEBEE.

Competish: Show-business slang for competition.

Complaint room: *see* OFFICE.

Con: 1. As a noun, an abbreviation for a confidence game. 2. As a verb, it means to persuade a person to do something against his own interest after the sucker's* confidence has been won. *see also* SHORT-CON GAME and SUCKER.

Con act: *see* BUILDUP.

Concert: 1. In the circus, an extra show after the main performance. This was usually a short program of an unusual or specially advertised feature. *see* AFTER SHOW. 2. Similar to the circus, the Toby show* often included a special performance called a concert, which was a brief show, either several vaudeville acts or a one-act farce, given, for additional money, after the main performance. The tickets were usually sold during intermission before the last act. *see also* BLOW OFF and TOBY SHOW.

Concert hall: The name given to many small-town theatres in the nineteenth century, along with other names such as town hall or the opera house, to give the theatres the aura of respectability and cultural acceptability. The names used had little to do with the type of entertainment seen within.

Concession: In the outdoor amusement business, a merchandise, food, or gaming booth or joint.* *see also* JOINT.

Concession agent: The operator of a concession,* in particular a sales or gaming concession. The agents of such gaming concessions as flat joints* or stores and hanky-panks* are paid like salesmen, in that they receive a small salary plus a commission. Flat store operators are called flatties.* *see also* CONCESSION, FLAT JOINTS OR STORES, FLATTIE, and HANKY-PANK.

Concessionaires or concessioners: Those who have bought the rights to operate various concessions* from a circus or carnival. A similar practice is followed in many theatres, where a person buys the right to operate a refreshment stand, hatcheck room, and so forth. *see also* CONCESSION.

Confederate: In a magic show, the equivalent to a shill,* a secret assistant who aids the magician in performing some trick or routine. To further the confederate's secret role, this person is often planted in the audience to appear later as a volunteer.* *see also* ASSISTANT, SHILL, STOOGE, and VOLUNTEER.

Conflict with: Carnival phrase to describe a grind show* duplicating another show booked by a carnival. *see also* GRIND SHOW.

Confusion: Magician's term for presenting so many details that an audience cannot tell the important secret moves from the innocent ones and is thus fooled. *see* MISDIRECTION.

Conjurer's choice: Magician's term for presenting only one choice—his own. *see* FORCE.

Conjuring: Generally considered synonymous with magic; thus, one who performs magic is a conjurer. Originally, conjuring was believed to be the calling up or conjuring of demons to gain supernatural help in performing miracles.

Connection: In a tent circus, the narrow, enclosed passageway between the menagerie and the main tent (the big top*), or between the pad room* or dressing tent and the big top. It sometimes is used to mean any areaway between any two tents, or the strip of canvas connecting any two tents. *see also* BIG TOP and PAD ROOM.

Connection box: Circus term for the ticket box in the connection.* *see also* CONNECTIONS.

Connection man: Circus slang for a grifter.* *see also* GRIFTER.

Continuous or continuous vaudeville: Used to describe a vaudeville show that repeated itself several times. The British termed such an arrangement continuous variety or nonstop variety. American performers sought freedom from continuous engagements in two-a-day* theatres. *see also* TWO-A-DAY.

(To) contract: In traveling tent-show lingo, to arrange for a lot* and a license or to play under sponsorship in a particular town. This is the job of the headman.* *see also* HEADMAN and LOT.

Contracting agent: A circus advance agent* or advance man* who, six weeks in advance of a date, spent one day at the site ordering provisions from local farmers and merchants, finding room and board for the advertising men, getting space for posting ads, and securing licenses for the show. *see also* ADVANCE AGENT OR ADVANCE MAN.

Conundrums: Riddles whose answers involve puns; used extensively in black-face minstrelsy.* *see also* MINSTREL SHOW and MINSTRELSY.

Convicts: Circus slang for zebras.

Cooch or cootch dancing: A precursor of the striptease,* called the hootchy-kootchy (or hoochie-coochie), from the belly dance but punctuated with bumps* and grinds* and a combination of exposure, erotic movements, and teasing. Found originally in both carnivals and circuses. *see also* BUMP, GRIND, and STRIPTEASE.

Cooch show or coochie show: A ''dancing girl'' show in which the female performers did the cooch or cootch. Once a common sideshow* or under canvas show featured at carnivals, circuses, and med shows.* *see also* COOCH OR COOTCH DANCING, MED SHOW, SIDESHOW, and UNDER CANVAS.

Cook top: *see* TOP.

Cookhouse: Circus or carnival dining facilities. In traveling tent circuses the cookhouse is usually a low-squatting tent called cookhouse by performers and the cookhouse by workmen. Most carnival cookhouses serve the general public as well, or, as DeBelle states it: ''Midway scoffery where early morning diners and knockers* meet.'' Also called crumb castles. *see also* KNOCKERS.

Cookhouse gang: Circus term for the employees in a cookhouse* who erect and take down the tent and its contents. *see also* COOKHOUSE.

Cookie-cutter or cooky-cutter: Circus slang for a policeman's badge; by extension, a policeman. *see* COP, DICK, FUZZ, SHAMUS, and TINS.

(To) cool him off: In a carnival, the act of taking a mark* or victim aside and consoling him when he has lost so that he will not complain to the police or cause a disturbance in close proximity to the joint* or concession.* *see also* COOL OUT, COOLING THE MARK, CONCESSION, JOINT, and MARK.

Cool out: Convincing a mark* that he has not been taken. *see also* (TO) COOL HIM OFF, COOLING THE MARK, and MARK.

Cooling the mark: Rewarding with a prize after taking a lot of money from a mark* is one way to cool him off.* *see also* (TO) COOL HIM OFF, COOL OUT, and MARK.

Coon: Deprecating term for a Negro; a survival of the old black-face* minstrel days. *see also* BLACK-FACE and MINSTREL SHOW.

Coon song: Popular songs around the turn of the century with racist overtones that helped to perpetuate negative images of Negroes. They combined ragtime rhythms with lyrics that ridiculed Negroes with a new vehemence. When sung in minstrel shows, the performers emphasized grotesque physical caricatures of big-lipped, pop-eyed black people, and added the menacing image of razor-toting, violent black men. Typical titles were: "Nobody's Lookin' But de Owl and de Moon," "He's Just a Little Nigger, But He's Mine, All Mine," "The Phrenologist Coon," and "Coon, Coon, Coon, How I Wish My Color Would Change."

Cop: 1. Carnival and circus word meaning, in verb form, to steal, cheat, or confiscate. 2. In carnival parlance, the noun form means a win; in circus circles, an officer. *see* COOKIE-CUTTER, DICK, FUZZ, SHAMUS, and TINS.

Cop-a-feel: Drawing upon the meaning of cop,* this slang expression means, as DeBelle defines it, a popular outdoor midway sport enjoyed mostly by concession agents. *see also* COP.

Cops: Midway term for small prizes or ballys* placed in boxes of candy or Cracker Jacks. *see also* BALLYS.

Cork opera or op'ry: A minstrel show,* so-called from the burnt-cork* makeup used. *see also* BURNT CORK and MINSTREL SHOW.

Cork up: To put on black-face in a minstrel show.* *see also* (TO) BLACK UP and MINSTREL SHOW.

Corn: A largely derogatory term applied to almost anything in writing, directing, or performing that is trite, ridiculous, old-fashioned, or used in the hope that it will be a crowd pleaser. Most likely, the term derives from the use of such methods before less sophisticated rural audiences in the so-called "corn belt."

Corn-game: A name for bingo in carnival lingo.

Corn punk or slum: Pitchmen's slang for any corn cure or orthopedic preparation sold in a medicine show.* *see also* MEDICINE SHOW.

Corner man: *see* END MAN.

Corporation show: A circus that belonged to the American Circus Corporation.

Coughed-up-skeletions: *see* PICKLED BASTARDS OR PUNKS.

Count store: A flat joint* requiring that the player score a specified number of points to win, something he cannot do because of the cheating lies in the count or add-up itself. Also called an add-up joint. *see also* FLAT JOINT.

Count the box: Theatrical expression for counting the ticket stubs in the box.* *see also* BOX.

Count the rack: Theatrical expression for counting the tickets left unsold in the box office.

Country routes: Circus routes laid out by the advertising car* manager into surrounding territory to be covered by a crew of two billposters in a day. *see also* ADVERTISING CARS.

Country store: Carnival concession* usually designed on a rotating wheel displaying inexpensive merchandise. *see also* CONCESSION.

Courier: A multipage circus advertising newspaper with two or more pages in color and full of photographs of the marvels in the attraction to come.

Cover-up: In burlesque, a concealment of lapses in the lines. *see* AD LIB.

Cowboy: Carnival jargon for one who comes on the carnival lot* looking for trouble. *see also* LOT and TOWNIE.

Crack: Carnival and less frequently circus slang meaning to speak.

(To) crack a wheeze: Expression used during the days of talking clowns;* the completion of a circus clown's patter.* *see also* PATTER and TALKING CLOWNS.

(To) crack the nut: Tent-show lingo for showing a profit or, more specifically, the point where expenses are made and profit begins. *see* GET UP THE NUT and NUT OR BURR.

Cradle: In the circus, an apparatus on which aerialists work when a trapeze is not used.

Crane bar: A metal bar suspended far above the circus performing arena from which apparatus for aerial performing, such as an aerial perch* or Roman rings,* is hung. *see also* AERIAL PERCH and ROMAN RINGS.

Crash: Circus slang meaning to change money.

Crashing: To get into a theatre without buying a ticket.

Crazy act: A circus expression that may be applied to any clown routine.

Creative flow: In magic, the linkage of points of focus so that the audience's attention flows smoothly from trick to trick.

Creep dive: A cheap saloon, so called because it is operated or patronized by creeps.

Creeper: A controlled spindle* of a carnival wheel.* It is named a creeper because a carnival wheel that utilizes such a spindle or arrow spins very slowly. *see also* CARNIVAL WHEEL, FLAT JOINT, and SPINDLE.

Crib: A theatrical and vaudeville word for a one-room brothel with one girl in attendance.

Crier: A term for a sideshow talker* used between the 1870s and 1890s. Frequently the crier followed the circus parade route encouraging patrons to see the exhibitions. *see also* TALKER.

Crime show: An old, traditional carnival exhibit displaying guns used in stickups or murders, pictures, or maybe wax figures of assorted criminals, and the like. *see* SIDESHOW.

Crimp: A method used by magicians and gamblers to mark a specific location in the deck of cards by secretly bending one corner of a card.

Croak: Circus slang meaning to kill or to die.

Croaker: Circus slang for a murderer; also used to signify a doctor.

Crocus: English slang for a patent medicine man. *see* MED MAN.

Cross cage: A small animal cage that could be loaded on a circus flatcar crosswise, thus conserving three or four feet of space.

Crossing: Railroad, street, or highway crossing where a circus is loaded or unloaded. Normally, this word refers to a railroad show that is loaded or unloaded. see CHUTES and RUNS.

Crotch row: A stock theatre and burlesque term for the row behind the baldheaded row,* which is so close to the stage that eye level is constantly on the performer's crotch. On occasion the ticket for this row is marked CRO. see also BALDHEADED ROW.

Crumb: Circus and carnival slang for body lice. see CIRCUS BEES.

Crumb box: In the circus, a wooden box, foot locker, or suitcase in which a circus man keeps his personal belongings. Since lack of traveling space prohibits a work hand from carrying a full-sized trunk, as do performers, a box about eighteen inches long, twelve inches wide, and fifteen to eighteen inches deep must suffice. In hobo cant, a crumb is a louse, due to close resemblance. It is also possible that the box got its name because it contained crumbs left from a sandwich or box of crackers or cookies.

Crumb castles: Circus slang for dining-room tents. see COOKHOUSE.

Crumb-up: Circus work-hand jargon for bathing, washing up, or any personal hygiene. Like crumb box,* the tramp or hobo use of crumb is applicable here. see also CRUMB BOX.

Cue: Like the traditional theatre term, cue in vaudeville (and in most other forms of stage entertainment, including the circus) meant a word or action regarded as the signal for some other speech or action by another performer, or for lights to change, a sound or music to be heard, or something to happen during the course of an act.* see also ACT.

Cue biter: In vaudeville and burlesque, a comic, straight man* or girl who jumped into the next line before it was completed or before the audience had a chance to laugh at the joke, thus killing the laugh before it had a chance. Similar in meaning to the expression "step on a line" in theatrical use. see also STRAIGHT MAN.

Cuff: To admit someone to a theatre free. Cuffo, then, would be on the cuff or for free. Cuff probably originated when men wore celluloid cuffs and made notes on them that could be wiped off, so that "put it on the cuff" came to mean to forget the matter.

Cuffo: *see* CUFF.

Cul, col, or cully: English circus expression for a friend or companion.

Cull: 1. Med-show* jargon for sir. 2. In card magic, to cull is to extract or assemble the desired number of cards, which are called "culls." *see also* MED SHOW.

Cups and balls: One of the oldest of magical apparatus in which sleight-of-hand* is exhibited. *see also* SLEIGHT OR SLEIGHT-OF-HAND.

Curdled in his cupola: Med-show* expression for one mentally weak. *see also* MED SHOW.

Curio hall: A room located in some dime museums* with platforms placed around the walls for the exhibit of freaks or other oddities. *see also* DIME MUSEUM.

Curtain: In vaudeville, since the curtain was dropped at the end of an act, this meant the finish.

Curtain raiser: An opening act in a vaudeville show.

Cush: Turn-of-the-century theatrical jargon for money.

Cushion: A small, sloping, wedge-shaped ramp used by some bareback riders in the circus to assist them when jumping up onto horses. *see* FORK JUMP, LIFT, RUNNING GROUND MOUNT, and VOLTIGE.

Cushy: *see* BONA.

Custard: The circus name for frozen ice cream.

Cut: 1. In the circus, a share. 2. In card magic, to divide the deck into two or more sections openly. 3. The British use cut to mean to leave, such as to cut the sawdust or leave the circus.

(To) cut cake: Circus jargon meaning to short-change. *see* CAKE CUTTER.

Cut from traces: In the circus, a phrase meaning to cut away dead baggage horses on muddy lots.

(To) cut him in: Carnival phrase (and some circus use) meaning to take another person into business temporarily.

Cut of flats: Circus jargon for the section of flatcars spotted in for loading or unloading.

Cut the buck: An expression used by old buck-and-wing dancers, meaning that the dancer or hoofer* can do it or "cut" it. *see also* HOOFER.

(To) cut the sawdust: *see* CUT.

Cut the strawberry cake: *see* CAKE CUTTER.

Cut-ins: Jargon in the outdoor amusement world for the fee the electrician collects for connecting electrical service.

Cut-up jackpots: Outdoor showmen's phrase for a discussion of past events, mostly lies. In the circus, this is performers' social talk, from the poker term (a pot that can be opened only by jacks or better, therefore apt to be a rich one).

Cut up pipes: Circus and carnival expression meaning to gossip or boast. *see* CUT-UP JACKPOTS.

Cuter: In carnival and circus slang, a quarter of a dollar. Borrowed from vagabond argot. Also called kuter.

D

Damp blanket: Show-business slang for a bad review.

Damper: In circus jargon, the front-door cash register or till.

Dancery: A dance hall.

Dangler: Slang name for a trapeze artist in the circus.

Dansants: A name for many dance halls (when they were the rage), from about 1909 through 1916.

Dansapation: Slang for syncopated music.

Darb: Circus word for excellent.

Dark: Term used in the theatre, the circus, and the carnival for a show that is not performing.

Dark ride: An amusement park or carnival ride attraction in which the patron is transported in some type of vehicle through a darkened enclosure and is greeted with surprises at every turn, designed to scare or startle the rider.

Date: General popular-entertainment term for a show's engagement in a town.

Date book: Book in which a show's route* is listed; used by most traveling entertainment forms. *see also* ROUTE and ROUTE CARD.

Date sheets: Printed circus advertising, used along with colored posters or lithographs,* which proclaimed the day the circus would be in town. *see also* CARDS and LITHOGRAPH.

Daub: 1. In the circus, a word for a space other than regular bill boards for posting circus posters or paper,* such as sides of barns, sheds, or fences. Also used to identify the advertising paper pasted on some structure. *see also* PAPER. 2. A paste used by card magicians for marking cards on the backs or faces.

Day and Date or Day-end dating: The simultaneous date and town of a circus with an opposition, or other show.

Day bill: An entertainment poster advertisement placed in a storefront window. *see* CARDS.

Dead cat: The name given a lion, tiger, or leopard that does not perform but is merely exhibited in a show. Until most circuses ceased traveling with tents, a menagerie of animals, including dead cats, was common. *see* TRAVELING MENAGERIE.

Dead man: Circus term for a wooden block made secure by stakes and connected to the rigging for aerial and high-wire acts. It received its name because it lies flat on the ground, has dead weight, and is thus very difficult to move.

Dead sell: Primarily, English usage for a successful show or act.

Deadfall: A kind of nightclub or all-night eatery considered a clip joint.

Deadheads: 1. In the circus, a nonworking member of a troupe. 2. A general term for those who sit in seats that would otherwise be unoccupied, having been given free tickets in compensation for some minor service for the troupe,* company, or management. Synonym for today's COMPS or FREEBEES. *see also* COMP, FREEBIE, and TROUPE.

Deadpan: A comedian who shows no facial expression, thus often more humorous to the audience because he does not indicate that he is funny. Like a Buster Keaton, such a comic is frequently an unusually subtle artist.

Dealing seconds: A gambling term also used in card magic to indicate a sleight* that permits the magician to retain the top card and deal cards below it in the deck as if they were actually from the top. *see also* SLEIGHT OR SLEIGHT-OF-HAND. .

Death trail: Small-time* vaudeville tours in the Midwest and Northwest, where distances between dates were long and performers frequently had to perform five or more times a day. Also used to describe, on occasion, any touring company, not just vaudeville. *see also* SMALL-TIME.

Deck: An American term for a pack of cards. Although an old English word as well, the English rarely use the word today.

Deckhand: Theatrical slang for a stagehand.

Deemer: Circus and carnival argot for a dime or ten cents.

Deluxes or De-Luxes: Circus box seats.

Demurred: Circus term for a railroad car that has been placed on a siding-track.

Den: 1. A circus cage for animals. 2. A consignment of snakes for snake eaters or snake shows. Dens once came in two sizes: a ten-dollar den with fifty snakes, or a five-dollar den with twenty-five.

Denari or denarlies: English circus slang for money.

Dentist friend: Circus slang for anything sweet to eat.

Detracting: What happens when one burlesque comic stooges* or plays straight man* for another. *see also* STOOGE and STRAIGHT MAN.

Deuce: 1. In carnival and circus lingo, a two-dollar bill. 2. In vaudeville, a two-night stand. *see* DEUCE ACT OR SPOT, SPLIT TIME, and SPLIT WEEK.

Deuce act or spot: In circus or vaudeville, second on a program or bill.* In vaudeville, playing the second spot, or deucing it, was a position few performers relished. *see also* BILL.

Deucing it: *see* DEUCE ACT OR SPOT.

Diachylon: A chemical substance used by some magicians for making two cards adhere together.

Dialect comedy act: A popular act, usually a two-man routine, in vaudeville. To differentiate ethnic backgrounds (especially Irish, German, Italian, and Jewish), comics stressed each group's unusual traits and exaggerated their dialects. The most famous of the two-man dialect comedy teams was Joe Weber and Lew Fields, who played Mike and Meyer (respectively). The period 1890 to 1920, the decades of major immigrations to the United States, marked the height of popularity for dialect comedy and ethnic humor.

Diamond Dye scenery: A traveling tent-repertoire-show method of using old-fashioned dyes available in any drugstore under the trade name Diamond Dye rather than conventional scene paint which would crack and flake when the scenery was taken down and rolled up.

Dick: Circus slang for a private detective or plainclothes officer, usually carried by the show. *see* COOKIE-CUTTER, COP, FUZZ, SHAMUS, and TINS.

Diddy: English circus word for gypsy. *see* GYP.

Die: In vaudeville and most forms of entertainment, when a performer or act failed to win applause or acceptance. *see* BRODIE, FLOP, and PASS OUT.

Die standing up: *see* DIE.

Digger: Theatrical slang for someone who buys large numbers of tickets to a successful show, especially musicals, and sells them to ticket brokers for profit. *see* RAT.

Diggers: A midway* gaming device in which a coin is inserted and a mechanical device scoops up merchandise and delivers it to the player. *see also* MIDWAY.

Dime museum: A major but little-known form of American entertainment established by 1875, offering crude and disorganized entertainments such as animals, freaks, mechanical and scientific oddities, wax figures, peep shows, and a so-called lecture room,* providing, under the guise of culture, extra "edifying" attractions running the gamut from jugglers and dioramas* to comics, musicians, and popular theatre fare. Dime museums came in all sizes and degrees of extravagance and existed in most fair-sized American cities up to World War I. *see also* CURIO HALL, BLOW-OFF, DIORAMA, LECTURE ROOM, and STORE SHOWS.

Ding: Circus slang meaning to borrow some money.

Dinge: Carnival and circus word, from "dingey," meaning a Negro.

Dingie: A theatrical term used at the turn of the century for a black actor. *see* DINGE.

Diorama: A form of optical entertainment originally referring to an illuminated show presented in a specifically designed building introduced by Louis Jacques Daguerre and Charles-Marie Bouton in France and England in the 1820s. In America, the diorama was largely diluted to mean an elaboration of a panorama* devised to show distant views on a painted canvas that rolled from one cylinder to another at the back of a stage. In some instances, as was true with the original dioramas, the scene remained still, and effects of movement or depth were created by means of changes in the direction and intensity of lighting and the use of cut-outs, translucencies, and transparencies. Like the panorama, the diorama was frequently little more than a peep show.* The true nature of the diorama is clearly explained in Richard Altick's *The Shows of London*. *see also* PANORAMA and PEEP SHOW.

(The) dip: 1. Used in the carnival and criminal worlds, a pickpocket. *see* (THE) SHOVE. 2. A term used in the 1920s and 1930s for what is today the advance agent or man* of a touring show. *see also* ADVANCE AGENT OR ADVANCE MAN.

Diskery: Show-business slang for a phonograph record manufacturer.

Dissimulation: Term in magic to describe one method of convincing an audience that something is not so when it actually is. *see* DIVERSION, DISTRACTION, and MISDIRECTION.

Distraction: In magic, a fairly violent way of shifting an audience's attention away from something it should not notice. *see* DISSIMULATION, DIVERSION, and MISDIRECTION.

Ditch: A slang word used by some magicians meaning to get rid of something.

Dive bomber: A novelty ride in the English fair in which two capsules, spinning on their own axes, rotate at the end of a revolving arm. The American midway has similar rides under various names, such as the Hammer.

Diversion: Magician's method of fooling an audience by taking their focus away from something they should not notice. *see* DISSIMULATION, DISTRACTION, and MISDIRECION.

Divertisement or divertissement: A short entertainment usually between the acts of a play. Although the word is originally French, the term, meaning "diversion," is used in the English-speaking world in this form.

Divinations: A type or class of magical effects in which the performer ascertains an object or objects concealed by the audience or discovers the order in which they were arranged.

Do a Brodie: *see* BRODIE.

Do black: Pitchmen's and vaudeville expression for acting the role of a Negro (in black-face*) in a show. *see also* BLACK-FACE.

Do it or did it: In Toby shows,* a phrase that meant an actor acted a part or hoped to act a part. *see also* TOBY SHOW.

Dobs: *see* CARDS.

Doc: Instead of using the title Dr., quack med show* operators or patent medicine pitchmen used "Doc" to avoid prosecution. *see also* MEDICINE SHOW and PROHANDLE.

Dodgems or dodg'em: An established English amusement park device with cars powered by an overhead electrically charged ceiling or grid. Same as the American bumper cars.

Dodgers: Small theatrical or circus handbills or throwaways.

Dog: 1. Circus slang for a hippopotamus. 2. Obsolete theatrical term for an audience outside New York City. To try out a play on the road was once to try it out on the dog.* *see also* TRY IT (OUT) ON THE DOG.

Dogs: Circus and carnival slang for frankfurters or hot dogs. Sometimes used to mean the legs.

Dog and pony show: A term applied to a small or modest-sized traveling circus, usually featuring small, domesticated-animal acts. Often used derisively by large shows.

Dog joint: A hot-dog or frankfurter stand. *see* JOINT.

Doggery: Early nineteenth-century American slang for a low drinking place.

Doll: Carnival term for a female friend.

Dolly: Carnival and circus term for a small, portable derrick, usually mounted on a motorized truck.

Dona: English circus term for a girl or woman.

Doniker, donniker, donnicker, donagher, donaker, or donegan: Circus and carnival word for an outhouse, privy, water closet, or restroom. A number of possible origins of the word have been postulated; the variants of the spelling suggest the difficulties, however. Irwin traces the word to the English low-slang equivalent, "dunnyken" or "dunnaken" (originally "dannaken"), meaning a water closet, from "danna" meaning human ordure, and from "ken," a place, especially a house. Danna and ken are seventeenth- and eighteenth-century thieves' cant. Ballantine suggests that the word may have come also from the Hindustani *"khan(n)a,"* meaning a house or room, which appears in various Gypsy dialects. *see* DONIKER LOCATION and IN DONIKER.

Doniker location: A spot on a midway* that is not especially good for business. *see also* DONIKER, IN DONIKER, and MIDWAY.

Doniker Sam: A man who plings* tips in restrooms on carnival or amusement park grounds. *see* PLING.

Doodle-a-squat: Slang expression in the carnival for money.

Dookie wagon: The office wagon in early traveling carnivals where money was handled.

Doors: A call or warn in the circus, meaning that the arena is about to open and the public will come in, thus warning performers rehearsing or visiting within the area to clear the space.

Double: A circus term that most commonly refers to a double somer-sault* but can also be used to describe double turns of juggled objects or a double trapeze act in which two aerialists perform together on the same trapeze. *see also* SOMERSAULT.

Double act: Sideshow slang for Siamese twins.

Double and triple booking: A booking method devised by theatre managers and owners in New York around the turn of the century whereby they would protect themselves from canceled attractions by booking two or more shows for the same date. The first show that arrived in town would then get the date.

Double-backer: Special magician's cards printed with a back on each side. *see* DOUBLE-FACER.

Double-banker: Outdoor amusement slang for a double-crosser, especially one who physically muscles in on an assault or an unsuspecting victim.

Double double: One of the more spectacular of circus acrobatic tricks from the flying trapeze. A double somersault* with a double pirou-ette.* *see also* PIROUETTE and SOMERSAULT.

Double-facer: Special magician's cards printed with a face on each side.

Double lift: A magician's sleight* in which two or more cards in a deck are lifted as one, thus making it possible to show the top cards as one. *see also* SLEIGHT OR SLEIGHT-OF-HAND.

Double pit: Theatrical term for working in more than one capacity. Literally, "to double pit" would be to play in the orchestra pit. *see* DOUBLING IN BRASS.

Double-saw or double-sawbuck: Circus and carnival slang for a twenty-dollar bill. *see* SAWBUCK.

Double-staking: *see* EXTRAS.

Double take: *see* TAKE.

Double trouble: A Negro dance of the early nineteenth century.

Double Willie: Fairly modern term for a stagehand who is not allowed normal lunch and dinner breaks but is required to work straight through these hours and is thus paid double or a Double Willie.

Doubling: Playing more than one part in the same play.

Doubling in brass: In general terms, an employee or performer who also plays in the band. In the circus, it now means to do any two different kinds of work. In the theatre, it came to mean playing two parts in one production. In the minstrel show, it frequently meant that musicians who played matinees and nights in the orchestra would also parade mornings in a brass band. Traveling repertoire companies often used the phrase to mean that an actor would be required to play a musical instrument and also to present a specialty* or variety act. *see also* DOUBLE PIT and SPECIALTY.

Douse: English circus term for extinguish.

Dovetail: Magician's term for shuffling cards by interlacing them. *see* RIFFLE.

Down: In some nightclubs, bars, and striptease lounges, a glass of cheap drink (disguised to look like the real stuff) sold to a male customer as whiskey and drunk by a female employee or the management.

Down yonder: In the American circus, an expression meaning the southern tier of states.

Downing: *see* RIDE FOREMAN.

Downtown wagon: A platform show carried on a circus train which could be exhibited in the town area during the day, thus attracting patrons to the main show. It also refers to a show ticket wagon stationed on the streets in the downtown area.

Drag: 1. The train or cars used to transport a circus or carnival; also in the same argot, a street. 2. Men dressed as women. These were popular acts in vaudeville and revues. *see* FEMALE IMPERSONATOR.

Drag the midway: An early carnival practice of some independent showmen on midways* of going to the front gate and enticing people down the midway to their attraction. *see also* MIDWAY.

Dramatic end tent: A type of tent used by dramatic tent-repertoire companies and tent chautauquas developed circa 1910 by a St. Louis tent maker. It was constructed so that the bothersome center pole* directly in front of the center of the stage was eliminated. It substituted two masts at either side of the stage opening for the last center pole with a cable stretched between the masts, in the center of which was a block and tackle for lifting the canvas at a point midway between the two masts. In tent-repertoire companies the stage end of the tent theatre was considered a separate addition to the tent, as was the marquee* or front entrance section of the tent. *see also* BALE-RING TENT, CENTER POLE, MARQUEE, PUSHPOLE TENT, ROUNDABOUT, and ROUNDTOP.

Drape: The overhang on a magician's table of a table cover or table-cloth.

Draw on: Primarily English usage, to move onto the fairground area in order to set up the fair or carnival on a specified date before the fair opens.

Drawback: An early nineteenth-century term for some kind of trick or performance.

Drawing-room magic: From the nineteenth-century practice of ama-teur magicians performing in the room where guests were entertained. The term became commonly used to describe magic shows given in intimate surroundings for small audiences, and now generally refers to tricks with small props. *see* CLOSE-UP MAGIC and PARLOR MAGIC.

Dressage: Circus term, more common in the English circus, for the art of showing trained horses in which the animal's movements are guided by subtle movements of the rider's body. *see* HIGH-SCHOOL HORSE.

Dressed: There are several variations of what dressed means. 1. In the circus, it means to emphasize the idea of distributing tickets so that all sections are filled with no obviously empty seats. 2. In the theatre, a similar meaning exists in which the audience is seated in such a manner so that it appears larger than it is, usually by leaving every other pair of seats vacant. 3. Another variation, however, is that of filling a theatre with pass holders who are likely to applaud.

Dressing movement: A principle of theatrical staging that applies to other forms of entertainment, including stage magic, vaudeville, and burlesque. Basically, the notion is that the actor or performer should be aware of balance on stage and keep the stage picture pleasing to the audience through subtle movements made in relation to other actors, scenery, and the like.

Dressing top: *see* TOP.

Drive: Term used for the artificial campaign used to plug a song into popularity. *see* PLUGGER and SONG PLUGGER.

Droll: During the Commonwealth period in England, a droll was usually a farce based upon a popular full-length play, a tradition that continued for some time. In the seventeenth and eighteenth centuries, a droll was a farce, puppet show, or some similarly amusing production. In more general terms, the word is used to denote a clown or comedian.

Drome: Slang abbreviation for a motordrome, a silolike wooden structure once found in most large amusement parks where men and women rode motorcycles and small automobiles on the straight-up-and-down wall. Although still in existence, their number is few.

Drop: 1. In vaudeville and theatre in general, a curtain of canvas painted with some scene and filling the full stage opening. 2. In card manipulation, it is the magician's ability to drop the balance of cards held in the hand during a shuffle, so that they fall upon the shuffled cards.

Drop tin: English term for a poor location for a show.

Droppers: Magician's device that is usually worn about the clothing, normally under a vest or coat, from which the performer can produce small objects, either in a bunch or successively. *see* HOLDER.

Drum-beater: A press agent* who beats the drum for a show. A very old tradition, dating from the medieval period and the common practice of the town crier or the banns (also bans). *see also* PRESS AGENT.

Dry up: To forget one's dialogue or song lyrics.

Dub: Abbreviation for double-sawbuck, or twenty dollars. *see also* DOUBLE-SAWBUCK.

Ducat or Ducket: Circus and carnival show, ride, and gate ticket. *see* SKULL.

Ducat or Ducket grabber or snatcher: A ticket taker or door tender.

Duck: Circus slang meaning to depart. *see* BEAT IT and SCRAM.

Duck a date: In circus lingo, this means to fail to exhibit as scheduled.

Duke: 1. Slang word used extensively at one time in both the circus and the carnival to mean the human hand (usually in a fist) or to applaud vociferously. 2. Also circus and pitchmen's slang for short-changing a person by palming a coin that is part of the change due to him. *see* SHORT-CHANGE ARTIST.

Duke 'em: Circus and pitchmen's practice of handing a child or young woman a confection, balloon, or novelty, and by means of this less than subtle pressure, force the person's companion or escort to buy. Duke alone sometimes is used instead of duke 'em for the meaning given here. Duke 'em is sometimes used as in duke* in its second meaning. *see also* DUKE.

(To) duke or duck him in: Pitchmen's phrase for steering a victim or drawing an unsuspecting victim into a game of chance.

Duke nightly: Circus argot meaning to pay off each night after the show is over.

Duke reader: *see* MITT READER.

Duker: 1. Carnival term for a fortune-teller. *see* DUKE. 2. Circus term for a meal ticket, because it was held in the hands or dukes. *see* DUKEY, DUCKIE, DUKIE, or DOOKIE.

Dukey, duckie, dukie, or dookie: Circus term for a snack or box lunch given to the working men* when the circus train had to make an extra long jump* between towns. Sometimes used to denote a ticket or chit for the sack or box lunch or as a general term for a handout at the cook tent for workmen. *see also* JUMP and WORKING MEN.

Dukey, duckie, dukie, or dookie book: Circus term for a pad of detachable tickets to be exchanged for meals. *see* DUKEY, DUCKIE, DUKIE, or DOOKIE.

Dukey, duckie, or dukie run: Circus and carnival slang for a long move between towns, usually longer than an overnight haul. *see*JUMP.

Dumb act or sight act: A vaudeville act using only acrobats, jugglers, and the like, and no verbal performances. An action-packed dumb act frequently opened the bill while the audience was still entering and being seated. *see* SILENT ACT.

Dumps: Theatre tickets returned to the box office by ticket agencies because they could not be sold, or to sell at a discount tickets on hand in an agency as a performance is about to begin.

Dummy:*see* FAKE.

Dwarf: Medically, a dwarf is someone with an average-sized torso and short arms and legs, whereas a midget's* body is in proportion to that of the normal adult. Most uninformed writers confuse the two, calling all little people midgets. Dwarfs are far more common in the circus, used as clowns, whereas most midgets in the entertainment world have been seen in sideshows.

Dynamiting: A tent repertoire term for dressing room gossip, which, if viciously motivated through petty jealousies and intense egotism by a performer, could destroy a show. Normally, dynamiting by an actor took the form of running down the show and everything about it, including the manager; in a short time the entire company would be angry and the consequent tension and dissatisfaction would spread like an epidemic.

E

East Indian Magic: Traditionally, the most mystifying of all conjuring* is that performed by East Indian fakirs, although the name is no longer limited to actual Indian fakirs. The branch of magic includes such effects as the "Indian Rope Trick," the "Indian Basket Trick," the "Indian Mango Trick," and "Levitation." It should be noted that in India the word fakir is applied to religious ascetics and not to magicians. *see also* CONJURING.

Eatery: Show-business slang for a restaurant.

Eccentric clown: A fairly uncommon clown in the American circus but quite popular in France and Russia. A solo clown whose comedy derives from the irrational or unexpected handling of or relationship to objects.

Eccentric dance team: *see* LEG MANIA.

Ecdysiast: A classy name for a stripper, coined by H. L. Mencken and attributed to the work of Gypsy Rose Lee, who denounced the term as snobbish. It was, on occasion, further refined to ecdysiste, apparently suggested by the word artiste.

Edition: A version or new revue* production (or part of one) based on a formula or concept that runs through all similar revue productions but differs from the original version. Sometimes the differences were so great as to have little resemblance to the original. *see also* REVUE.

Educate: Circus argot meaning to teach a lesson or to wise up.

Educator cracker: Med show* slang for one who makes wisecracks. *see also* MED SHOW.

Effect: In magician's terminology, the apparent magic seen by the audience for any given trick, or the description of a trick from the vantage point of the audience.

Elbows: Pitchmen's word meaning to be friendly with someone.

Eleven forty-five: Theatrical and minstrel-show term used around the turn of the century to describe a tall silk hat, so called from the fact that eleven forty-five was the hour that minstrels donned their silk headgear and reported for a street parade. It sometimes was used to mean the daily parade of a minstrel company. Also called Hi Henry. *see* (AN) OSCAR HAMMERSTEIN.

Elmer: A derogatory term used by tent shows for any resident of a rural community. *see* TOWNIE OR TOWNEY.

Elope: Circus word meaning to marry and leave the show without giving notice.

Embryo shows: *see* PICKLED BASTARDS OR PUNKS.

Emcee or emsee: Abbreviation for master of ceremonies, especially in vaudeville.

En Douceur or En Pelotage: European circus terms adopted internationally for presenting wild animals in such a way as to appear tame. *see* EN FEROCITE.

En Ferocite: European term used to describe American wild-animal acts, as opposed to their "tableau" or tame presentations. *see* FIGHTING ACT.

End grip: Magician's term for holding a deck of cards with the thumb at one end and the fingers at the other.

End man: One of the comic performers at either end of the seated semicircle in a black-face minstrel show.* In England, where the popularity of minstrel shows still persists, the end man is called the corner man.* *see also* BONES, CORNER MAN, MINSTREL SHOW, and TAMBO.

Entr'acte: An intermission or, more commonly, a brief entertainment, often of variety, presented during an intermission.

Entree: An extended circus clown act performed by clowns (often a white-face clown* and an Auguste*) or group of clowns and containing a good deal of dialogue. *see also* AUGUSTE, FILL-IN CLOWNS, and WHITE-FACE CLOWN.

Entry: *see* SPEC OR SPECTACLE.

Eppice: Pitchmen's term for nothing or no good.

Equestrian drama or hippodrama: A type of spectacular entertainment in which horses (or by extension, other animals) were used prominently, not only as additional spectacle but as actors, often with leading actions of their own to perform. The animals, in other words, became the homified heroes of the plays. The term was ultimately used to describe any play in which horsemanship was prominently displayed, not just those specifically written to feature animals. The form was particularly popular in the nineteenth century in England and to a lesser degree in the United States.

Equestrian director: Frequently confused by the layman with the ringmaster,* this position in the circus is actually that of the performance manager who controls a circus performance from the arena floor and serves as master of ceremonies. He is usually a dignified gentleman equipped with a whistle to alert audience and performers of changes about to take place. Also called a whistle tooter. *see also* ANNOUNCER and RINGMASTER.

Equestrian juggler: A circus performer who juggles while standing on the back of a moving horse.

Escape: A type of magical effect, usually one item in a program.* Classes of escapes include ties, handcuffs, and the like, bags, boxes, and containers. *see also* PROGRAM and RELEASES.

Ethiopian delineator: Name used by early black-face entertainers who claimed that they authentically portrayed American Negroes. With the rise of the minstrel show, this phrase was used less and less. Also called Ethiopian minstrelsy or opera.

Ethiopian minstrelsy or opera: An early name for black-face minstrelsy. *see* ETHIOPIAN DELINEATOR and MINSTREL SHOW.

Ex: An exclusive concession or right of a pitchman or circus worker to sell a product. Also known as an X.* *see also* X.

Excess baggage: 1. In the circus, this means anyone in an act who takes no direct part in a presentation but who is in the ring* with the act to add style or assist by posing or pointing to the star performer during key moments or as a bow is being taken. *see also* RING. 2. In vaudeville, it was a wife or some other woman traveling with a male performer but not working in the show. 3. In minstrel shows and as a general theatre term, it once meant a poor performer.

Excursion car: An advance circus railway car used by large circuses in order to arrange for special trains to bring patrons to the circus. A special fare usually included a ticket to the circus. Without excursion trains, many towns on the circus route would have been unprofitable.

Exec: Circus name for executives.

Exhibition room: One of the earliest terms used in the United States instead of theatre or playhouse to avoid possible censorship or other legal difficulties. *see* LECTURE ROOM OR HALL and MORAL LECTURE.

Exotic costume: In magic circles, this refers to authentic Chinese, East Indian, or Egyptian garb worn by magicians. In recent years such dress, as well as formal attire, has largely been abandoned. The prime example is the simple, skin-fitting costume of Doug Henning. Such a costume eliminates special pockets and "body work" so frequently depended upon in the past.

Exotic dancer: A term that modern strippers frequently apply to themselves and use for advertising.

Exposures: In magic, this means the revealing of magical secrets, a practice much debated in magic circles. Apparently, exposure is simply explaining a trick or its mechanics, while making some honest attempt to teach performance. It is thought of as a means of bringing new recruits to the art.

Extension front: In architectural terms, the definition given to the entrance to a ride or show. Used most extensively in England but similar to the American marquee* of a tent show. *see also* MARQUEE.

Extra man or woman: In vaudeville, a person used for parts that do not require speech; not a regular member of the company. *see* THINKING PART.

Extras or double-staking: In circus terminology, this describes the practice of putting extra (or two) stakes in the ground to hold ropes, especially in threatening or windy weather. *see* FUNNY ROPES.

Extravaganza: A confusing form of American and English entertainment especially popular in the nineteenth century. Basically, a light entertainment in dramatic form, with music, often improbable in plot, and spectacular in presentation. Many productions at first resembled literary burlesque.

F

Face card: *see BOTTOM CARD*.

Fag show: Carnival expression for a show with female impersonators.* *see also* FEMALE IMPERSONATOR.

Fair shuffle: In card magic, a genuine shuffle of cards rather than a false shuffle.* *see also* FALSE SHUFFLE.

(To) Fairbank: In carnival and general midway slang, to make a cheating move in favor of the player in order to entice him to continue playing or to increase the size of his bets. *see* FLASH and THROW A COP.

Fair-ground theatre: Rarely used term in the United States for a booth or other temporary theatre erected at a fair; common in the seventeenth and eighteenth centuries, especially at English fairs. *see* BOOTH STAGE OR THEATRE.

Fake: 1. Once used in the theatre and circus to mean a complimentary ticket. 2. Some circus and carnival use to mean to be hit by an unexpected blow. 3. In magic, a piece of apparatus, seemingly unprepared, that has been fixed in some way, such as with a secret container or dummy.* Frequently the presence of the apparatus itself is unsuspected by the audience, although some magicians distinguish between the fake, seen but not understood by the spectators, and a gimmick,* which is not seen. *see also* DUMMY and GIMMICK.

Fakir: *see* EAST INDIAN MAGIC.

Fakirs: The name given to shady operators on fair and circus grounds during the period 1890 to 1905.

Fall guy: Primarily, a circus term for anyone who is blamed for anything wrong or anyone who can easily take the responsibility for the wrong, real or imaginary. This person is usually an easy mark.* *see also* MARK.

Fally Markus: A vaudeville expression named after a small-time theatre booker who paid small salaries. Performers would thus break in new material on Fally Markus dates.

False count: In magic, the counting of cards, coins, or other items so as to indicate that there are more or less than their real number.

False cut: A move in card magic whereby the performer appears to cut the cards but actually keeps them in the same order.

False shuffle: In card magic, the act of shuffling a deck of cards in such a way as to retain the whole deck or certain cards in a desired order.

Fan: 1. In the circus, an enthusiast (noun) or to search hastily (verb). 2. In card magic, to manipulate playing cards into the form of a fan.

Fan dancer: A type of exotic dancer popularized by the late Sally Rand, who in 1933 introduced her fan dance at the Chicago World's Fair. Rand's peekaboo dance depended on her adroitness with two big ostrich plumes, which she flashed, exposing and concealing her body, to the music of Chopin or "Clair de Lune." In addition to fans, bubbles were sometimes used to tease the crowd.

Fancy wagon: Pitchmen's term for the truck or trailer that carried the show and was highly decorated.

Fanner: Slang abbreviation for a fan dancer.* *see also* FAN DANCER.

Fantoccini: An Italian word for a kind of puppet operated by machinery on hidden strings or wires, used in English-speaking puppetry, although often anglicized to fantocine.

Farce: A broadly humorous species of dramatic composition, or a portion of one, usually distinguished from comedy by its improbable situations, broadly drawn characters, and intricacies of its plotting. The dividing line between farce, a perennial form of popular theatre, and pure comedy has never been clear. Most farce, however, because of its lack of subtleties and physical humor, has appealed to a broad audience.

Fat: Theatrical word for a part that gives the performer a good chance to show off his talents.

Fat show: Carnival expression for an attraction featuring corpulent persons, either men or women, or both.

Feed line: In comedy, and especially in a vaudeville comedy act with two persons, a line of dialogue, usually delivered by the straight man* to the comic, the purpose of which is to elicit a funny reply. *see also* FEEDER and STRAIGHT MAN.

Feeder: A straight man* who serves a comedian by delivering lines that result in comical replies. *see also* FEED LINE and STRAIGHT MAN.

Feeliers: English circus term for children. Also called chavies.

Feet jump: In equestrian riding and as used in some circuses, the term for standing with the feet together and jumping from the ground or teeterboard onto the back of a running horse. *see* TEETERBOARD ACT.

Feet-to-feet: Circus term for a somersault made from the feet back to the feet. *see* FEET-TO-FORK.

Feet-to-fork: Circus term, more frequently used in the English circus, to describe when on horseback the rider lands astride. *see* FEET-TO-FEET.

Female impersonator: A man who plays the role of a woman, especially popular in the United States during the first thirty years of this century. Among the more famous American female impersonators were Julian Eltinge (probably the greatest in the history of American show business), Francis Leon, Bothwell Browne, and Bert Savoy. *see* MALE IMPERSONATOR.

Femcee: Show-business abbreviation for mistress of ceremonies.

Femme: General show-business and circus slang for girls or women.

Femme looker: Slang for a physically beautiful female. *see* FEMME.

Ferris wheel: A power-driven vertical wheel, steel-framed and with freely pivoted passenger cabs with seats mounted at the extremities. The amusement ride was developed by G. W. G. Ferris and introduced at the Columbian Exposition in 1893. This original Ferris wheel, destined to become a fixture in all outdoor amusement forms, was 250 feet in diameter and had thirty cabs suspended from its girders. In England, it is also called "Big Wheel" or "Eli Wheel." Also called a chump heister or hoister.

Fifth wheel: Term used by carnivals when the show traveled by wagon. Refers to the section that connected the front wheels to the show wagon and enabled the wheels to turn.

Fighting act: Circus term for a big-cat act that moves rapidly and has lots of bounce, thus giving the sense that the trainer is dealing with a group of jungle-wild animals. *see also* BOUNCE and EN FEROCITE.

Fill-in clowns: Circus clowns who perform between turns or acts but do not work an entree,* or a clown with no gags of his or her own. *see also* ENTREE.

Filling-station town: *see* TANK TOWN.

Fin: A late eighteenth-century term for hand, used in the circus and carnival world for a five-dollar bill.

Finale bend: Theatrical slang, rarely used today, for the final bows.

Finger: In the circus and carnival, to accuse or identify someone who has violated laws and thus cause an arrest.

Finish or finish trick: The last "trick," usually the most impressive number by a performer or rider in the circus, for example, and the one that draws the most applause.

Fink: 1. In the circus, a broken novelty or a torn balloon. *see* LARRY. 2. In most outdoor amusement forms, a nonmember or a showman who is no good. Supposedly the word was coined in memory of one Mike Fink, a no-good guy who betrayed his sharpshooting act partner by plugging her square between the eyes at a matinee.

Fireball or fireball outfit: A third-rate outdoor amusement show or operation allowing dishonest tactics to abound so as to burn up* the towns in which it played for other attractions. *see also* BURN UP.

Fireman drama: A type of popular drama of the nineteenth century focusing on the firefighting activities and social life of volunteer firemen, including the most popular of these characters, Mose the firebouy.

First card: In card magic, the first card to be dealt, whether face up or down, or the top card of the deck when the deck is held face-down.

First count: The initial tabulation of money taken in by the various circus attractions after a performance. The employee responsible for this task frequently kept a portion of the take before turning his revenue over to the owner.

First entrance: In vaudeville, an entrance to one.* *see also* ONE.

First-of-May or First-of-May guy: In the circus, a rookie or newcomer who has just joined the show and is thus the most inexperienced, or a first-season trouper. The term was also used by tent-repertoire companies to mean a beginner. The term derives from the fact that traveling tent circuses began their season around May 1.

First opening: *see* OPENING.

First-part ladies: The name given to female minstrels who opened early variety theatre shows. After sitting in the ensemble, they then sold drinks on commission (and other favors on occasion) to patrons of the horseshoe circle of boxes.

Firstie: A black-face minstrel novice.

Fish: Medicine-show lingo for a sucker.* Also a guy, bird, or bozo. *see also* SUCKER.

Fish unpickled: Medicine-show slang meaning of a studious habit.

Fishplate: The metal connecting bridge between two flatcars that enables a circus to unload equipment and assorted paraphernalia lengthwise.

Fit-up: A traveling or portable company, or, in the fair world, especially in England, a traveling theatrical booth or show.

Fix: In carnival language and some circus use, a license received or protection money paid to the local authorities or county or state official for permission to operate a carnival. At one time the fix or ice* implied permission to include illegal gambling enterprises. Fix is also used to denote a dishonest lawyer or a shyster. *see also* BAG MAN and ICE.

Fixed: Carnival and pitchmen's term meaning ready for work, with the implication of buying off the police. *see* FIX and FIXER.

Fixer: 1. A legal representative of a circus or carnival who handles legal adjustment for damages, accidents, claims, or unfair claims. Such a position, often a former lawyer, also acts as mediator between the show and the local officials. 2. An illegal or diplomatic agent who buys protection from local officials and sometimes pays licenses, fees, or adjusts. Also known as a squarer. *see* ADJUSTER, BAG MAN, ICEMAN, MENDER, PATCH, and VULCANIZER.

Flack or flak: One of several terms for a press agent, as well as the material sent out in great volume (publicity) by the press agent.* *see also* PRESS AGENT.

Flag: The signal raised over the cookhouse* in a circus when a meal is being served; meals may be had only as long as the flag is up. *see also* COOKHOUSE and FLAG'S UP.

Flag's up: Circus expression for "soup's on," when the flag* has been run up over the cookhouse while meals are being served to employees. At one time on the Ringling Bros. and Barnum & Bailey Circus, the employees called out Joe Blow,* because the man whose duty it was to run up the flag was named Joe Blow.* *see also* FLAG.

Flag waver: Literally, a performer who brandishes the flag for easy applause; figuratively, one who seeks easy applause with something other than talent or the excellence of the performance.

Flannel-mouth: In vaudeville and burlesque, this term had the following meanings: 1. A straight man* with false teeth. *see also* STRAIGHT MAN. 2. A straight man who acted as feeder* to the comic. *see also* FEEDER. 3. A comic or straight man or girl who came in after the matinee with a few drinks in him or her, thus mushy mouthed with a thick tongue.

Flash: 1. In general, a smart, showy, or well-dressed person; a good appearance, not only of an individual, but also merchandise or an act upon the stage or in a circus. *see* SLUM. 2. In pitchmen's terms, the flashy display of merchandise on a gaming concession, or any striking bally* to attract prospective purchasers. None of the above definitions to the people who are concerned has any context of vulgarity or ostentation. *see also* BALLY, (TO) FAIRBANK, and THROW A COP. 3. In verb form, in carnival terms, either to set up a display of merchandise or prizes or to show a stolen article to one capable of evaluating it. 4. In the striptease, to expose any part of the body, especially the pubic area. *see* FLASHING.

Flash act: A type of act in vaudeville comprised of a man and woman or a good single performer (a dancer, for example) backed up by a line of women or men (or both) who sing and dance, plus some attractive scenery of their own, and often with their own conductor. The act, using the full stage and attempting to present a mini-revue, made a "flash." Some of the better chorus men became stars of their own vaudeville flash acts. A number of the acts were quite lavish.

Flash back: In vaudeville comedy, the situation when a straight man* turned a laugh which a comic had won into a laugh for himself. *see also* STRAIGHT MAN.

Flash effect: A magic trick with a fast and highly visible climax.

Flash for the crowd: To give a valuable prize at a carnival set-joint* for the purpose of attracting the crowd. *see* (TO) FAIRBANK, SET-JOINT, THROW A COP, and THROW-AWAY.

Flash paper: Extremely useful piece of magical tissue paper chemically treated with mildly explosive chemicals so that it disappears with a brilliant flash when touched with anything hot.

Flash wand: A magician's wand that emits a bright flash of fire when the control is triggered.

Flasher: A modern carnival game of chance in which electrical circuits and lights have replaced the old wheel of chance. In some places where Percentage or P. C. store* games are disallowed, the authorities permit flashers and convince themselves they are outlawing carnival wheels.* *see also* CARNIVAL WHEEL and PERCENTAGE OR P. C. STORE.

Flashing: In the striptease, the lowering or removal of the G-string* so that the pubic area is revealed. Although the G-string may be lowered to the knees or ankles, its complete removal was apparently considered obscene by many strippers in the past. It is now commonplace, if, indeed, a G-string is even used. *see also* G-STRING.

Flashing it up: In the circus, the adding of fancy touches, spangles, sequins, and the like, to the wardrobe* (never called costumes). *see also* WARDROBE.

Flat: In carnival slang, pertaining to any carnival gambling game, especially one in which money is the prize. *see* FLAT JOINT OR STORE.

Flat joint or store: A carnival gaming concession operated by control where gambling is the attraction. Originally, a flat joint was a horizontal wheel of chance that actually employed an arrow or spindle* instead of a wheel and got its name because it lay flat rather than suspended vertically like most carnival wheels. Not found in the most reputable carnivals today. *see also* SPINDLE and TWO-WAY JOINT.

Flatfoots: The nickname of a group in New York City who in 1835 established a trust, which was to become the Zoological Institute, with the intent of preventing circus competitors from performing in New York, albeit unsuccessfully. They were called flatfoots because, when an outside exhibit attempted to invade their territory, they put their feet flat down and refused them entry.

Flat riding: *see* HIGH RIDING.

Flats: In circus terms, the flatcars of the show train.

Flattie or flatty: 1. Carnival meaning is that of the operator of a carnival gambling or con-game, such as a flat joint,* alibi store,* two-way joint,* or G-joint.* Flatties are considered, even among carnival performers, as common thieves and unlike the performers who give the marks* something for their money. Today, their numbers are limited because carnival owners often restrict (or disallow altogether) the number of flat stores and the like on their midways. *see also* ALIBI STORE, FLAT-JOINT, G-JOINT, MARK, and TWO-WAY JOINT. 2. In the English circus, a flattie or flatty is one of the public or a member of the audience. Also called josser, gajo, and yob.

Flea bag: A disreputable, dirty, and ragged circus show.

Flea circus: An exhibition, once found in carnivals and some circuses, of performing fleas with human traits.

Flea powder: Pitchmen's term, used by med showmen especially, for powdered herbs.

Flesh: Actors who appear live (in person).

Flesh peddler: A booking agent who handles actors for a fee.

Fleshings or fleshing tights: Skin-colored tights frequently worn to make the performer appear naked. Adah Isaacs Menken, in the latter half of the nineteenth century, helped to establish female sexuality as part of the mainstream of show business by wearing fleshings under a brief costume in the role of Mazeppa.

Flic-flac: *see* FLIP-FLAP.

Flip-flap: Circus term for an acrobatic trick, called by gymnasts a "back handspring." The trick is to flip from a standing position to the hands. It can be done on the ground or in the hands of a bottom man.* It is also called a flic-flac and is seen in various forms depending on the culture and country. *see also* BOTTOM MAN.

Flirtation act: In vaudeville, an act presented by a man and woman playing lover-like scenes.

Flivved: Theatrical slang for flopped.

Floaters: Slices of lemon or orange, made of colored wax, that floated on the top of bowls or tanks of imitation orange or lemonade sold on the circus or carnival midway.

Floating stage: A stage in a floating theatre or showboat.* *see also* SHOWBOAT.

Flock of hungry eggs: Medicine-show expression that refers to bums and, on some occasions, sailors.

Flookum, flukem, flukum: 1. Carnival slang for a midway-mixed soft drink made of powder containing synthetic flavor and color. 2. In pitchmen's terms, it is any of various kinds of cheap, nearly worthless, but classy-looking and apparently useful merchandise. Most often it refers to nickle-plated ware but can also mean a pitchman's metal polish. *see* FLOOZUM.

Floor show: The name for an entertainment presented in a nightclub, some cabarets, and other similar places of amusement.

Floozum: A pitchman's metal ware. *see* FLOOKUM.

Flop: 1. Outdoor amusement-business term for a night's lodging, usually a cheap room or bed. In verb form, to flop means to sleep or stay overnight. It has also been used to mean to beg on city streets by sitting on sidewalks. *see* FLOP-HOUSE. 2. General show-business word for a failure.

Flop-house: Outdoor amusement-world term for cheap rooming house or hotel. *see* FLOP.

Flop sweat: A vaudeville term used when a comic went out and flopped* or laid an egg to a tough audience. This obviously describes the perspiration that appeared over his body. *see also* FLOPPED.

Flopped: A performance that failed.

Flopperoo or floperoo: A slang term for a failure, applied to a person or thing, especially a spectacularly unsuccessful stage show or film. Typical of slang popularized by *Variety*.

Floss: Circus term for pink spun-sugar or cotton candy. Also called sweetened air.

Flossy: Circus word for showy.

Fluff: Originally, probably a medicine-show term for a sap.

Fluff off: In the jargon of the chorus girl,* this signifies getting rid of an unwelcomed admirer. *see also* CHORUS GIRL.

Flunkey: Waiter in the circus cookhouse. *see also* COOKHOUSE.

Fly: *see* BREEZE.

Fly gee: Carnival-originated slang for a wise guy.

Flyer or flier: An aerialist, especially those in flying return acts, who literally leaves his trapeze to fly through the air. Although flying is among the most glamorous of circus acts, it is actually one of the youngest, having been invented about a century ago by the Frenchman Jules Leotard, who also gave the flyer's distinctive costume its name. *see also* CATCHER, FLYING RETURN, and LEOTARD.

Flying frame: The aerial rigging for trapeze aerialists.

Flying horses: Carnival term used at some southern amusement parks and carnivals for the carousel* or merry-go-round. *see also* CAROUSEL.

Flying machine: English fair term for any riding device simulating flight.

Flying return: The return trip by a flyer* from the catcher's* hand by way of the trapeze to the pedestal or perch from which he originally started. *see also* CATCHER and FLYER.

Flying squadron: The first section of a circus to reach the lot.

Flying trapeze act: A circus aerial act in which flyers* fly from one swinging trapeze bar to another or to the hands of a catcher*. *see also* CATCHER and FLYER.

Foil: *see* STOOGE.

Foldee: Theatrical jargon for a show that folded or closed.

Folding stuff: Carnival slang for paper money.

Follow the animated: To open the bill in a vaudeville show. *see* OPEN THE SHOW.

Foo Can: A magician's device allowing a container to be shown empty even though it holds liquid. A partition keeps the liquid inside when the container is tilted one way but a reverse tilt allows the liquid to pour out.

Footlights: Although originally footlights were the row of lights with reflectors lining the front edge or apron of the stage, the word has come to indicate a point of view as much as the literal objects (especially since most theatres have eliminated footlights), that is, the mysterious line between the performer and the audience.

Force: Magician's term for the ability to restrict or control a spectator's choice to one item, especially a playing card. Numerous methods are used, e.g., a glide,* a glimpse,* or a thought force. *see also* FORCING, GLIDER, and GLIMPSE.

Forcing: In magic, in some way compelling a spectator to choose a known object from among a number of items, though the spectator believes he has had freedom of selection. *see* FORCE.

Fore-runner: *see* HEADMAN.

Fork: An iron rod used to place meat in circus animal cages.

Fork jump: In a circus equestrian act, a leap from the ground to the back of a horse, landing astraddle. *see* LIFT, RUNNING GROUND MOUNT, and VOLTIGE.

Forty-miler: A carnival term of comparatively recent origin meaning a trouper new to the outdoor show world; a person who joins a show but quits after making a few moves; a trouper who does not possess real showman's spirit; or one who never takes his concession, show, or ride more than a few miles from his home base. *see* HOME GUARD.

Forty-nine camp (49 camp): A carnival concession patterned after the old-time western dance halls of the gold rush days, in which girls danced with the customers at so-much-a-dance and then usually steered them to the bar to buy drinks. By the late 1920s, such concessions were virtually a thing of the past.

Found: A tent-repertoire term used as a synonym for food.

Fountain: A one-hand juggling pattern creating an effect in which the objects rise and fall. It can also be called a one-hand shower.* *see also* SHOWER.

Four: In vaudeville, the stage space six or so feet behind the upstage (away from the audience) line of three.* *see also* IN ONE, ONE, THREE, and TWO.

Four and three: Tent-repertoire and Toby-show* phrase to describe the typical makeup of some repertoire shows, that is, four men and three women, although many companies actually had larger troupes. *see also* TOBY SHOW.

Four-man-high: A circus teeterboard* trick in which an acrobat, usually the lightest of the troupe, catapults to the top of a three-person pyramid. *see also* TEETER BOARD ACT and THREE HIGH OR THREE-MEN-HIGH.

Four-way(s): In circus slang, a way is a code word for five cents used by boss butchers* to keep each other informed and the public in ignorance of the price of their wares. Prices can constantly fluctuate above an official rate according to what the traffic will allow. *see also* BOSS BUTCHER.

Four-way joint: A carnival game that can be played from four sides. *see* JOINT and THREE-WAY JOINT.

Fractional Kale: *see* KALE and ROW OF CHICKEN FEED.

Frail: Medicine-showman's term for a woman.

Frame: In carnival terminology, to build, prepare, or set up anything, especially a new concession, midway, or show. *see* BUILD UP.

Frame a joint: *see* FRAME and MAKE A JOINT.

Frame-up: The display of a pitchman's stock.

Framing or framing a show: Circus word for planning a circus production or starting a new show.

Freaks: *see* HUMAN ODDITIES.

Free act: A free carnival or amusement park midway show or added attraction given in the open air on the show grounds to draw a crowd that will ultimately attend the paid attraction. Frequently free shows are of a sensational, death-defying nature. *see* BALLY.

Free chorus: An early twentieth-century practice of having a chorus girl paid by her friends rather than by a producer. Obviously, talent was of little concern so, if fortunate, a popular chorus girl, one of a large number, would depend on one or more male friends to help pay her way.

Freebees: Complimentary tickets given away to help fill a house. By extension, a person is a freebee. *see* COMP.

Freeloader: Show-business term for a chiseler or, literally, one who loads up on free drinks and food.

French drop: A magician's sleight or sleight-of-hand* enabling the performer to retain a small object in one hand while pretending to pass it on to the other. *see also* SLEIGHT OR SLEIGHT-OF-HAND and TOURNIQUET.

French leave: Tent repertoire and touring-company slang expression meaning to leave a job without giving notice and usually secretly. Originally, the term was used in World War I for one leaving a navy ship or army post without authorization.

Friend of show: One who enjoys special privileges around a circus, such as a member of the Circus Fans' Association.

Fringe: A decoration on a stripper's or show-girl's panties or G-string comprised of many thin strips of gold or silver material.

Fright wig or hair: In burlesque and vaudeville, a wig worn frequently by comics. By pulling a string the hair stands on end and underscores moments of surprise or fear. Sometimes called a scare wig. *see* SCRATCH WIG.

Frisco: Show-business abbreviation for San Francisco.

Frisk: Term used in outdoor amusement areas meaning to explore thoroughly or to search. In general use today.

Frog: A circus contortionist. *see* BENDER and LIMBER JIM.

Frog salad: Slang expression for a girlie show* or some other female entertainment that provides a ready opportunity for studying the female form. *see also* GIRLIE SHOW.

Frohman: The name given to the manager of a country opera house or theatre in general. Named after the famous New York manager Charles Frohman (1860-1915). Now obsolete.

Frolic: An entertainment or performance; originated by professional entertainers to indicate the number of times they appeared in any one day.

Front: In both the circus and carnival, this can mean a good appearance or one's wearing apparel, although it most frequently refers to the front of a midway show or attraction, such as a sideshow, including the lineup of banners* and platforms. *see also* BANNER.

(On the) front: To be before or in front or a joint* of store* in order to either make an opening* or grind on the front, which means to keep up a continual and repetitious spiel* for the joint. *see also* BALLY, JOINT, MAKE AN OPENING, SPIEL, and STORE.

Front and back, timber and town: Phrase used to describe the types of backdrops a touring theatre company, especially a small one, would expect to find in any small-town theatre, thus eliminating the necessity of carrying the same. The terms meant parlour, kitchen, woods, and street backdrops.

Front door: 1. The main entrance to the circus tent used by patrons. 2. A circus term for a person stationed at or near the front door for running errands. 3. The administrative staff of a circus, as opposed to the performers. *see* BACK YARD.

Front-end: Generally thought of as pertaining to that portion of a midway near the main entrance, most frequently used on carnivals but also some circuses. The front-end usually refers to the games, the refreshment and souvenir concessions, and not to a geographical location or physical patterning, although there is some correspondence. Small rides and shows, for example, are usually part of the front-end, although a ride can be at the geographical rear of a carnival and still be considered part of the front-end. *see* BACK-END.

Front-end people: Carnies* who work games, food, and other concessions, as opposed to back-end people,* who are concerned with shows, such as freak shows, gorilla shows, walking-zombie shows, and girlie shows. *see also* BACK-END PEOPLE, CARNIE, and FRONT-END.

Front grandstand: Reserved circus seats on the side opposite from the bandstand. The performers took their bows to these seats and focused their acts to that side of the big top.* *see also* BIG TOP.

Front room set: *see* CENTER OR CENTRE DOOR FANCY.

Front row: The foremost line of a chorus or dancing ensemble; also, the line of seats nearest a stage.

Front track: Hippodrome track* on the side of the big top* opposite the back door* and the bandstand. *see also* BACK DOOR, BIG TOP, and HIPPODROME TRACK.

Front-worker: On the midway, a confederate who mingles with the crowd and plays a gambling game, walking off conspicuously with a large prize or a bundle of money, thus enticing customers to try their luck. *see* BOOSTER, CAPPER, COME-ON, OUTSIDE MAN, SHILL, and STICK.

Frost: A turn-of-the-century word for a theatrical failure.

Fruit-machine: The English fair equivalent to the one-armed bandit once found at amusement parks and carnivals; a coin-operated gaming machine. Still to be found in altered forms.

Full stage: In vaudeville, the stage space was usually divided into four areas running parallel with the footlights and going toward the back of the stage. Full stage, then, was the same as four.* *see also* ONE, TWO, THREE, and FOUR.

Full three: A feat attempted by circus leapers* in which three complete somersaults were attempted in the air after the leap. *see also* LEAPER.

Funambulist: A circus rope walker, rope dancer, or wire walker. From the Latin "funis" (rope) and "ambulare" (to walk).

Funny Old Gal: The American version of the "dame" in British pantomime, played by end men* in a minstrel show. Comic men played the part of females in drag. *see also* END MAN and FEMALE IMPERSONATOR.

Funny ropes: Extra ropes added to a regular one, usually at angles, to give extra stability, strength, and spread to canvas circus tents. *see* EXTRAS OR DOUBLE-STAKING.

Fuzz: Term used by carnies and pitchmen for the police or a policeman. When police first used to interrupt carnival games of chance (and some circus games), they appeared on the grounds in smaller towns and rural areas as rustics with chin whiskers, and thus the name, based on these fuzzy chins, came into the carnival language. *see* COOKIE-CUTTER, COP, DICK, SHAMUS, and TINS.

G

G or G-Note: Show-business term for a grand or $1,000. *see* GRAND.

Gabber: A radio commentator.

Gabbing act: A vaudeville act with dialogue.

Gadget: 1. In pitchmen's terms, any household article, or articles in general. 2. In striptease, the device worn by some performers to enhance the illusion of their performance, or the G-string.

Gaff (also gimmick or "G"): 1. In carnival, circus, and amusement-park terminology, a concealed device or secret method that controls the play of such mechanical gambling devices as a flat joint* or gaffed joint or G-joint.* As a verb, it means to install such a device, or by extension, to cheat someone (specifically to short-change a customer or withhold money from the sale of admission tickets that should go in the till). *see also* FLAT JOINT, GAFFED JOINT, and TWO-WAY JOINT. 2. Limited use, in circus parlance, for the manager. 3. In English fair slang, a fairground site or a cheap place of amusement. 4. The English circus uses gaff to mean a fairground booth. 5. The British once used gaff to mean a portable or improvised theatre or music hall and, by extension, any cheap, low-class theatre or music hall. A number of these theatres were referred to in terms of their admission charges, such as penny gaff, twopenny gaff, and so on. Gaff street meant any street with several theatres.

Gaff lad: English fair term for a casual laborer who builds up and pulls down rides and collects the money.

Gaff wheel: A gambling wheel controlled by a secret device, such as a board built into the platform upon which the operator is standing. By pressing hard on the board the wheel can be stopped at any desired point. *see* CARNIVAL WHEEL and GAFF.

Gaffed: A rigged carnival game. *see* GAFF.

Gaffed joint or G-joint: A carnival game that can be operated dishonestly. *see* GAFF.

Gaffer: Circus term for a manager. Also called colonel, governor, and main guy. Also used for the big boss in a carnival or on a midway. (In the movie industry, this is the head electrician.) *see* GAFF.

Gaffs on the joint: In circus, carnival, and amusement-park slang, a spindle* or some other device on a mechanical gambling game that is working crooked. *see also* GAFF, GAFF JOINT, and SPINDLE.

Gag: 1. In the American circus, all clown routines. A production gag, for example, is a full-scale act with elaborate props lasting about five minutes. 2. In general terms, a gag can be a comic remark, trick, prop, scene, stunt, and so on, used in a performance. 3. In vaudeville, a gag was any joke or pun. *see* POINT. 4. In carnival (and sometimes circus) lingo, this can mean an effective come-on. *see also* COME-ON.

Gag card: English fair term for a poster attempting to make humorous observations that relate to a ride or attractions, thus helping to attract customers. *see* BANNER.

Gajo: English circus term for an outsider. Also called josser, flattie or flatty, and yob.

Gallery gods: Theatrical term, used frequently during the first quarter of this century, to mean those in the upper balcony who could only afford the less expensive tickets and were often rowdy and disorderly. *see* POST IN THE GALLERY.

Galop: Circus word, used mostly in English circuses, for fast band music used for certain exits and entrances.

Gams: Once a common word for a girl's legs as used in carnivals, circuses, and most entertainment forms. One explanation for this usage is that, when groups of circus workers casually chatted about a show (having a "gam" or talk), the most frequent subject was the legs and general attractiveness of the girls and women who passed. The word actually comes from eighteenth-century low slang, "gambs," meaning thin, unshapely legs, and a corruption of the French "jambes." In heraldry, "gamb" is the technical word for a leg.

Gander: Circus slang meaning to look.

Gandy dancer: From the motion of a railroad section hand or track laborer, with his rhythmic dancelike movement in straightening rails and smoothing gravel. In carnival slang, this has come to mean a seller of novelties.

Garbage stand: A circus or carnival novelty booth.

(The) Garden: Madison Square Garden in New York City, which has become the traditional first and longest stand of the season for Ringling Bros. and Barnum & Bailey Circus. Circus performers, who now winter in Florida, use the Garden to denote the wet, cold, dark North, expensive meals and hotel bills, and other derogatory notions. However, the word also reminds performers of spring and a new rebirth, thus it can be also a hopeful and optimistic expression.

Garland entry: A circus equestrian act in which the riders use garlands of artificial flowers.

Garter: Circus term for tape or narrow ribbon over which a performer, usually a bareback rider, leaps or jumps.

Gas: The name given to trucks and tractors used by railroad-transported circuses by the workmen and bosses in the 1920s and 1930s.

Gasoline bill baker: Pitchmen's stock name for any editor of the pitchmen's department of *Billboard*.* *see also* BILLBOARD.

Gate money: Admission paid at the door or gate of a house or field of entertainment; used primarily for a sporting event.

Gather a push: *see* PUSH.

Gathering back: Circus term for a back somersault ending in front of the starting point.

Gawks: Townspeople who watch the loading and unloading of circus trains or who throng the show lots. Also called lot loafers.

Gazoonie or gazooney: Used in most outdoor forms, including the circus, as a name for a man who works cheaply or for nothing. Often, it is used more specifically for a young working man or a kid. *see* GUNSEL and PUNK.

Gazukus: Medicine-show and pitchmen's term for either authentic speech or the goods (the real gazukus). Also called Skookum.

Gazuntheit: One of a number of classic burlesque comic retorts to a Bronx cheer or heckle.

Geedus: Circus, carnival, and pitchmen's term for money. Also called gelt, Jack, kale, and scratch. *see* TAKE.

Geegaws: Carnival slang for trinkets, novelties, or domestic tools sold by pitchmen. *see* FLUSH and SLUM.

Geek: The most frequently used meaning of this term is that of a carnival or circus pit show* snake-eating wild man. The geek, virtually nonexistent today, was considered a freak, usually a fake, who performed sensationally disgusting acts that normal people would not. A geek would swallow live mice or snakes or bite heads of live chickens and usually regurgitate them. The geek's status in the carnival world was quite low and even among carnies* he was usually considered perverted or mentally deranged. Maurer in "Carnival Cant" says the word is reputed to have originated with a man named Wagner of Charleston, West Virginia, whose hideous snake-eating act made him famous. His ballyhoo* included this verse:

> "Come and see Essau
> Sittin' on a see-saw
> Eatin' em raw!"

see also BALLYHOO, CARNY, GLOMMER, and PIT SHOW.

Gelt: Circus and carnival slang for money. Also called geedus, Jack, kale, take, and scratch. *see* TAKE.

Gelt on the lease: Pitchmen's phrase for money on hand, or money which is readily available. *see* GELT.

General agent: Carnival or midway slang for a person whose nerve or courage is in his boss's name.

General business: Used in tent shows, in particular Toby shows,* for actors who could play whatever was required of them. *see also* TOBY SHOW.

General card: Name for a group of card routines used by magicians. Usually performed with a chosen card, in which the entire deck seems to be made up of one card. At the conclusion, the deck is shown to the audience, and this card is the only one missing; the card is then produced by the magician in some mysterious way. Also known as the "Ambitious Card" and "Everybody's Card."

Generally useful: A phrase in a circus performer's contract that indicates that he or she is available for whatever work the management chooses.

Genre: In the circus, this refers to a performing specialty defined by the skills involved or the use of a particular apparatus or prop. Examples would include such genres as foot juggling, wire dancing, and pole acrobatics. Genres exist within broader classes of circus arts, such as aerial, clown, wire, and acrobatics. In the history of the circus, genres pass away and others are newly created. The introduction, for example, of new apparatus and materials will open new possibilities to inventive circus performers. Normally, a new genre becomes more complex, demanding, and specialized until, when it surpasses the ability of those performing it, it dies out. Still, one genre will influence other genres and can pass from one class to another. Many circus acts will incorporate several genres.

Gentling: The process in the circus of subduing by patience and bribery wild animals and teaching them to perform tricks or take part in group acts. The term was apparently coined by the animal trainer Carl Hagenbeck around the turn of the century.

George Spelvin: A fictitious name, said to have been in *Karl the Peddler*, written by Charles A. Gardiner in 1886, used in a theatre program to indicate that either an actor does not want his real name used or that the actor playing a particular role is not known at the time the program deadline arrives. Also used for an actor doubling (playing two or more roles) when it is wished to have that fact concealed.

Sometimes George X. Spelvin is given when the character dies in the course of the performance. Other variations on the first name have appeared, such as Georgiana (although this is less frequently used because of the porno star with a similar name). Less prominent but serving the same purpose as George Spelvin is the mythical Harry Selby.* *see also* HARRY SELBY, JOE HEPP, and WALTER PLINGE.

Gerry Society: A movement that had a noticeable effect on both the legitimate stage and especially vaudeville. The Society for the Prevention of Cruelty to Children, headed by Elbridge T. Gerry, did not permit children to perform on the New York stage unless a permit was granted by the society. The movement spread to many other states.

Get a grouch on: *see* GROUCH BAG.

(To) get a hand: To receive applause.

Get across with a bang: Vaudeville phrase to indicate when an act (or turn) is a rousing success. *see* CLICK.

Get away stake: Medicine-show expression for having the means to move from one place to another.

Get in (or out): Order given in a carnival to sticks* or shills* indicating whether or not they should actively win at a game in order to attract business or move aside because the number of marks* has increased adequately. As the number of players decreases, once more the sticks are ordered to get in. *see also* CLEANER, LIVE ONE, MARK, SHILL, and STICK.

(To) get over: In vaudeville, to make a speech or entire act a success.

(To) get the hook: In vaudeville, to remove prematurely an inferior or unsuccessful act. In some vaudeville houses, actual hooks on long poles were used.

(To) get the McCloskey: Turn-of-the-century theatrical phrase meaning to be jilted.

(To) get the wrinkles out of your belly: Carnival and circus expression meaning to get adjusted to a new show and become accustomed to the show life.

Get the show on the road: Circus phrase for "let's get going." Used today in many contexts.

Get up the nut: To raise funds adequate enough to cover the overhead and operating expenses of a carnival, circus, theatre production, or other form of entertainment. *see* (TO) CRACK THE NUT and NUT OR BURR.

(To) get with it: Circus expression specifically referring to returning to one's business with the show. By extension, it is also used to mean to get busy, to work harder, to hurry, or to step lively.

Getaway day: The last day of a circus engagement.

Getaway night: Similar meaning to getaway day.* Touring companies used this term to mean the night on which the company played its last performance in a particular theatre. In some smaller tent shows, including traveling Toby shows,* it was not unusual for the scenery and props to be struck (by the actors during the performance) and loaded onto the truck by the time the final curtain fell. Apparently, this was one of the fascinations for the audience on this night. *see also* GETAWAY DAY and TOBY SHOW.

Getting a ride: Primarily a circus expression for unpaid and unfavorable publicity in newspapers.

Ghost: The treasurer of the theatre or a theatrical company. The title possibly came from the ghost in *Hamlet*, an actor in this role having refused to play until he was paid. *see* GHOST-WALKING OR THE GHOST WALKS.

Ghost-walking day or the ghost walks: Theatrical phrase for payday. As H. L. Mencken states it, "The ghost* is said to walk on payday." To receive one's salary is to see the ghost walk; when not paid, the ghost fails to walk. *see also* GHOST.

Ghost's window: Theatrical pay window. *see* GHOST and GHOST-WALKING DAY OR THE GHOSTS WALKS.

Ghost show: A particular kind of magical entertainment, often performed at midnight, which consists of such attractions as horror movies, mind reading, staged torture, suspense plot magic, and a short sequence in darkness in which "ghosts" float over and through the audience, a gimmick incorporated recently in the off-Broadway production of *The Passion of Dracula*. *see* REACHING RODS.

Ghost train: An English fair ride and show combination. At regular intervals, cars on energized rails carrying no more than two passengers penetrate a darkened enclosure. A labyrinth of hair-raising spectacles, optical illusions, and sudden cloying tactility await them. Similar to numerous rides in American amusement parks, some carnivals, and most modern theme parks (such as Disney World's "Haunted Mansion") that operate under less identifiable names. In technique, the same as the Tunnel of Love.* *see also* TUNNEL OF LOVE.

Ghost tube: The name of a popular piece of magical apparatus that can be shown apparently empty, while later producing goods, scarves, and the like.

Gig show: Circus slang for a minstrel show.

Gill or gills: Circus and pitchmen's slang for customers, usually with the connotation of suckers, outsiders, or rustics. *see* GILLY.

Gillipin: *see* GILLY-GALLOO.

Gilly, gilley, and gillie: 1. In its verb form, gilly has been used to mean the renting of a few cars and moving a small show by rail, and also the handling of a show's equipment and paraphernalia by hand or moving in a vehicle not built for the equipment being moved (when the ground was soft and muddy, a circus sometimes had to be "gillied" on the lot). 2. As a noun, gilly has several possible meanings: anyone uninitiated or not connected with the circus; in the English circus, a member of the audience; a small circus moving in cars or a vehicle hired to transport circus or theatrical equipment. The gilly or gilly wagon is perhaps the most common use of the term in the American circus. Small one- and two-car shows, in particular, used a knockdown wagon or gilly wagon and carried everything to and from the train. Larger shows always used gilly in the meaning of an extra wagon or vehicle or any method of carrying (to shuttle, relay, or tote) that was different from that usually used. The extra wagons, when rented, were usually used to carry lighter pieces of equipment around the lot. The word originated from British sailor jargon, "gilguy," a wrong rope on a boat, hence wrong guy. *see* GILL.

Gilly-galloo or gillygaloo: An insulting circus slang expression for an outsider because of the addition of "galloo," a corruption of "gelubt," Dutch for eunuch. "Galoot" was used circa 1835 to mean an inexperienced marine and was probably added to gilly* after that date. The phrase as compounded implies a jerk or a stupid person. Also used are gillipin and scissorbill. *see also* GILL and SCISSORBILL.

Gilly show: Term most frequently associated with carnivals, meaning a small carnival loaded in boxcars, carrying very little, and having to gilly* its equipment back and forth by trucks to and from the railroad. This type of gilly show has not been in existence for several decades. On the other hand, the meaning has been extended to refer to a rag bag* show or one that "burns the lot" and doesn't return; a cheap show that is often extremely dishonest and holds great contempt for its customers. *see also* GILL, GILLY, and RAG BAG.

Gilly wagon: *see* GILLY.

Gimme some light, Slim: In the circus, midway, or carnival, the cry of the teardown* boss to the one remaining light plant. *see also* TEARDOWN.

Gimmick: From gimix, a small tool or machine, a gimmick in the carnival and, as used by pitchmen, refers to any trick, secret device, or gadget that can cheat the public or stimulate business. In games of chance, it is a dishonest device for controlling or regulating the outcome. In the circus, it is a mechanical aid, not apparent to the audience, for making a difficult trick easier to perform. Magicians use the word to indicate a secret piece of apparatus or preparation that is largely responsible for the success of a trick. Prepared articles in each form are "gimmicked" or gaffed.* In magician's lingo, this is also known as a fake.* *see also* FAKE, GAFF, and GAFFED.

Gimp legged: Circus slang for a cripple. Also called a gimpy.

Ginger: Theatrical usage current around the turn of the century to denote suggestive lines or some risqué significance.

Gink: Medicine-show and pitchmen's word for a person in a crowd.

Gipsy Lee: In the English fair, the name frequently given the fortune-teller's booth or concession. *see* GYPSY CAMP and MITT CAMP OR JOINT.

Girlesk: A carnival tent show featuring girls.

Girlie show: Originally used for crude, somewhat illegal shows, tending toward the obscene, whose main attractions were scantily clad girls. Now used to apply to any show featuring attractive females, usually with a great deal of nudity. Sometimes used as a synonym for a burlesque or a striptease show.

Gismo or gizmo: A term probably originated by Joe Weber and used in the Weber and Fields act to mean any mechanical contraption; it was also used by Kolb and Dill, another German dialect act in vaudeville.

Give 'em the iggy: *see* IGGY.

Give him the skull: As used in various forms of entertainment, a skull* means a take.* In burlesque, a skull or (to) skull a line meant a slow reaction to a line, with the skull being the face or facial expression. To be effective, the skull was done as a carefully timed delayed reaction, and if the face did much of the work, this was called *to skull a line*. Give him the skull, then, was the process used by the comic in reaction to a straight man or vice versa. *see also* SKULL, STRAIGHT MAN, and TAKE.

Give out the play: An obsolete theatrical practice of announcing the play to be performed the following night on very short notice.

Give the office: *see* (TO) OFFICE.

Giveaway: *see* HIGH PITCH.

G-joint: A carnival concession that has a controlled device. *see* GAFFED JOINT.

Gladway: A southern term for what is called the midway in the North.

Glass house: A crystal maze and a house of mirrors on a carnival midway.

Glass joint: Carnival concession in which glass articles are sold or awarded as prizes. *see* JOINT.

Glide: A magician's sleight-of-hand* that allows the performer to hold back a card and deal the next card to it from under the deck. *see also* DEALING SECONDS and SLEIGHT OR SLEIGHT-OF-HAND.

Glim: In the English circus, the word for light.

Glimpse: In magic, to secretly catch sight of some article that is supposed to be hidden from the audience.

Glims: Circus, carnival, and general pitchmen's slang for eyes or eyeglasses. Also called cheaters. *see* GOOGS.

Glittergals: Carnival term for female show performers. *see* BIMBOS.

Glommer or glommin' geek: "Glaum" or "glom" means to seize or to snatch. In this context, a glommer is a sideshow or pit* attraction who uses the hands to "glom" an item to eat instead of having it pushed into the face. *see also* GEEK, PIT, and PIT SHOW.

Glorifier of the American Girl: The name given to Florenz Ziegfeld, producer of the Ziegfeld Follies, which featured the beautiful, alluring Ziegfield girls. *see* REVUE.

Glove or hand puppet: A hollow cloth figure, fitting the hand, with a wooden head and hands moved by the fingers. It is usually manipulated by the operator from below. *see* MARIONETTE.

Go-ahead: Nineteenth-century English circus term for an advance agent.* *see also* ADVANCE AGENT.

Go big: In vaudeville, when a performer, act,* gag,* song, or the like, is very successful and receives a great deal of applause. *see also* ACT and GAG.

Go clean: To sell all tickets to a performance.

Go gilly: Traveling theatrical troupe term for motorizing a show. *see* GILL and GILLY.

(To) go in the back way: Carnival phrase meaning to practice pederasty. Also (to) go up the dirt road.

(To) go in the bushes: Carnival phrase meaning to have sexual intercourse.

Go out with or go south: Circus and tent-show slang expression meaning to embezzle or to conceal below; to hold out on the receipts. *see* TOOK THE FENCE.

Go rotary: Circus expression meaning emotionally hysterical or very enthusiastic.

Go to Cain's: Theatrical phrase meaning to close a show. Cain's Warehouse was a storage establishment in New York City operated by Cain's Transfer Company (1886-1937), which sold and rented scenery to road companies. *see* CAIN'S.

Go to the runs: In circus lingo, this meant to go to the railroad crossing where the train was being loaded or unloaded. *see* CHUTES, CROSSING, and RUNS.

Go up in the air: Theatrical phrase for missing a cue or forgetting one's lines. Today, simply "go up." *see* BALLOON.

(To) go up the dirt road: *see* (TO) GO IN THE BACK WAY.

(To) go wrong: Carnival and pitchmen's term for losing money. In a carnival concession, this would usually mean that the customer had won a prize that the operator did not intend him to win. *see* BLOW.

Goes to the barn: An outdoor show that goes into winter quarters.* *see also* WINTER QUARTERS.

Gold brick: Circus term sometimes used for a pass to the show.

Gone to the Charley: Circus phrase meaning that something has been thrown in the wastepaper receptacle carried in the bill car. *see* AD-VERTISING CARS and CHARLEY OR CHARLIE.

Gone Sunday school: A circus that has eliminated dishonest games or grift.* Virtually all circuses today are Sunday school* shows, as are a large number of carnivals. *see* GRIFT and SUNDAY SCHOOL.

Gonk: Paste used for posting circus bills. Also, (to) serve up the gonk. *see* HOKUM.

Goobers: Peanuts in circus lingo.

(A) good call: A mark* on a carnival midway who can easily become involved with a particular hustle.* *see also* HUSTLE and MARK.

Good head: Principally a circus expression for a good man, a smart person, or someone who is reliable.

Goofus: Carnival and circus use for a rustic or an easy mark.* *see also* MARK.

Googs: Pitchmen's term for spectacles or eyeglasses; from "goggles." Also called cheaters and glims.

Goose: Theatrical and vaudeville term for a Hebrew or Jewish impersonator. *see* YID.

Goosey: Circus term that can refer either to an individual who is sensitive to being touched on his body, in particular his rear, or to wagon poles used to help push wagons across a railroad flatcar.

Gorge: Circus slang for food. Also called chuck. *see* SCOFFINS.

Gorgio: Outdoor amusement-business word, from the Romany, for a nongypsy.

Gorilla: A muscular or tremendously ugly person who intimidates people; possibly originated in vaudeville.

Governor: Manager, owner, or main guy of a circus or carnival. Also called colonel and gaffer.

Goy: Yiddish expression once used by some theatrical performers for a Gentile.

Grab a handful of boxcars: *see* CATCH OR GRAB A HANDFUL OF BOXCARS.

Grab joint: A circus or carnival food or snack stand that is usually centrally located, especially in a carnival, and often is a stand-up joint with no place to sit, although a few stools may be provided. In the circus, the grab joint is often a quick lunch stand for circus employees. Since circa 1940, the term has been used also to denote a booth or stand that sells souvenirs. *see* JOINT.

Graft: An English circus term meaning to sell at street markets.

Graft the markets: English fair term meaning to sell at street markets.

Grafter: Gambler or "short-changer"* who traveled with a circus or carnival, or who "trailed" the show on the same route* so as to work* the large crowds. Few grafters are allowed on a circus lot today. By extension, a grafter is one who lives by his wits. Also known as a lucky boy* or a slicker. *see also* LUCKY BOY, ROUTE, SHORT-CHANGE ARTIST, and WORK.

Grai: *see* PRAD.

Grand: Show-business slang for one thousand dollars; borrowed from the underworld. *see* G OR G NOTE and HORSE.

Grand entreé: English circus name for the now-defunct circus parade.* *see also* MARCH and PARADE.

Grand guignol: "Guignol" originally was a puppet in a sort of French Punch and Judy show.* This term derived from the Théâtre du Grand Guignol in Paris where a genre of short, sensational horror plays flourished in the 1890s and 1900s. Used in general terms for a type of play built around a sensational situation, such as a murder, rape, or supernatural occurrence, and exploited in terms of the pleasurable horror it can incite in the audience. *see also* PUNCH AND JUDY SHOW.

Grandmother's necklace: An old magic principle of threading beads in such a way that they can be unthreaded instantly; the principle is the basis of many modern string, tape, and rope tricks.

Grandstand: The seats located nearest the rings on each side of the circus big top* and sold for an extra price. *see also* BIG TOP, BLUES, and STAR BACKS.

Gravediggers: *see* CLOSS.

Gravy: Slang for old-time minstrel jokes. Also called oakum.

Grease: 1. Circus and carnival slang for protection money. 2. Pitchmen's word for salve. 3. English circus term for butter.

Grease joint: A circus or carnival hot-dog or hamburger stand. Sometimes used in circus lingo to mean a quick lunch wagon or stand serving circus people and their guests exculsively. *see* GRAB JOINT.

Greaseball: 1. A circus hamburger stand or concession. *see* GREASE JOINT. 2. A term of opprobrium for a clown who does not powderdown his shiny, grease-painted face. *see* SHINE. 3. An actor who uses too much makeup.

Great mogul: An affectionate name for the owner of a carnival.

Green folding: Pitchmen's slang for paper money.

Greyhound: Circus lingo for a fast-working salesman or pitchman. *see* BUTCHER.

Greatpole: English term for center pole.* Also called the king pole.* *see also* CENTER POLE and KING POLE.

Grift: Carnival and, especially, circus term for crooked games of chance, short-change artists,* shell games, or any similar unlawful and dishonest concession or gambling joint.* *see also* GRIFT CONCESSION, GRIFT SHOW, GRIFTER, JOINT, and SHORT-CHANGE ARTIST.

Grift concession: Circus and carnival term indicating that the right to pick pockets, swindle, defraud the marks,* operate a crooked gambling joint, and so on, had been sold to a grifter.* *see also* GRIFT, GRIFT SHOW, GRIFTER, and MARK.

Grift show: A circus that carried grift,* that is, permitted crooked gambling. A circus term, but it should be noted that most early carnivals also carried grift. *see also* GRIFT, GRIFT CONCESSION, and GRIFTER.

Grifter: 1. One who buys concessions of grift* on a circus or carnival site, or is given permission to practice some other dishonest con or swindle. Most grifters were card sharks, pickpockets, or petty swindlers, although they were often well organized and quite successful. The grifter lived by his sharp wit and skilled hand and, unlike big-time operators, did not depend on the threat of force or violence. *see also* GRIFT and SHORTING. 2. Used, on occasion, for a con artist or pitchman who worked on the streets by himself.

Grind: 1. To spiel* at a concession or joint* or talk to a crowd in front of a sideshow or tent attraction about the attraction to be seen inside. *see also* JOINT, SPIEL, and TALKER. 2. Used also to mean the talk of the talker* or spieler* in a carnival or circus, as well as a pitchman's spiel.* If a show has ballys,* the spiel between them is the grind. *see also* BALLYS, GRINDER, SPIEL, SPIELER, and TALKER. 3. A stripteaser's slow, circular gyrations of the pelvic areas. *see* COFFEE GRINDER. 4. A show that runs continuously without intermissions. *see* GRIND HOUSE and GRIND SHOW.

Grind auction: Sales by a low-class pitchman who hires a store and stages auction sales of phony jewelry, silverware, and the like.

Grind house: A continuous performance, show, or theatre, either without intermissions or for a long daily run and without closings on holidays. *see* GRIND and GRIND SHOW.

Grind on the front: *see* (ON THE) FRONT.

Grind joint: A sideshow, pitchmen's concession, or some other carnival concession or show where lectures or spiels are given continuously. *see* GRIND STORE and SPIEL.

Grind show: A carnival show, such as a sideshow or pit show* that plays continually but has no regularly repeated performances. It usually opens when the carnival opens and closes at the end of the carnival day. *see also* GRIND HOUSE and PIT SHOW.

Grind store: A carnival or midway game in which everyone wins small prizes. The operator, however, pays a pittance for a gross of these prizes and thus always makes a profit. *see* GRIND JOINT and SLUM.

Grinder: 1. The one who grinds; a person with a set spiel* or lecture delivered in front of a show or joint.* Generally, the grinder often talks continuously until the show or concession closes. Irwin explains that a good grinder, in addition to having a voice that can be made to express every nuance of expression, must be a "keen student of human nature, and know just when to stop his 'grind' and enter upon the exhortation." *see also* GRIND, JOINT, SPIEL, and SPIELER. 2. A stripper or burlesque dancer.

Grinds on the front: *see* (ON THE) FRONT and MAKE AN OPENING.

Grip: In vaudeville, the man who set scenery, or gripped it.

Grocery wheel: A carnival game or wheel of fortune with food as its prize. *see* CARNIVAL WHEEL.

Groggery: A late eighteenth- and nineteenth-century term for a low drinking place; also known as a grog-shop.

Grotesque: In the circus, this is a type of clown who wears exaggerated costume, carries outlandish props, and has an eccentric style of performing. It also refers specifically to a genre of comic acrobat popular in France during the first half of the nineteenth century.

Grouch bag: A tent-show and circus term for a money bag usually made of chamois, suspended by a string around the neck, and worn under clothing. The performer would frequently place some of each week's wages in the bag so that in case of an emergency, getting fired, or quitting (get a grouch on), it would be possible to move on to another town or get home. Another possible meaning of the term is that of a reserve fund kept by a tent-show manager to meet unexpected emergencies. If the grouch bag had to be used, the manager was then grouchy. In its more general usage, it is an actor's purse.

Ground and lofty tumbling: Acrobatic feats without and on the rope; used together and separately. Term dates from the eighteenth century.

Ground man: *see* WEB.

Group game: Another carny* name for a percentage game.* *see also* CARNY and PERCENTAGE or P.C. STORE.

Group jugglers: More than one person juggling the same objects back and forth.

G-string: A thin strip of cloth passed between the legs of stripteasers and supported by a waist cord or band. Ann Corio claims that the term was originated by the early striptease artist Carrie Finnell. Presumably, when she tossed the apparatus on her dressing table one night it fell in the Shape of a "G." *see* CHICAGO G-STRING and PASTY.

G-string role: A stock role in Toby shows* of a shrewd, honest, brash, inventive, old eccentric. The origin of the name is unclear, although one interpretation suggests that it was so called because of the customary chin whiskers worn by the actor; another proposes that the name comes from the strident timbre of the actor's voice, like that of the G-string on a stringed instrument. *see also* TOBY SHOW.

G top or G-top: A carnival tent behind the public tents where show people gather for social purposes of one kind or another. *see* PRIVILEGE CAR.

Guide: *see* HEADMAN.

Gummy: A pitchman's glue or cement; also the pitchman who sells the glue. The pitch is that this glue would join any broken item or material, similar claims to today's super glues.

Gump: Carnival slang for a chicken (of the fowl family).

Gun: Carnival and underworld term for a pickpocket. By extension, a gun has come to include any thief. *see* CLAW and DIP.

Gunsel: Outdoor show-business term for a young person, usually a boy. *see* GAZOONIE and PUNKS.

Gus Edwards units: Children's vaudeville acts produced by the best known of this ilk, Gus Edwards. Many stars graduated from such units as "School Days" and "Kiddie Kabaret" acts.

Gut: A circus billposter's term meaning the main business street in a town.

Gutbucket or gut-bucket: Early term for a cheap saloon or gambling house where musicians played for patrons' contributions.

Guttenburg: At one time, the word for good-looking secondhand costumes, after the name of what was the largest secondhand theatrical costumer in New York City.

Guy: *see* FISH.

Guyed-out: Originally, a circus term meaning to be drunk or tight as a tent; connotation apparently was something more than being in an average drunken state. *see* GUYS.

Guying-out crew: *see* ROPE CALLER.

Guys: In the circus, heavy ropes or cables that guy up or help support poles or high wire rigging.

(A) Guy's from Dixie: Burlesque and striptease expression for a performer who was no good. *see also* (A) GUY'S FROM HUNGER.

(A) guy's from hunger: *see* A GUY'S FROM DIXIE.

Gyp, gip, or jip: A contraction of gypsy which, as a noun, means a person who shows the characteristic sharp business techniques of the typical gypsy in all his dealings. As a verb, it means to "beat out of" or to "outsmart." In its carnival and circus context, a gyp is a cheater or swindler, or a fake or swindle. Despite popular lore, gypsies are not particularly popular among carnies and circus people. *see* RAG-HEADS.

Gyp 'n' take: A noncarnival phrase for a larcenous show or a carnival.

Gypsy: 1. In the carnival, an unreliable carnival employee or operator; frequently used to mean a drunk. 2. In musical theatre, a gypsy is a chorus member or dancer who is mobile, prepared to move quickly, and travels from show to show or town to town. Also denotes that they travel as a tribe, like gypsies.

Gypsy camp: The tent, booth, or concession of a fortune-teller in a carnival. *see* GIPSY LEE, MITT, MITT CAMP OR JOINT, and MITT READER.

H

Half and half: A carnival sideshow performer who claims to be half-man, half-woman.

Half-yard: Carnival slang for fifty dollars. *see* YARD.

Hall show: An indoor entertainment as distinguished from an outdoor amusement.

Ham: Pitchmen's and some circus use for food or meals.

Ham or ham actor: An amateur or professional actor who is affected, self-indulgent, or conceited, and who tends to strive for attention over the other actors on the stage by overplaying.* A number of theories to the origin of this unflattering epithet have been posed. Two possibilities involve the operation of Tony Pastor, the early vaudeville manager. He had an act in his downtown establishment called "The Hamtown Students," a black-face quartet known for their exaggerated movements and the overblown nature of their act. Supposedly, whenever Pastor saw an actor who was overplaying he described him as a "ham." Others apparently used the full name, "Hamtown Student." Another theory is that a poster at Pastor's Opera House in New York announced "Sixty hams distributed on Monday evening." This offering of free hams, according to the theory, began to reflect poorly on the actors until they were known as "ham actors." H. L. Mencken suggested that it came from *Hamlet*, since all actors either claimed to have played Hamlet to great applause—or wished to play Hamlet. He further pointed out that an old name for an amateur was hambone. It has been said that the term actually came from a name associated with Hamish McCullough (1835-1885), who toured the "pig-sticking" towns of Illinois with a fit-up* or portable company. His nickname was

Ham and his troupe was called Ham's actors. The most sensible origin is that the word is short for hamfatter,* the emollient or lard derived from pork and ham used by old-time actors and minstrel men to remove their makeup. It was common before the advent of cold cream and later, when cold cream was available, was just as effective and cheaper. *see also* FIT-UP, HAMFATTER, and OVERACT.

Hamalama: Circus term for wardrobe* (never costumes) that is tacky, in extremely bad colors, or in poor taste. *see* FLASHING IT UP and WARDROBE.

Hambone: *see* HAM OR HAM ACTOR.

Hamburger outfit: Circus slang for a carnival.

Hamfatter: A term used for an inferior, obvious entertainer or entertainment. Since black-face minstrels used hamfatter, the term in its figurative meaning was applied to actors whose subtlety was like that of a minstrel show or a performance or act that was unbelievable and frequently ludicrous. *see* HAM OR HAM ACTOR.

(The) Hammer: *see* DIVE BOMBER.

Hammer gang: Men who drive the stakes in erecting a circus tent. A stake-driver in circus lingo is usually the machine that drives stakes. *see* STAKERS.

Hand puppet: *see* GLOVE PUPPET OR HAND PUPPET.

Hand-to-hand: A type of circus balancing act in which the two performers involved balance with hands touching.

Hand-to-hand music: Show-business expression for applause.

Handbill: A small printed theatrical or other form of entertainment notice of a forthcoming production, attraction, or performance, identifying the location, title or description, players or attractions, date, and hours.

Handle: To direct or instruct the stick* or shill* during the time they are playing at a gambling concession so that the real customers do not suspect anything. *see also* SHILL and STICK.

Handling: Medicine showman's word for a remonstrance.

Hanging his own: Circus slang for a braggart, so called from hanging paper or circus posters. *see* BUTTON-BUSTER, PUTTING UP PAPER FOR YOURSELF, and THREE-SHEET OR THREE-SHEETING.

Hanky-pank or Hanky: 1. A carnival gaming concession offering simple games of skill and rewarding its patrons with a prize each time he or she plays. The payoff is usually cheap merchandise. Such games are more amusement devices than gambling games, if they are operated honestly. Typical examples include fish-pong, the ring-toss, dart throwing, cigarette shooting gallery, the string game, and pitching coins or Ping-Pong balls into a receptacle of some kind. A hanky-pank can also be the type of grind joint or store,* which operated on a nickel-and-dime play (often to women and children) and required a great deal of action in order to grind out a profit. By extension, the term is used for the spiel* to get customers to take a chance in such a game and to mean, in a general way, a trivial thing that is basically no good. *see also* GRIND JOINT, GRIND STORE, SLUM, and SPIEL.

Hard or hard money: Circus term for silver money or a coin.

Hard-nosed: Originally carnival slang for stubborn.

Hard tickets: Circus term for general admission tickets; so named because these seats were hard and not upholstered. McKennon, in *Horse Dung Trail*, suggests that the name came from the cardboard general admission tickets used and reused before World War II and the governmental order that all tickets must have serial numbers. *see* BLUES.

Hardass: The process of working the big circus teams for several hours each day before a show opened its season or during week stands in order to condition them for the one-day stands to come.

Hardest boiled: Medicine showman expression for the least sentimental.

Hardwood: Theatrical slang for standing room.

Harps: Turn-of-the-century theatrical slang for those who played Irish parts, including Irish comedians in vaudeville.

Harry Oliver: *see* H. O. OR HARRY OLIVER.

Harry Selby: *see* GEORGE SPELVIN.

Has-been: An actor who has lost his popularity.

Haul: In circus lingo, this refers to the distance from runs* or the railroad to the circus lot.* When circuses commonly traveled by train, the haul was marked both night and day with ball-torches that indicated right turns. The circus hand, if smart, knew the length of the hauls, how far the animals, especially the horses and elephants, had to walk, and sometimes even the street names. *see also* LOT and RUN.

Haunted house: Common amusement park and carnival attraction in which insatiable curiosity becomes the draw. In modern theme parks these have reached new heights of extravagance and elaborateness. In the English fair, they are called "Haunted Castle," "Crazy House," and "Frankenstein's Castle."

Have you seen Oscar?: A warning in the circus for the approach of a fireman patrolling dressing rooms and looking for illicit smokers. If the fireman is in close proximity, the warning is shortened to Oscar.

Hay animals: Circus name for bulls, camels, zebras, horses, and other similar hoofed animals. Also known as hay burners.

Haywire: Outdoor amusement-business term for one who has gone a bit crazy or something that is spoiled or ruined.

He has gone with Barnum: Phrase indicating that a performer or showman is deceased; after the first great American showman P. T. Barnum.

He went up: *see* BALLOON and GO UP IN THE AIR.

Head-to-head: A type of balancing act in which one acrobat balances vertically on the head of another acrobat.

Headline: Used principally in vaudeville, to obtain star billing.

Headliner: An outstanding actor or act, whose name usually appears at the head of the list of acts in the theatre's billing, usually in larger letters than the others. In England, it is called the top liner. *see* BILLING.

Headlining: Appearing as the leading performer. In England, this is called topping the bill. *see* HEADLINE and HEADLINER.

Headman: In a traveling tent show, the advance agent* for the troupe. Also known as the ad man, forerunner, and guide. *see also* ADVANCE AGENT or ADVANCE MAN.

Heads up: Although in general use today, this probably originated in the circus and means to look out for something that is about to hit you unknowingly.

Heart: Originally, a type of padding used in tights worn by actors, acrobats, and the like. Also a term used instead of falsies by chorus girls during the prestriptease age. *see* SYMMETRICALS.

Heat: 1. In vaudeville, slang word for a performance. 2. In carnival terms, heat is trouble with those not carnies and the violence that ensues due to a squabble with the law or due to the resentment of people over their losses on the games. During the early days of the American carnival, most of the heat was generated by the games, the at show(s),* or the strong* dancing girls. *see also* AT SHOW, CARNY, STRONG, and STRONG PERFORMANCE.

Heavy or heavy man: An actor, playing serious roles, who looks or can act villainously or in a tough manner. The heavy almost always appeared in old-time melodramas.

Heavy blacksmithing: Carnie* argot for the act of taking care of an elderly (and usually buxomy) widow with money. *see also* CARNY.

Heavy section: The section of the circus, or trains, that carried the heavier properties and animals.

Heavy sugar: Circus slang for a large amount of money.

Hebe comic: Show-business slang for a Jewish comedian. *see* GOOSE and YID.

Heel: A member of a theatrical company who is unpopular. In vogue early in this century.

(To) heel: Carnival expression meaning to leave without paying a debt or bill. *see* (TO) HEEL A HOTEL and (TO) HEEL A JOINT.

(To) heel a hotel: To slip into a single hotel room of a friend and stay the night, leaving in the morning without paying. *see* (TO) HEEL.

(To) heel a joint: To walk out of a hotel or restaurant without paying the bill. *see* (TO) HEEL.

Heel and toe: A dance combination, popular in vaudeville, derived from folk dancing.

Heel beater: A dancer in vaudeville.

Heel box: The last ticket stand inside a circus big top. *see* INSIDE BOX.

Heel out or heel a room: To leave without paying; to behave like a heel. By extension, to heel a meal, and so forth. *see* (TO) HEEL, (TO) HEEL A HOTEL, and (TO) HEEL A JOINT.

Heeler: Outdoor amusement-business slang for a political henchman.

Hefty: Circus term for a performer who does a strong-man act.

Hell driver: Name given to an auto daredevil seen as a midway attraction or special show at an amusement park.

Hellstromism: *see* MUSCLE READING.

Helter skelter: An English fair ride, also found in some American amusement parks. Also known as "Alpine Slip," "the Glide," and "Mat Slide." It is basically a towerlike structure contained within an unwinding spiral chute. The tower encloses a staircase by means of which the riders climb to the top of the chute. While sitting on individual mats, the riders then descend by gravity to the bottom.

Hep or hepp: Circus and carnival argot for road-smart, wise, informed, or well traveled.

Herald: Circus and outdoor show advertising paper printed on colored newsprint, approximately 9 inches by 20 inches, which can be pasted down, handed out, mailed, or placed in a person's car or front door.

Herbalists: A type of med man or quack doctor whose specialty was medicines made from herbs and plants.

Herd: Circus method of naming any two elephants. Twenty herds, in typical circus exaggeration, are better than forty elephants. *see* BULL.

He's carrying her bags: A vaudeville and burlesque expression meaning that the comic or straight man and the chorus girl or principal girl* were keeping company. *see also* PRINCIPAL GIRL.

Hey Rube!: Once used by both the circus and carnival, although virtually obsolete since the 1880s, this was known as the war or rallying cry of the circus. It was more common among the shadier operations and was used as a cry for help when toughs or irate townspeople, for one reason or another, decided to start a fight with carnies or circus workers. At one time such a fight was not uncommon and picking on smaller circus troupes was a favorite sport, although in time the show people could not afford the reputation that ensued from such fights and were rarely the aggressors, even if strongly tempted. It has been suggested that the origin of Rube came from the first lawyer employed by a circus to protect it. His first name was Reuben and when trouble approached they called out "Hey Rube!" *see also* CLEM and RUBE.

Hi Henry: A theatrical term for a tall silk hat. *see* ELEVEN FORTY-FIVE and (AN) OSCAR HAMMERSTEIN.

Hick: Originally from English cant, this was used by pitchmen and med men to mean a sucker or a small-town, countrified person.

High ball: A signal in the circus that the show was loaded and ready to move.

High boy: A circus clown who performs on stilts.

High C: Minstrel term for cornetist.

High grass: In circus parlance, high grass means small-town or rural American, so named because this is where the grass is not mowed. *see* LOW GRASS.

High pitch: This is a pitchman's term for the delivery of the sales talk or a demonstration from behind a high counter, on the tailgate of a truck, or on a platform. This is usually a short-con game* involving the sale of cheap merchandise, the price of which is refunded by the operators, who then sell worthless goods at a high price and then leave or drive away. *see also* SHORT-CON GAME.

High pitchman: A leading salesman in the line in which he pitches. *see* HIGH PITCH.

High riding: Circus bareback riding including standing or jumping on the horse, as opposed to flat or seated riding.

High roller: Outdoor showman's term for a flashy gambler.

High-school animals: Circus and carnival expression for trained animals. *see* HIGH-SCHOOL HORSE.

High-school horse: In the circus, a horse trained to execute fancy steps in special riding academies, such as the Spanish Riding School. *see* DRESSAGE.

High seating: In the circus, the inducement of patrons to move up to the highest tiers of blues* or general admission seats so that latecomers can be more easily seated. *see also* BLUES

High striker: A carnival midway device whereby the patrons are invited to swing a sledgehammer or wooden maul at a springboard, which then sends a weight on a track fastened to the face side of a verticle timber about thirty feet toward a bell or gong on the top. The object is to demonstrate one's strength. The catch, of course, is that an assistant or shill* can control one of the guy wires that actually serves as a continuation of the one that forms the runway for the weight. When taut, the bell will sail to the bell; when relaxed, the weight slows due to the vibration set up by the slack wire. *see* RING THE BELL, SHILL, and STRIKER.

High wire act: A circus wire-walking act performed at a great height with or without a net.

Hill horses: Name given to chorus girls in burlesque before 1900 because of their size. *see* BEEF TRUST and BIG HORSE.

Him-hammin': Circus term for hemming and hawing, or stumbling and stammering, circumventing a subject rather than speaking the truth.

Hindu shuffle: A shuffle used by some magicians whereby the deck of cards is held on the long sides by each hand; one hand draws out a batch of cards and then replaces them elsewhere in the deck.

Hip or hippo: Circus abbreviation for a hippopotamus.

Hip-flinger: Fairly recent slang expression for a cooch or cootch dancer.* *see also* COOCH OR COOTCH DANCING.

Hip-kick: Carnival and circus slang for the rear trouser pocket.

Hippodrama: *see* EQUESTRIAN DRAMA.

Hippodrome track: The oval track running around the inside of a circus big top between the tiers of patrons' seats and the rings and stages.

Hiring fair: An English country fair at which domestic staff or farm-hands were hired for a season. *see* CHARTER FAIR, MOP FAIR, and STATUTE FAIR.

Histe or heist the rag: Gallery gods'* cry to raise the curtain. *see also* GALLERY GODS.

Hit the bell: *see* RING THE BELL.

Hits: Circus word used for places (such as barns, buildings, and fences) on which heralds* and posters can be pasted. *see also* HERALD.

H. O. or Harry Oliver: Circus and carnival expression or short-form for a holdout.

Hobo clown: *see* CHARLEY OR CHARLIE and TRAMP CLOWN.

Hod: An assortment of lithographs,* date sheets,* and other types of circus advertising made into a bundle so that each billposter or litho-grapher would have the amount needed for his route that day. *see also* DATE SHEET and LITHOGRAPH.

(The) Hog Show: In the circus world, this was the inside name for the Mighty Hague Circus.

Hogger: Circus slang for a greedy showman.

Hoister: Circus and carnival term for a Ferris wheel. Also called a chump heister. *see also* FERRIS WHEEL.

Hoke: Outdoor showman word, short for hokum,* which infers some-thing composed of or containing hokum, as well as trite talk, cajolery, or something illusionary. *see also* HOKUM.

Hokey-pokey or hoky-poky: Cheap ice cream, candy, confections, and the like, sold primarily to children at circuses and carnivals. Also used for the name of the seller, and, by extension, to mean anything cheap, gaudy, or useless. *see* HOKUM.

Hokum: 1. Cheap, sugary candy, useless and inexpensive souvenirs, and the like, sold at carnival booths. *see* HOKEY-POKEY. 2. Any time-worn gag, speech, situation, piece of business, line, and such, that is foolproof and can be relied upon to produce a predictable response, usually applause or tears, from any audience. Also called gonk* or hoke.* *see also* GONK and HOKE.

Hold your horses: An old-time circus warning, given because the smell of elephants frightened city horses.

Holder: A magician's device that is worn under the clothes to keep some small article in readiness for a steal.* Unlike the dropper,* which releases objects automatically, a holder must be pulled away. *see also* DROPPER and STEAL.

Holding: A circus term meaning, "do you have cash?" Employed troupers frequently helped out unemployed colleagues who were broke.

Holdout: A magician's secret device for holding articles, most frequently playing cards, so they are concealed and still at the disposal of the performer when needed.

Home guard: In pitchmen's terms, someone who is a resident of a town where the carnival or circus is playing and puts up a concession near the lot, thus giving the traveling pitchmen competition; or, pitchmen who work only in their home area, normally not working outside a radius of about forty miles. Sometimes, the term is used to refer in general to a native of the town where a show is playing, to a retired circus worker, or to a street beggar. *see* FORTY MILER.

Home run: The trip the circus makes from its last performance to winter quarters.* *see* HOME SWEET HOME, RUN, and WINTER QUARTERS.

Home Sweet Home: The concluding date or performance of the season for a circus. *see* HOME RUN.

Homing: A magician's term for the magical return of an object to its original place after it has been previously removed.

Homy: English circus term for a man. A "bona homy," for example, is a good man. *see* OMNEY.

Honey: A stripper's greeting to virtually anyone.

Honky-tonk: A cheap saloon, featuring gambling games and dancing. The honky-tonk became a kind of cheap, small-town theatre, offering drink, entertainment, and frequently containing a brothel or areas where women were readily available. An important precursor of American burlesque. *see* RINKY-DINK.

Hooch or hootch: *see* COOCH OR COOTCH DANCING.

Hoochie-coochie: *See* COOCH OR COOTCH DANCING.

Hoofer: Name given a professional step or clog dancer,* originating probably in ministrel shows where a minstrel dancer was called a hoofer (by extension, the word was used for a Negro). Irwin suggests that the name originated from the joke that pictured the unfortunate member of a stranded show walking home. In any case, the word later was used to denote a dancer on the vaudeville stage or one working on a cheap circuit, and, in time, any actor on the road. Today, it is used synonymously for any dancer on stage or in a dance chorus. To hoof it, then, means to dance. *see also* CLOG DANCE.

Hoofery: A dance hall. *see* HOOFER.

Hook: Pitchmen's term for snaring an audience. *see* POKE.

Hook-ring: Collective term for pitchmen.

Hook ropes: When circuses traveled by wagons, these were stout ropes with hooks on ends that were hooked into rings on wagon sides and used to hitch extra teams onto the wagons in order to aid in mud and soft ground. *see* CHAIN TEAM.

Hook-up teams: Men used in loading and unloading circus wagons at the trains. Also know as pull-up teams or pull-over teams. *see* HOOK ROPES.

Hooking: Working an elephant with a bull-hook.* *see also* BULL HOOK.

Hooks: In magician's lingo, this is a needle point soldered near the edge of a coin, handkerchief hand box, or similar small piece of apparatus, at an angle pointing toward the center. This serves to attach the object temporarily to the performer's clothes, hand, or other convenient place for easy access.

Hooligan: Originally, a hoodlum, ruffian, or tough guy. This use of the word led to a circus association where it referred to a Wild West tent in a circus or the dressing tent of the Wild West show cowboys and Indians, usually a rowdy bunch.

Hoop or hoople: Pitchmen's slang for a ring; usually the kind of slum* sold by a pitchman. *see also* SLUM.

Hoopla or Hoop-la: Originally, from the exclamation associated with the carnival concession in which the player tosses embroidery hoops over blocks; later it became the name of such a game. In the English fair, it is still used specifically for such a game but has been extended to mean any round stall or booth. In the American carnival, it can be used today to mean any concession or a ballyhoo.* *see also* BALLYHOO.

Hoosier: Carnival and circus word for a yokel or unsophisticated person, especially one from the state of Indiana.

Hootchy-Kootchy: *see* COOCH OR COOTCH DANCING.

Hop: *see* BREEZE.

Hopjoint: A cheap saloon, from "hops." Also an opium den.

Hop-scotchers: Independent carnival concessionaires who move around the country on their own without any permanent connection to a specific show. *see* INDIE.

Horn nuts: Pitchman's argot for flower bulbs.

Horse: Some circus use for one thousand dollars. *see* G OR G NOTE and GRAND.

Horse feed: Circus expression for poor returns from poor business, or simply poor attendance.

Horse-laugh: Med-show term for a laugh of derision.

Horse opera or opery: Used to denote a circus in a joking manner; a Western show (either a Wild West show or a rodeo); or a carnival that includes a show using horses.

Horse piano: An old-time name for the circus steam calliope when it was drawn by horses in the circus parade. *see* CALLIOPE.

Horseshoe runway: *see* RUNWAY.

Horse top: *see* TOP.

Hose: A fairly rare carnival term meaning to cheat or cajole in order to win a favor.

Hot: Carnival and underworld term for something that has been stolen. Now in general use.

Hot spot: Pitchmen's term for an excellent business location. *see* OPEN.

Hot-stove and radiator leagues: Pitchmen's expression for the men who gathered in groups around various types of stoves in order to keep warm during the off-season and told stories of past glories in pitchdom.

Hot wagon: An electrical transformer wagon carried by most carnivals to run the midway before generating plants were built compact enough to be feasible.

Hotel Ringling: These words appear on some of the yellow pennants that are flown from one of the circus cookhouse's* center poles to announce meals. As long as the flag is up, meals are served. *see also* COOKHOUSE, FLAG, and FLAG'S UP.

Hotscotch: A grease joint* that is located at the greatest distance from a circus lot. *see also* GREASE JOINT.

Hotter 'n-a-pistol: Used mostly in reference to carnival concessions that have caused disturbances or complaints from the public.

House board: A fairly obsolete term for the boards or frames located on the front of a theatre, usually on each side of the main entrance, that announced the name of the attraction, performers, and other relevant information. *see* MARQUEE.

House curtain: In vaudeville, this is the curtain that ran flat against the proscenium arch and was raised at the beginning and lowered at the end of the performance. It was sometimes used to close-in on an act. *see also* (TO) CLOSE-IN.

House of mirrors: *see* MIRROR MAZE.

Hawdah, howdy, or houdah: A seat, often with a canopy, carried on the back of a circus elephant or camel.

Hulligan: A corruption of hooligan,* which, in turn, derives from "Hooley Gang," a group of young toughs of late-nineteenth-century London. Sergel suggests that it was a mispronunciation of the word "Hungarian" and dates from the days when some of the first foreign circus artists came from Hungary. In either case, it is used as a derogatory designation of a foreigner, in particular a European circus act, by intolerant American circus performers. *see also* HOOLIGAN.

Hulligan family: By extension of the meaning of hulligan,* this refers to a foreign circus family. *see also* HULLIGAN.

Human blur: Med-show and pitchmen's term for an unlucky person.

Human oddities: Circus term sometimes used instead of freaks; refers to a side-show of abnormal or deformed persons.

Humbug: Used by the American showman P. T. Barnum to mean a practical joke played on the public. At his American Museum, Barnum practiced such deceptions to the delight of his customers. It has come to mean a hoax, fraud, or deluding deception in order to cheat, swindle, or trick.

Humps: Circus slang for camels.

Humpsti-bumpsti: Primarily an English circus term for a knockabout acrobatic act.

Hurdy-gurdy: A hand organ such as those used by street organ grinders.

Hurry music: Music that was played very rapidly in order to enhance and underscore the swift action of a melodrama. *see also* MELODRAMA.

Hustle: As a carnival term, this means either to peddle or sell something temporarily or to prostitute oneself. *see* HUSTLER.

Hustler: In carnival lingo, this is a peddler or pitchman with no special line, or a prostitute. *see* HUSTLE.

Hustling the leaf: *see* LEAF.

Hymn hustler: Carnival lingo for a sky pilot.

Hype: As used in vaudeville, hype referred to the practice of stimulating or creating special interest in a product, song, or act. *see* PUT ON THE HYPE.

Hype guys or hypers: A short-change artist* with a carnival. *see also* CAKE CUTTER and SHORT-CHANGE ARTIST.

I

I hope it rains today: An expression originating when burlesque depended more on the weather than on its talent to sell tickets. Even with tickets as low as ten cents, it was frequently necessary to fill burlesque houses with drifters off the street who would pay a dime to get out of the rain.

I hope the gentleman sits on it!: Typical burlesque comic's retort to hecklers, especially to a Bronx cheer.

I hope you break a leg: A superstitious good luck wish used by various types of performers, especially actors.

I love you, darling, but the season's closed: In vaudeville companies, traveling theatrical troupes, and even circuses and carnivals, members of the company frequently paired off for the season. This was the good-bye or exit line when the season was over and the performers went their separate ways.

I'll send you the birdseed next week: Stock burlesque comic's retort to a Bronx cheer from someone in the audience.

I think I'll phone in the act today: A phrase used by vaudevillians meaning the performer was sick, drunk, or hung over.

Icarian: A name given to an antipodist who juggles another performer with the feet while the latter performs somersaults and other acrobatics. *see also* ANTIPODIST.

Ice: A tip, commission, or bribe given by a ticket agent to a box-office treasurer, attendant, or producer for theatre tickets. It can also be a premium charged on a ticket purchased from a ticket agent. Today, ice is a particularly difficult problem in the film industry. *see* FIX.

Iceman: *see* BAG MAN and FIXER.

Ice-packed juice bowl: In pitchmen's lingo, a soft drink concession.

Iggy: Slang for being ignorant and indicative of an attitude feigned by circus people (playing dumb) when confronted by an overly curious towner* or the local police. This is known as to give 'em the iggy. *See also* TOWNERS.

Illusion: Any magical trick may be called an illusion, but among magicians it is almost always limited to large stage effects, usually involving a person or large animal, or large, expensive, bulky apparatus.

Illusion show: A midway presentation (a magic show) featuring illusions.* *see also* ILLUSION.

Impresario: A producer, usually of musical entertainments or other forms of entertainment other than legitimate* drama. *see also* LEGITIMATE.

Impression clipboard: An irreplaceable piece of apparatus used in mentalist* acts, especially of the question-answer variety. The clipboard looks like a common sort but actually has secreted, on its face, carbon paper and extra clear paper. A spectator records questions on the clipboard and removes the paper. The performer then has, unbeknownst to the spectators, an impression in carbon of what has been written. *see also* MENTALIST.

Impressment: A magician's technique used in enlisting an audience member as a secret assistant. Usually a secret visual or auditory cue is given the spectator to alert him or her to the moment when the amateur shill* is needed. *see also* SHILL.

Impromptu magic: Ever-ready tricks that can be done virtually anywhere at any time. Especially important to the magician for publicity purposes.

In center: A circus act playing the middle ring.* *see* RING.

In doniker: Circus, carnival, and pitchmen's slang for a bad location, lot,* or the wrong side of town. *see also* DONIKER, DONIKER LOCATION, and LOT.

In one: An expression used in vaudeville, burlesque, and, less frequently, the theatre. Refers to a scene or act played in the stage area closest to the audience with a demarcation created by an imaginary line across the stage from the left side farthest downstage (toward the audience) to the right side farthest downstage, or, in the days of footlights, the area nearest to the footlights (usually in front of a drop hung across the stage or the stage curtain). *see* ONE.

In the patch: *See* PATCH.

In the test tube: A theatrical tryout.

In two, three, or four: *See* IN ONE, TWO, THREE, and FOUR.

Indexing: Method used by magicians for covering all possible choices a spectator might make in a mental effect. For example, if a spectator chooses a specific card, the magician or mentalist simply reaches into a small index or file in his pocket and produces the correct card. *see also* POCKET INDEX.

Indian clubs: *see* CLUB(S).

Indie: An independent carnival exhibitor. *see* HOP-SCOTCHERS.

Indifferent card: A card not being used by a magician in a card trick.

Info: Outdoor show lingo for information, or, as a verb, to inform, notify, or write a message. Also used are scribe,* pipe,* pen or pencil, wigwag, typewrite, signal, and postcard. *see also* PIPE and SCRIBE.

Ingenue: The sweet young woman in many predictable dramas and comedies, especially melodramas. In some of the tent shows, they were played by older actresses who had always played the ingenue.

In-jog: In card magic, the technique of replacing a card on the deck so that its end projects toward the performer. *see* JOG.

Ink sticks: Pitchmen's term for fountain pens.

Inside box: The ticket office inside the tent of a traveling theatrical tent show where audience members could purchase chair seats.* *see also* CHAIR SEATS and HEEL BOX.

Inside lecturer: In a circus or carnival sideshow or pit show,* a talker* or spieler* who directs the attention of the audience to each attraction and points out special features. *see also* LECTURER, MAKE AN OPENING, PIT SHOW, SPIELER, and TALKER.

Inside man: The operator of any carnival game.

Inside stand: A circus or carnival concession on a midway.

Inside stuff: Show-business expression for the real lowdown or the true story.

Inside talker: *See* INSIDE LECTURER.

Interlocutor: The master of ceremonies in the black-face minstrel show who served as the straight man and onstage director. He sat in the center of the semicircle and posed questions to the end men* known as Tambo* and Bones* and called for the walk-around.* He was also known as the middleman.* *see also* BONES, END MAN, MIDDLEMAN, TAMBO, and WALK-AROUND.

Internal douche: An orange- or lemon-flavored drink served at a carnival grab joint.* *see also* GRAB JOINT and JUICE.

Interpreter: An early name for the collector of donations for a puppet show—a man who stood in front of the stage to describe what was going on and to backchat with the puppets. Necessary, perhaps, because puppets spoke a corrupt and often unintelligible speech, or the puppeteer used an impediment to give the puppet a unique voice. *see also* SWATCHEL OR SWAZZLE.

Interpretive dancer: High-class name given to a stripper or a cooch* dancer. *see* COOCH or COOTCH DANCING.

Invisible deck or pack: Card magic trick in which a selected card appears as the only face-down card in a deck of face-up cards.

Irish justice: The classic burlesque bit in which a judge hits the defendant with a rubber bladder. *See* BLADDER.

Irish nightingale: In vaudeville, a tenor, especially a countertenor, who sang Irish ballads with an Irish accent.

Irish sluggers: Circus argot for a kind of under-chin whiskers.

Iron or irons: Iron stakes used by a tent circus on hard lots.* "Irons at the door" would signify a hard lot at the next stop and "irons inside" would mean a soft lot ahead. *see also* LOT.

Iron-jaw: An aerial acrobatic stunt in which the performer is suspended by clamping the jaws to a metal mouthpiece attached to an apparatus from above. Also known as the butterfly suspension act.

Iron men: Med-show and pitchmen's argot for dollars. *see* JACK.

It's the nuts: Phrase coined by *Variety* for anything spurious.

It will be all right on the night: A reassuring comment among theatrical people, dating from the nineteenth century, meaning that by opening night everything will be fine, despite disasters up to that point.

Itchy feet: Used to describe a retired circus trouper's desire to get back with a show.

J

Jack: Med-show term for money. Also called geedus, gelt, iron men, jack, and scratch. *see* TAKE.

Jack-pot: A carnival gambling device working on the same principle as a three marble tiv,* except that it uses a coin. *see also* TIV.

Jackpots: 1. In the circus, tall tales, gossip, and reminiscences about the circus. *see* CUT-UP JACKPOTS. 2. Large earnings for a pitchman.

Jackeroo: A cowboy; term sometimes used in Wild West shows. The word possibly came from the Australian slang "jackroo" (young fellow), although it more likely is from the Spanish "vaquero."

Jacks and stringers: In traveling tent shows, the supports for the stage, orchestra, and candy pitch platform floors. The jacks are supports or trestles (similar to sawhorses), and the stringers are two-by-fours placed across them and set in notches on the jacks. The platform boards are then laid across the stringers.

Jacob's ladder: Circus slang for a cheap flophouse with no elevator.

Jagger: Carnival word for a tattoo artist.

Jakes or to be jaking: This is one of the oldest circus words still in use (circa 1530) and refers to a clown who takes water or allows himself to be squirted or doused by another clown in a gag. *see also* GAG.

Jam or jamb: 1. In circus lingo, a difficulty or an uncomfortable fix or condition. Also a squeeze. 2. In pitchmen's terms, high-pressure tactics or illegitimate selling tactics.

Jam-man: A pitchman with no professional ethics. *see* JAM.

Jam pitch: An indoor stand for a pitchman.

Jam show: Circus expression for a spectacular or showy method of attracting crowds.

Jam store: A pitchmen's sales concession that builds up the customer's confidence by giving away lots of cheap (slum*) merchandise. Also called an auction store. *see also* SLUM.

Jamming: Forcing sales through trickery, or a pitchman's selling to a whole crowd at once rather than to an individual. *see* JAM.

Jane: Although this is a common word in general use for a girl or young woman, in the circus it is an extremely uncomplimentary noun used for a woman. *see* JILL.

Jay towns: Early twentieth-century term for smaller cities played by a theatrical company. It comes from the meaning of a simpleminded, inexperienced, or gullible person.

Jazbo, jazzbo, or jasbo: Used to mean either a rough and vulgar comic bit* or a Negro performer in a minstrel show. *see also* BIT.

J. C. L.: *see* JOHNNY-COME-LATELY.

Jeff: In the English circus, a rope.

Jenny: Circus and carnival name for a merry-go-round or carousel.* *see also* CAROUSEL.

Jerk(s): In the carnival, a jerk is a no-good person; in burlesque, the audiences were called jerks.

Jig: 1. A lively dance, or a humorous song accompanying such a dance. Probably derived from the kind of tap dancing common to southern plantations and later incorporated into minstrel shows and other theatrical entertainment. 2. By extension, jig was used synonymously for a male Negro. 3. In the Elizabethan theatre, surviving into the English Restoration, a jig was a kind of comic afterpiece including songs, often ribald and libelous, accompanied by dances.

Jig Band: An obsolete term for a Negro sideshow band in a circus.

Jig show or jig opry: A Negro minstrel show in a carnival.

Jigaboo: Derogatory carnival jargon for a Negro, usually a woman.

Jill: English circus term for a girl. *see* JANE.

Jim Crow song and dance: An Afro-American song and dance devised in the nineteenth century around 1825 by Thomas D. Rice after seeing a crippled Negro stableman do the catchy little song and dance as he worked. Rice, who became famous for his Jump Jim Crow routine, made a career from this simple act. Jim Crow became the slang word for the white-created system of racial segregation that was aimed at eliminating contact between blacks and whites.

Jit or jitney: In circus and carnival jargon, a nickel or five cents.

Jittery: . In the carnival world and other outdoor forms of amusement, nervous or hysterical. Assimilated into general use today.

Joan: *see* JUDY.

Jockey act: Circus horseback acrobatics performed, normally, by several people on a single mount.

Joe Blow: *see* FLAG'S UP.

Joe Hepp: In the circus world, an imaginary person or character. Bill Hepp is Joe's brother. *see* GEORGE SPELVIN and WALTER PLINGE.

(Do a) Joe Jefferson: The declaration of intent by a performer (especially an actor) to have a good long sleep. Named after the famous actor Joseph Jefferson (1829-1905) who was closely identified with the role of Rip Van Winkle, which he played for over thirty years.

Joe Miller: An old joke. Named for Joseph Miller, an eighteenth-century English comedian. To tell an old joke, then, is to Joe Millerize.

Joe Morgan: In burlesque, the show drunk.

Joebreened: A script that has been cleaned up or censored. Named after Joseph I. Breen, at one time the film industry censor.

Joey: A nickname for a circus clown. It is so named after the famous Joseph Grimaldi (1788-1837), a great British clown who performed exclusively (in the role of "Clown") in English pantomime.

Joey walk-around: Circus clown stunts performed around the hippodrome.* *see also* JOEY, HIPPODROME, and WALK-AROUND.

Jog: In card magic, this describes a card protruding a little from any part of the deck in order to fix the location of a particular card or cards. In-jog means the card protrudes over the little finger of the left hand toward the magician; out-jog means the card protrudes over the first finger of the left hand away from the performer. *see also* IN-JOG and OUT-JOG.

John Law: Originally, hobo and circus use for the police or any law enforcement officer.

John Orderly: Circus jargon meaning to depart, to go, or to hurry it up.

John Robinson: In circus lingo, this is either an abbreviated performance, or the cutting short of anything. Also known as a quick show. *see* (THE) JOHN SHOW.

John Robinson layout: An arrangement of circus tents on the show grounds or lot* so that they are all end-to-end or in a single file, and thus create an impression of massiveness to the spectators. *see also* (THE) JOHN SHOW and LOT.

(The) John show: Brief form for the John Robinson Circus, a well-known circus operation during the golden age of the American circus.

Johnny: The callow youth who is inclined to haunt the stage door, known in the theatre as a stage-door Johnny.

Johnny-come-lately or J. C. L.: Either a novice or greenhorn pitchman, or one who is in his second year with the circus and believes he has all the answers.

Johnny Sap: A performer, especially in vaudeville, who was in his first season.

Johnny Tin Plate or tin plate: Circus name for a small-town constable or marshall.

(To) join out, to join, or to join up: To accept a job with a circus and go on tour.

Join out on wire or join on wire: To be called to a circus job by telegram.

Joint: 1. An outdoor amusement concession stand or booth. It has been suggested that it is so called from the racetrack bookmaker's stand, which is hinged or jointed to pack up more or less flat. *see* RACKET OR TRICK and STORE. 2. In the English fair, it is used as a generic term for any form of portable sideshow of the ground booth variety but not for shows with raised platforms for performers. 3. In theatrical jargon, a joint is a nightclub, hotel, or restaurant, no matter how exclusive.

Jonah: Circus name for one who brings bad luck to a show. Also called Jonah's luck. *see* JONAH'S BAD LUCK.

Jonah's bad luck: Wagons stuck in the mud or, in general, to wallow in bad weather or unusual mud. Also called Jonah's luck.

Jonah's luck: *see* JONAH'S BAD LUCK.

Jonathan: The central character in many Yankee plays. It came to mean an individual American, particularly a "Down-Easter." *see* YANKEE.

Jongleur: From the Latin *"joculator"* and the Old French *"jogleour."* This word has had a number of meanings from the ninth century, including a wandering or itinerant performer, a minstrel, a sleight-of hand* magician, and, during the past one hundred years, a juggler, or one who keeps several objects in the air by tossing and catching them or balances and spins objects. *see also* SLEIGHT or SLEIGHT-OF-HAND.

Jongleurs de force: *see Kraft-jugglers.*

Joseph Grimaldi: *see* JOEY.

Josser: An English circus term for a circus outsider. Also called yob. *see* FLATTIE OR FLATTY, and GAJO.

Juba: A Negro dance accompanied with patting or slapping. The early form was used in Ethiopian minstrelsy or opera* and full-fledged minstrel shows. *see also* ETHIOPIAN MINSTRELSY OR OPERA.

Judy: Punch's wife in a Punch and Judy puppet show.* Until the nineteenth century, she was called Joan. *see also* PUNCH AND JUDY SHOW.

Juggler: *See* JONGLEUR.

Juice: 1. Lemonade and other fruit drinks sold at a circus. *See* INTERNAL DOUCHE. 2. Theatrical nickname for a stage electrician; also used in most entertainment forms to mean electrical current.

Juice joint: A circus or carnival midway concession or inside stand* that sells beverages, usually lemonade.

Juice worker: One who sells fruit or fruit juice in a circus or carnival; or a vegetable-squeezer.

Juke or jook: A regionalism of western Pennsylvania and Ohio used in the circus to mean to duck or dodge a blow.

Juliets: Long, floppy clown shoes; these were frequently worn by burlesque comics.

Jumbo: P. T. Barnum bought "Jumbo," the largest elephant on record, from London's Royal Zoo in 1883; in America the animal quickly caught the public imagination, advertised as "the largest and heaviest elephant ever seen by mortal man either wild or in captivity," and became the first major attraction of the Barnum circus. It has come to mean anything large or extra large, such as jumbo jets or jumbo hamburgers.

Jump: The distance between points of performance of a circus, traveling carnival, vaudeville troupe, Toby show,* and other forms of popular entertainment that travel. A jump is sometimes used to denote the distance between one-night stands but should not be limited to this. *see* DUKEY, DUCKIE, OR DUKIE RUN and TOBY SHOW.

Jump Jim Crow: *see* JIM CROW SONG AND DANCE.

Jump stand: In the circus, an extra stand or ticket booth near the front entrance from which tickets can be sold when there is a big rush.

(To) jump through: In theatrical circles, henpecked husbands were spoken of as having to jump through, an expression that referred to the manner in which trained animals are compelled to jump through hoops and other objects at the command of the trainer (or master).

(To) jump or dangle up the line: Primarily, a circus expression meaning to journey or to move on to the next town. *see* JUMP.

Jumping the cut: *see* PASS.

Jungle buggy: Circus and carnival jargon for a house trailer.

Jungle layout: Circus expression for sleeping cars that are stationed outside of town.

Jungle show: An outdoor show-business description of a trained animal show.

Junk: Theatrical slang for a monologue. *see* STRING OF TALK.

Junker: A word used in the outdoor show world, especially on midways and in amusement parks, to mean an old car an auto daredevil rolls over, jumps to land on its nose, or otherwise demolishes.

Juve: Slang for a juvenile actor. *see* JUVENILE.

Juvenile: 1. In theatrical jargon, a young male actor or an actor who plays clean-cut, rather simply drawn young men. 2. A burlesque juvenile is either a young singer or dancer who can do a specialty on his own, double as a second straight man (or woman), and also work as a general utility performer.

K

Kale: Money. Also called geedus, gelt, jack, take and scratch. *see* TAKE.

Keister (also keester, keyster, kiester, and kister): In pitchmen's lingo, a satchel or case in which a pitchman carries his stock, and which opens out to form a display case. In general terms, it also can mean simply a traveling bag, grip, or suitcase. *see* TRIPES and TRIPE AND KEISTER OPERATOR.

Kerosene camps: Primarily, a med-show term for settlements of less than three thousand population.

Kerosene circuit: A circuit of theatres in small towns with relatively ill-fitted playhouses, usually lit with kerosene instead of gas or more sophisticated stage lighting.

Key or locator card: In card magic, a distinctive or marked card that can be readily identified by the magician and thus assist in the discovery of a chosen card.

Keystone: Carnival and some circus use for a prosecutor. *see* PROS.

Kibitz: Used by carnies* to mean to talk things over in idle conversation. *see also* CARNEY.

Kick: *see* SPRING.

Kickin' em: Most likely originated as a minstrel-show expression meaning to make the daily street parade.

Kicking sawdust: Circus slang for following a circus or becoming part of it. *see* TENT-SQUIRRELS.

Kid money: Circus admission for children "under age" collected at the front door.

Kid show: Carnival and circus term for a sideshow or annex to the main circus tent, so called because it is usually the smaller of the attractions on the lot. Also used to denote a circus job on which the majority of the workers are young and without experience. *see* KID TOP.

Kid top: A sideshow tent. *see* KID SHOW and TOP.

Kid workers: Circus bosses who oversee boys of local towns picked up to aid in getting a tent show ready because of a late arrival.

Kiester: In the circus, a trunk or wardrobe box. *see* KEISTER.

Kife: Circus jargon meaning to swindle the suckers.

Kinetoscope: *see* VITASCOPE.

Kill time joint: Fairly recent show-business phrase for a cocktail lounge.

(The) King: Nickname of Otto Ringling, the financial brains of the Ringling brothers during their rapid climb to the top of the circus world.

King pole: English circus term for the center pole* of the American circus; the center mast or masts of the main circus tent. *see* CENTER POLE.

Kinker: Originally, this referred to a ground tumbler from the stretching of acrobats and contortionists to get kinks out of their muscles. Now it is used to denote any circus performer, usually one experienced. Spangles once was used with the same meaning. *see* GROUND AND LOFTY TUMBLING.

Kinker talk: The special language of the circus.

Kinodromes: The name given to small buildings for the showing of early motion pictures in amusement parks at the turn of the century. Between 1894 and 1902, early movies became part of programs in virtually all variety entertainment, including dime museums,* amusement parks, and vaudeville theatres, as well as in the penny arcades and all movie nickelodeons. *see also* DIME MUSEUM.

Kip: Circus word for a bed or sleeping. Originally underworld and vagabond use.

Kiss ride: A 1911 version of the later and more exciting whip ride introduced by the magician Howard Thurston.

Kisser: In the outdoor amusement world, slang for the mouth or lips. *see* MUSH.

Knife force: In magician's jargon, this is a way to force a card on a spectator by means of a knife thrust into the deck.

Knights of the tripes and keister: Slang expression for pitchmen. *see* TRIPE.

Knock them in the aisles: To overwhelm an audience with one's talent; to entertain an audience with truly hilarious humor. Also used is the phrase "laid 'em in the aisles." *see* TAKE THREE BENDS AND AN ENCORE and PANIC 'EM.

Knock-down wagon: *see* GILLY.

Knockabouts: Comedy acrobatics in which falls and slaps predominate. Used primarily in the English circus.

Knocked 'em bowlegged: Theatrical phrase for a rousing success.

Knocker: 1. Theatrical slang from the turn of the century meaning one who is disposed to say unkind things about a fellow actor. 2. Someone in a crowd who warns others that a pitchman is dishonest and the product is a "fake" or faulty.

Knockout: Med-show term for a surprise.

Knocks herself out: A stripper who works especially hard. *see* STRONG PERFORMANCE.

Kosh: English circus term for a whip or weapon.

Kraft-jugglers or jongleurs de force: Early jugglers in the modern sense who specialized in the manipulation of heavy objects and weights. Almost obsolete today.

Krenk: Theatrical expression derived from the Yiddish for a pain or sickness.

Kush: Money. Also called geedus, gelt, jack, take and scratch. *see* TAKE.

Kutch: Word sometimes used in carnivals for a hoochie-coochie attraction. *see* COOCH DANCING.

Kuter: *see* CUTER.

L

Lacing: Small rope loops by which sections of the main circus tent (middle-pieces) are securely tied together, creating the illusion of one large piece of canvas. Bust the lacing is an order to untie or separate the lacings when dismantling tents.

Ladder swing: A circus aerial act on a swinging ladder.

Ladies free: An admission practice in some tent shows whereby ladies accompanied by a ticket-holding male would be admitted free.

Lag: In carnivals and circuses, used as a noun to mean a leak; as a verb, to send to jail.

Laid 'em in the aisles: *see* KNOCK THEM IN THE AISLES.

Lam: Criminal word used in the circus to mean depart hastily or to run.

Lancashire clog: A form of wooden clog dancing,* brought to America from Lancashire, England, popular in early variety. *see also* CLOG DANCE.

Larry: Circus and carnival word for any small worthless or broken article or merchandise (such as a punctured balloon), or a bad date. It can also refer to a customer who does not intend to purchase anything. Thus, by extension, as an adjective it means worthless, second-class, bad, or phony. *see* LEARY.

Larry spot: A place where business is poor for a pitchman. *see* BLUE ONE, COLD, and LARRY.

Lash whip: A whip used in the circus in animal training and performing. It is not a crop or quirt but a long rawhide lash connected to a heavy stock with a cord cracker at its tip. *see* POPPER.

Laundry queens: Circus slang for female dancers.

Law: Carnival term for any local policeman, sheriff, constable, or the like. *see* COOKIE-CUTTER, COP, DICK, FUZZ, and TINS.

Law and outlaw show: A carnival wax works exhibition in which the wax effigies of famous bandits, train robbers, and other criminals were displayed.

Lay an egg, lay an omelet, or lay a bomb: To fail or flop. Used in reference to a production, actor, comic, and the like, that fails miserably.

Lay down: A diagram of betting spaces or a numbered painted cloth on the counter in front of some carnival games on which the players place their bets. *see* SLEEPER.

Lay 'em in the aisles: *see* KNOCK THEM IN THE AISLES.

Lay it on the line: Put money into a pitchman's hand.

Lay of the land: Featured female dancer in a carnival girlie show.* *see also* GIRLIE SHOW.

Lay off: An actor out of work, or at liberty.* *see also* AT LIBERTY.

Lay-out: A kind of somersault, used in the circus, in which the body remains straightened out. *see* BALLED UP.

Layers out: A circus advance man* who arrived in town a day before the circus in order to make final arrangements and to confirm that the grain and hay contracts were fulfilled. *see also* ADVANCE AGENT OR ADVANCE MAN, ADVERTISING CAR, and OUTRIDERS.

Laying the leg: Carnival jargon; putting the make on or seducing a female.

Laying the note: Pitchmen's term for short-changing a customer by removing money while putting more in the hands of the customer. *see* SHORT-CHANGE ARTIST.

Layout man: One of the first men on a circus lot* who measures off the area and directs the placing of iron pins to designate the final locations of stakes for tents. *see also* LOT.

Lazzo (lazzi): Term used in the Italian commedia dell'arte for a short piece of comic business, either physical or verbal. Still used today to denote a comic bit of business* or gag.* *see also* BUSINESS and GAG.

Lead bar: The double trees used in the rigging of the circus teams.

Lead bar detective: A circus employee who picked up all broken lead bars and body poles each day, dragging the worn and broken rigging to the blacksmith shop, where it was repaired and delivered back to its proper place on the lot

Lead joint: A carnival or circus shooting gallery.

Lead-sheet: Musical notation that provides the melody or outline of a song. Extremely important use in vaudeville.

Lead stock: Circus animals that are haltered or do not require confinement in cages, such as camels, zebras, llamas, and horses. Elephants are not included. *see* RINGSTOCK.

Leaf: Pitchmen's term for the "paper business." It can also refer to the gold-leaf pitchmen used for engraving fountain pens, wallets, and the like. Hustling the leaf would mean selling gold-leaf engraving. *see* PAPER BOY OR MAN.

Leaf-worker: *see* PAPER BOY OR MAN.

Leap tick or leaptick: 1. A mattress on which circus clowns and acrobats leap and fall. 2. Used in vaudeville in much the same way, but also for the false fat belly of a comedian, stuffed with mattress ticking or straw. *see* LEAPING TICK.

Leaper: Prior to the late nineteenth century, this was an acrobat, commonly seen in the circus, who sprinted down a ramp, catapulted off a springboard into the air, and somersaulted over horses, camels, elephants, or some other barrier, hopefully landing safely in a soft mattress or a net. Such acts are rare today. Later, a leaper was used as a synonym for a flying trapeze aerialist who did not catch. *see* CATCHER and FLYER.

Leaping tick: A nickname for the circus fat lady, said to rival in size the large mattresses upon which clowns and acrobats fell. *see* LEAP TICK.

Leaps: 1. Acrobats leaping over each other and tumbling. 2. Acrobats and clowns performing as leapers.* This was frequently the opening feature of older circuses. *see also* LEAPER.

Leary: Pitchmen's term for damaged goods. *see* LARRY.

Leather: Pitchmen's and carnival term for a pocketbook.

Leather-lunged: Carnival term for the talker* on the bally platform* before electric amplification, and they became known more frequently as talkers. With amplification, to be leather-lunged was no longer necessary in order to be heard. Also called a sounder. *see also* BALLY PLATFORM OR STAND and TALKER.

Leblang: Joe Leblang was an early twentieth-century ticket promoter. Leblang or Leblanged came into theatrical slang to mean the selling of theatre tickets at cut rates, or a show that was supported by ticket sales through cut-rate agencies such as Joe Leblang's. Now obsolete.

Lecture room or hall: Name given to a theatre space located in many so-called museums* in the nineteenth century so as to give the play-house greater respectability and acceptance to a public that otherwise might shun a real theatre. *see also* DIME MUSEUM, EXHIBITION ROOM, MORAL LECTURE, and MUSEUM.

Lecture store: A pitchman's concession equipped with a loudspeaker. The pitchman stands on an elevated platform while he makes his speech.

Lecturer: An inside talker* for a circus or carnival show, such as an illusion show,* a sideshow of freaks, a pit show,* and so forth. *see also* ILLUSION SHOW, INSIDE LECTURER, PIT SHOW, and TALKER.

Left-hand side: Since most Americans tend to move to the right, carnival midways are laid out to take advantage of this, with shows catering to children on the right-hand side, if possible, and shows for adults in the back-end,* and so forth. *see also* BACK-END and RIGHT-HAND SIDE.

Left-legged pony: *see* PONY.

Leg mania or legmania: A type of act in vaudeville and other variety forms that featured an eccentric dance team or group in close-fitting, one-piece black tights, who, painted like demons, twisted their elongated forms and legs into almost unbelievable shapes, performed high kicks above their heads, and doubled up their bodies so that they could disappear into ordinary barrels. "The Three Lorellas" were an outstanding success in such an act. Used in general terms to mean a dancer possessing special acrobatic skill or an intricate routine.

Leg piece or show: Terms used for girlie shows or any performance or show of girls dressed or undressed so as to show their legs and bodies. In burlesque and revues,* the main appeal was mild sexual excitation. *see* NUDIE and REVUE.

Legerdemain: A term literally meaning "light of hand" and referring to manual manipulation or sleight-of-hand.* By extension, it has come to mean any performed magic. *see also* SLEIGHT OR SLEIGHT-OF-HAND.

Legit: Short for legitimate.* Used to distinguish the professional New York commercial stage from traveling and nonprofessional shows. The inference is that legit means stage plays as serious art versus popular fare. It also is used for the serious artist (performer, writer, painter, composer, and so on). *see also* LEGITIMATE.

Legit actor: A performer in legit* theatre. *see also* LEGIT and LEGITIMATE.

Legitimate: H. L. Mencken explained this was any theatrical enterprise devoted to the production of actual plays by living actors, and excluding musical comedy, vaudeville, burlesque, melodrama, and the like. In vaudeville, the term referred to the stage, actors, theatres, and so on, that presented a full-evening play. *see* LEGIT.

Legitimate road: Tent-show term for the circuit and stops made by New York traveling theatre companies. *see* (THE) ROAD.

Leotards: Skin-tight singlets worn by acrobats and named after the inventor of the flying trapeze act,* Jules Leotard. *see* FLYER and FLYING TRAPEZE ACT.

Letting out the traces: When traveling troupes moved by wagons between small towns, they would parade down the main street upon their arrival. To make the parade seem longer and more important, the traces would be let out on the wagons so that the horses or mules were farther out in front of the wagons than normal. This would give the appearance of a parade larger than it actually was.

Letty or lettie: English circus term for a bed or lodging. Scarpering letty is an expression meaning an unpaid bill for lodgings. *see* SCARPER.

Levitation: A magical trick in which a person or object is raised into the air without any visible means of support. *see* SUSPENSION.

Liberty act: A circus act in which a group of horses perform without riders, displaying muscular control and obedience from the command or signal of a trainer who stands in the ring. The horses usually do changing group formations that resemble a drill.

Liberty horse: A horse that works in a liberty act.* *see also* LIBERTY ACT.

Lie down to rest: A theatrical failure, or to fail.

Lift: In circus terminology, the natural bounce that propels a bareback rider from the ground to the back of a running horse. *see* FORK JUMP, RUNNING GROUND MOUNT, and VOLTIGE.

Light on a show: To join a circus and be accepted for employment.

Light opera: *see* COMIC OPERA.

Light section: The section of the circus train, or trains, that carried the cages, lighter properties, and the ringstock.* *see also* BAGGAGE SECTION, HEAVY SECTION, and RINGSTOCK.

Light up: In burlesque, the opposite of a blackout.* A scene beginning in the dark with the lights coming up at a given point in the dialogue so as to discover the actors on stage, in place. Usually such a discovery serves as a punch line* set up by the dialogue in darkness. *see also* BLACKOUT and PUNCH LINE.

Light wagon: In the circus, the electric power unit. It was the last wagon loaded on the circus train and thus became a kind of symbol. When it was loaded, the circus was ready to move.

Limber Jim: Circus name for a contortionist. *see* BENDER and FROG.

Limelight: A performer in a position of prominence is said to be in the limelight. So identified after the actual limelight spotlight, one of the earliest forms of bright, focused stage lighting.

Limped into town: The description used for a bankrupt or poorly organized circus moving into a town.

(The) line: The chorus of dancing girls performing in an act or show.

Line of business: The type of part chosen as a specialty by most nineteenth-century actors, e.g., juvenile, old man, walking gentleman, and so on.

Line up joint: A local girl who came on the show grounds of a circus or carnival and took on all comers, usually for a dollar a lay.

Lion's leap or lion leap: English circus term for an acrobatic jump. *see* MONKEY JUMP.

Lithograph: Any and all circus posters or bills, irrespective of the method by which they were printed.

Little Caesar: The right-hand man of the owner of a carnival.

Little People: Circus name for midgets or dwarfs.* *see* DWARF.

Live one: A player with money at a carnival game. Used especially when referring to a set-joint. *see also* GET IN, SET-JOINT, and STICK.

Live paper: Circus advertising that is good until the exhibition date. *see* PAPER.

Liver-head: Burlesque slang for a performer who has great trouble learning dialogue, a routine,* or a bit.* *see also* BIT and ROUTINE.

Living statuary: Phenomenon of the last half of the nineteenth century (preburlesque) in which women wearing only revealing tights appeared on stage posing as living statuary portraying classical subjects and famous sculpture.

Load: A technical term used by magicians in referring to an article (or collection of articles) prepared so that it can be introduced into some container, such as a hatbox, usually with the purpose of producing the article or articles afterward by "magic." Loads are frequently classified in relation to the location from whence they are produced, such as body loads, table loads, hat loads, and so on.

Load of hay: A group of nonpaying customers who see a show or entertainment on free passes.

Lobsterscope: A wheel used by a projectionist with a burlesque show for a dance specialty or ensemble number. By rotating the wheel in front of light, the impression was created of a slow-motion act; a pre-strobe-light effect.

Locater: Outdoor amusement-business term for one who assigns or allots spaces for shows, rides, and concessions on the lot.* *see* LOCATION, LOT, and LOT MAN.

Location: The space allocated to a concession, show, or ride on a midway. *see* LOCATOR.

Locator: A playing card, specially prepared in some secret way, used by a magician in locating other cards. *see* KEY CARD OR LOCATOR.

Lofty tumbling: *see* GROUND AND LOFTY TUMBLING.

Long: A circus pass with a reserve seat coupon.

Long card: A playing card used by card magicians which is slightly longer than the rest in the deck. Also a name for a joke card, which is considerably larger than a normal card. *see* SHORT CARD.

Long con: Slow, deliberate persuasion on the part of a pitchman.

Long green: Pitchmen's slang for money; most specifically, folding money.

Long-line skinner: *see* LONG-STRING DRIVER.

Long season under canvas: An ad used by a tent-show owner looking for actors. Such an ad would frequently indicate that the boss wanted no drinkers and would indicate further that he was looking for people who had worked for him before.

Long side: The side of the circus cookhouse* in which the workmen eat. *see also* COOKHOUSE.

Long-string driver: A person who drove four, six, eight, or more horses in the circus. Sometimes called a long-line skinner.

Looker: Show-business slang for a beautiful woman.

Lookout: An outside man* in a carnival who took unhappy losers aside and tried to console them so as to prevent complaints. *see also* OUTSIDE MAN.

Loop-the-loop bicyclist: A circus and fair attraction, rare today, in which a bicyclist or motorcyclist descended a ramp and then did a 365° turn around a loop at the bottom of the ramp. By riding at top speed on a track, it was possible to rise sharply in a full backward loop, with the rider completely upside-down, and then, having gone full circle, to ride off in the original direction. A number of performers, however, died or were injured attempting this feat. *see* LOOPED THE GAP.

Looped the gap: To remove a piece of the track at the top of the loop in a loop-the-gap act and then to jump it. *see* LOOP-THE-LOOP BICYCLIST.

Lot: The grounds where carnivals, circuses, and traveling tent shows are held. Small towns once reserved, near the business district, a show lot which, during other periods of the year, could be used as a baseball field, fairground, or space for revival meetings or a chautauqua.* Also used is site; the English equivalent is the tober* or pitch. *see also* CHAUTAUQUA and TOBER.

Lot lady: A carnival groupie.

Lot lice: Circus and carnival hangers-on who follow the show but are not a part of the salaried employees; also, townspeople who hang around a circus or carnival watching it being erected, stay late, but spend no money. They are true vermin to the show people and once were only tolerated by the smaller, less reputable establishments. *see* CARNIVAL LOUSE.

Lot loafers: *see* GAWKS.

Lot man: A person responsible for surveying the grounds ahead of the carnival and deciding where to place the various attractions. *see* LOCATER.

Lot reader: The person in a circus or carnival who, after the show has packed, is responsible for making sure that nothing is left behind and that everything is cleaned up satisfactorily. *see* READ THE LOT.

Lota vase or bowl: A piece of magical apparatus which appears to be empty or full at the magician's whim.

Low back: Defined by H. L. Alexander as an "underslung differential" in describing a stripper.

Low grass: Circus slang for big cities and towns where, because they are sophisticated, cosmopolitan places, the grass is mowed. *see* HIGH GRASS.

Low-life farce: A popular form of nineteenth-century American drama, best exemplified by the knockabout farces of Edward Harrigan, especially the "Mulligan Guard" plays. Also applicable to the earlier Bowery B'hoy plays and the works of Charles H. Hoyt and George M. Cohan, although the focus in these is on ethnic neighborhoods and not necessarily low life. *see* FARCE and FIREMEN DRAMA.

Low pitch: A pitch* set on the ground or pavement. *see also* PITCH.

Lucky bag: A kind of lottery with few prizes; once offered in English circuses.

Lucky boy: There are two possible meanings of this appellation in the carnival world: 1. A manly but lazy young man who travels with a show but lives off a woman who works; thus, a male gold digger. 2. A gambler, grifter,* or operator of a rigged game or gambling privilege* who can't lose and thus is called lucky. *see also* GRIFTER and PRIVILEGE.

Luey: Apparently, a corruption of Joey,* one name for a circus clown. *see also* JOEY.

Lug: Carnival and circus word for a round-faced person, or, as a verb, to borrow.

Lugger: In pitchmen's terms, someone who is paid to "lug in" or steer customers to a certain show or joint.* *see also* BOOSTER, CAPPER, COME-ON, JOINT, and STICK.

Luken: An unsophisticate. *see* CHUMP, MARK, MOOCH, MONKEY, RUM OR RUMMY, and SUCKER.

Lumber: Generic circus term for virtually any group of items containing wood, such as seats or tent poles.

Lumber-buster: A minstrel show term for a wooden-shoe dancer. *see* LANCASHIRE CLOG.

Lump: Circus slang for a small, tightly packed lunch carried in a pocket.

Lumper: *see* BOOSTER, SHILL, and STICK.

Lunge: A safety device used to prevent performers from falling and injuring themselves when learning or practicing difficult tricks. Better known in the American circus as a mechanic.* *see also* MECHANIC.

Lunge line or rope: The name used in the circus for a rein attached to a horse's bridle or a restraining rope or chain attached to a wild animal's collar or harness.

Lush: Carnival slang for liquor and beer.

Lush hound or lusher: Carnival and pitchman's lingo for an habitual drinker.

L'ville: Show-business abbreviation for Louisville.

Lyceum: A kind of chautauqua* circuit during the winter months when it all went inside, into lodges and halls or any large meeting rooms. There was less pure entertainment in Lyceum than in the chautauqua. *see also* CHAUTAUQUA.

M

Macher: Outdoor amusement-business word for the big boss.

Machine: Term used in the English fair for any form of mechanically propelled riding device.

(A) Macready: Named for the English actor William Charles Macready (1793-1873), this term referred in acting to a marked pause plus a catching of the breath before certain words, characteristics of Macready's vocal delivery.

Madball: The glass globe used by a carnival fortune-teller. *see* MITT READER.

Magic carpet: The huge carpet on the lobby floor of the Sherman Hotel in Chicago where old-time showmen always met when in Chicago. Also, the name of a carnival midway riding device.

Magic lantern: A simple projection machine used for optical effects, once a popular form of entertainment in itself.

Magic ring or arena: Nineteenth-century English term for the circus ring.

Magician's choice: A forcing* technique in which a magician actually picks an object to be selected, although the spectator believes a free selection has been offered. Also called Magician's force. *see also* FORCING.

Magician's force: *see* MAGICIAN'S CHOICE.

Magician's milk: *see* MILK SUBSTITUTE.

Magician's rope: A very soft cotton rope with the core removed, used by magicians because it is pliable and easy to work with in cut-and-restored tricks and rope escapes.

Magician's wax: A variety of beeswax available in various colors for causing objects to adhere to each other or to something else or to make small objects "float" in air.

Magoo: A custard pie used by comic performers or clowns to throw at one another in comic sketches or routines.

Mags: Circus short form for programs (in a magazine format).

Mahout: Infrequently used term for a circus elephant attendant. In India, the mahout is the keeper or driver of an elephant.

Main drag: Carnival slang for the main street in a town. Sometimes called the main stem. *see* GUT and STEM.

Main guy: 1. Owner or manager of a circus or carnival. Also called governor, colonel, and gaffer. 2. A guy rope that holds up the center pole* in the circus big top. The first meaning given here probably derived from this definition. In other words, the person who holds up the show. *see also* CENTER POLE.

Main mast: The main support of the circus tent structure. Also called the main pole. *see* CENTER POLE, KING POLE, QUARTER POLE, and SIDE POLE.

Main-most-man: A carnival owner.

Main pole: *see* MAIN MAST.

Main stem: *see* MAIN DRAG.

(To) make: 1. In carnival parlance, to rob or to accomplish anything. 2. In traveling tent shows, such as a Toby show,* this meant to be hired by a show. *see also* TOBY SHOW.

Make a bally: *see* BALLY.

Make a joint: Carnival phrase meaning either to set up or frame a joint,* or to call at a hotel or place of business. *see also* FRAME A JOINT.

Make an opening: To make the first spiel* or lecture in front of a carnival or circus show. *see also* INSIDE LECTURER and SPIEL.

Make a stall: Carnival expression meaning to stop anyone and engage him or her in conversation. It is used especially in reference to prostitutes.

Male impersonator: Not to be confused with a breeches part in which a male role was played by an actress, a practice popular in the seventeenth and eighteenth centuries. This is a woman who specialized in male impersonation, most often in a variety act. Male impersonators, such as Vesta Tilley, Hetty King, and Kathleen Clifford, were especially popular in the English music hall and to a lesser extent in vaudeville. *see* FEMALE IMPERSONATOR.

Maline: Very thin, virtually transparent material used by strippers for bras and pasties. *see* MERKEN and PASTY.

Mammy: A woman backstage who helps dress strippers and waits in the wings to catch clothing as they disrobe.

Manege: A circus act with horses and riders, most specifically the riding of a high-school horse* so that it shows off properly all its tricks. "To ride a high-school horse" would mean "to work a menage act." On occasion, the term is used to refer to the horse or elephant production number of a circus. *see also* HIGH-SCHOOL HORSE and MENAGE OR MANEGE RIDER.

Manipulator: *see* WEB.

Map: Pitchmen's and medicine-show slang for a face or one's countenance.

March: The now obsolete circus street parade.* Usually termed "the March." *see also* PARADE.

Marinelli bend: A position taken up by a contortionist.

Marionette: A full-length jointed figure, usually made of wood and fashioned to simulate a person, animal, or object, originally moved from above by a stout wire to the head and strings or wire to the hands and legs. The all-stringed marionette evolved in the nineteenth century.

Marionette show: A puppet show in which the figures are usually manipulated by wires or strings from above by marionettists who also speak the dialogue, if any. Originally the figures were carried in a show box, which could be opened and used as a stage for producing the play in any park or village square.

Marionettist: *see* MARIONETTE SHOW.

Mark: A victim of a confidence man or swindler; among carnival workers, any outsider or member of a local community. Rarely, if ever, used on a circus. *see* CHUMP, LUKEN, MONKEY, MOOCH, RUM OR RUMMY, and SUCKER.

Marquee: 1. In theatrical terms, a projection above a theatre entrance usually displaying the names of attraction and performers. 2. In tent shows, in particular a circus or a traveling tent theatre, the main canopied entrance to the show. A tent rep-marquee, and those of most tent circuses, is actually an addition to the main tent itself, attached to it in some way, housing a box office and often decorated with posters, bills, and the like.

Masking principle: Magic term for covering secretly an object with something that matches its surface exactly so that an audience is not aware of its existence.

Mat: Circus abbreviation for a matinee performance.

Matinee idol: A male actor whom female audience members admire extravagantly.

M. C.: Show-business abbreviation for master of ceremony. *see* EMCEE.

Meat-show: The name sometimes given to a burleque show offering stripteasers, or a cabaret* of some sort with scantily clad or nude dancing girls in the floor show. *see also* CABARET and FLOOR SHOW.

Mechanic: 1. A dice hustler in a carnival. 2. An apparatus used by the circus as a safety device in training acrobats and aerialists to prevent beginners from falling off a horse. It is a simple leather harness or belt to which is attached a rope and pulley system and is then controlled by someone below who can break the fall of the person in the belt. When, on occasion, it is used during a show for the performance of a very dangerous trick, it is only to protect the performer in the event of a fall and can in no way assist the performer in completing a trick, in contrast with a gimmick.* *see also* GIMMICK and LUNGE.

Mechanic's grip: The way a cardsharp holds cards when dealing.

Med man: In pitchman's argot, and at fairs or carnivals, a medicine man or bogus doctor; one who peddled proprietary remedies, most of which were absolutely worthless if not actually harmful. *see* MEDICINE SHOW and PHYSIC MAN.

Med opry: In pitchmen's argot, a medicine show consisting of a short motion picture, some Indians, dancers, singers, and usually a few comedians in black-face, plus the "Doctor," who acted as interlocutor,* master of ceremonies, and finally as salesman or pitchman. *see also* INTERLOCUTOR.

Med show: Short for medicine show.

Med worker: Anyone who sells medicine, as used in the outdoor amusement business. *see* MED MAN.

Medallion: The name given to a rug on the floor of a center door fancy* set or a front room set in a Toby show.* Possibly named so because of medallions in the center of many rugs. *see also* CENTER OR CENTRE DOOR FANCY and TOBY SHOW.

Medicine show: A very American institution, as it evolved, designed to sell patent medicines and other miscellaneous cheap articles. It flourished in the mid-nineteenth century, although the tradition continued well into this century. Many medicine shows provided the only entertainment in small, out-of-the-way towns and were greeted by the townspeople with great eagerness when the wagon of the show rolled into town. The size and extravagance of these shows ran the gamut from a quack and a single musician performing on the tailgate of a wagon to very elaborate productions with large numbers of entertainers, Indians, and such, performing on more sophisticated stages erected in tents or surrounded by canvas walls. Ultimately, of course, the important moment was the spiel* by the "Doc" and the sale of goods (often involving a shill* who would buy the first bottle of patent medicine, salve, or the like). *see also* SHILL and SPIEL.

Medium: In a mental act, an assistant who receives coded messages and reveals them dramatically to the audience. Actually, a stage medium is so central to the act that the person is a full partner to the mentalist.* *see also* MENTALIST.

Medium show girl: *see* SHOW GIRL.

Medzies: *see* DENARI.

Meller: Twentieth-century term for plays with extravagant theatricality; melodrama.* Use of the term and contemporary plays that fit it indicate little understanding of the real genre. *see also* MELODRAMA.

Melodrama: Probably the most popular form of drama ever conceived. Originally either, in Germany, a passage in an opera spoken with musical accompaniment, or, in France, a passage in which the character says nothing while music expresses the emotion. Circa 1780, the modern meaning emerged of an extravagantly theatrical drama using all the possibilities inherent in music, lighting, stage machinery, and so forth, for the artificial enhancing of emotion. Popular theatres continued to exploit the form until it came to mean a straight drama of an unusually sensational nature, implausible in characterization, dialogue, and situation, normally abounding in thrilling struggles between exaggerated heroic and villainous figures and ending happily with the triumph of virtue. Its predictability accounted in large measure for its success, as did its reinforcement of middle-class values. For a time, especially during the Victorian period, melodrama succeeded as a kind of naive popular entertainment, as well as a more elevated drama for the middle classes. By the late nineteenth century, the term began to be used derogatorially. Today, although it is still extremely popular, it usually appears under other guises.

Menag. top: The circus animal tent. *see* MENAGERIE TOP.

(The) menace: The villain in a drama or melodrama.* *see also* MELODRAMA.

Menage or manege rider: A circus equestrian performer working with high-school horses.* *see also* HIGH-SCHOOL HORSES and MANEGE.

Menagerie top: The circus tent where the animals are exhibited. *see* MENAG. TOP and TOP.

Mender: A carnival and sometimes circus term for a claim adjuster who travels with a show and takes care of any claims or complaints customers may raise against the show. Also called iceman. *see* ADJUSTER, BAG MAN, PATCH, and VULCANIZER.

Mene tekel deck: A trick deck of cards made up of twenty-six pairs of cards arranged face to back with every other card cut short. The magician, by having the deck cut and the top card chosen, can then identify the chosen card since the mate of the top card will appear on the bottom after the cut. *see* SVENGALI DECK.

Mejarie or monjarie: A English circus term for food.

Mental magic: *see* MENTALISM.

Mentalism: Magician's term for the branch of conjuring also popularly known as mental magic, thought-reading, and clairvoyance. *see* MIND READING.

Mentalist: An alleged mind reader.

Merchandise joints: *see* STOCK JOINTS.

Merken: A material that looks like "fuzz" placed under the G-string by a stripper to look like pubic hair. *see* MALINE and PATCH OR IN THE PATCH.

Merry-go-round: *see* CAROUSEL.

Middleman: 1. Another name for the interlocutor* in the minstrel show. *see also* INTERLOCUTOR. 2. The performer between the bearer,* bottom man* or understander* and the top mounter* in a column of a three-men-high* acrobatic act. *see also* BEARER, BOTTOM MAN, THREE HIGH, TOP MOUNTER, and UNDERSTANDER.

Middle-piece: *see* LACING.

Midget: *see* DWARF.

Midway: In general terms, a midway can be defined as the area where shows, rides, or games are located on the lot* of a circus, carnival, or amusement park. Specifically, a circus midway, although few circuses still have them, is the area near the main entrance, a kind of wide avenue fronting the circus big top* and leading to its entrance-way and containing sideshows, concession stands, and ticket and administrative wagons. A carnival midway is its main street and includes all the public areas. Most amusement parks can also be considered midways, although the large ones, in particular the modern theme park,* might include one major area of games and concessions which they call the midway. *see also* BACK-END, BIG TOP, CARNIVAL, LOT, and THEME PARK.

Midway bonus: Carnival term for a big, artificial promise; usually a chance or promise on last year's sweepstakes.

Midway snitch: A carnival press agent* who reports the news. It is not uncommon for this agent to write bad weeks into good ones or reds.* *see also* PRESS AGENT and RED.

Milk: To wring applause and encores from an audience. Used in most forms of performance, especially prevalent in burlesque. *see* STEAL A BOW.

Milk jump: A one-night stand* accessible to a company only by a milk train, inconveniently early. *see also* ONE-NIGHT STAND.

Milk man: Slang for an actor who milks* an audience for extra laughs, applause, and the like. *see also* MILK.

Milk substitute: A substance used by magicians which, when added to water, resembled milk but does not spoil. The most common substitutes in the United States are Oil of Milk (OOM) or Magician's Milk.

Milkmen's matinee: In early western mining camp theatres, variety shows that ran till four in the morning.

Milky way: A frozen custard machine stand or location on a carnival lot.

Minches: Dull and nonspending patrons at a carnival.

Mind reading: A catch-all term in magic covering a wide variety of effects, including the divination of the thoughts of a spectator or group of spectators. *see* MENTALISM.

Mini-tramp or minitramp: A small trampoline used in circus rebound acrobatics.

Minsky's burlesque: A type of burlesque show so named after the Minsky brothers, who popularized the striptease. In 1908, Abe Minsky founded the first Minsky Burlesque operation, joined in partnership by his brothers Billy and Herbert.

Minstrel: 1. Originally, the generic name for a professional traveling entertainer of the middle ages who sang, played musical instruments, told stories, juggled, clowned, and tumbled. 2. In the nineteenth century, the term came to mean in America a form of entertainment and the performers in this entertainment, the black-face minstrels. Most performers were white in black-face makeup, although in the latter part of the nineteenth century there were a few black minstrels, yet they, too, normally wore the traditional black-face makeup. *see* MINSTREL SHOW.

Minstrel black: A cosmetic used in making up for Negro roles on the stage. Originally this was composed of burnt cork* and glycerine but was superseded by brown or very dark greasepaint. *see also* BURNT CORK.

Minstrel Show: A type of American entertainment, usually considered the first uniquely American show-business form, which, beginning in the 1840s, literally swept the nation, producing, in time, a tremendous impact on subsequent forms, in particular burlesque* and vaudeville.* It reached its peak in 1870 and was virtually over by 1896, although changes after the Civil War prolonged its life well into the twentieth century. Today, for obvious reasons, especially its perpetuation of black stereotypes, it is extinct. Most frequently the performers were whites in black-face.* The show was ultimately divided into three major parts: repartee between the master of ceremonies or interlocutor* and the end men,* Bruder Tambo and Bruder Bones, sitting on either end of a semicircular arrangement of the company, followed by the "olio"* or the variety section, and culminating with a one-act skit. This comic stage entertainment, consisting of dialogue, song, and dance in its set pattern, claimed to imitate Negro manners and speech, though the portrayal had little realism to it. Even the all-Negro minstrel shows after the Civil War could not gain popularity with a realistic impersonation of Negro life and ways. Despite its negative connotations, the minstrel show was terrific entertainment and dominated American popular entertainment for over fifty years. *see also* BLACK FACE, BURLESQUE, END MAN, INTERLOCUTOR, MINSTREL, OLIO, VAUDEVILLE, and WALK-AROUND.

Minstrelsy: Collectively, minstrel shows.

Mirror maze: English fair name for a house of mirrors, a labyrinth of mirrors, plane and distorting, with some clear glass thrown in to add to the confusion. Traditionally, this has not been a good money-maker in England or the United States, and thus few are found with traveling fairs or carnivals.

Mirror McGimp: Defined by DeBelle as an illusion show gal's* jockey in a carnival. *see also* ILLUSION SHOW.

Miscount: *see* PEEK.

Misdirection: The magician's art of diverting the audience's attention from some secret maneuver or device involved in making an illusion or trick work.

Missing a tip: English circus expression for missing a trick. The term tip dates, at least, from the nineteenth century. It seems to have originally meant to fall or fail at a jump.

Mitt: A palmist in carnival argot; short for mitt reader.* *see also* MITT READER.

Mitt camp or joint: A palmist's or fortune-teller's concession at a carnival. *see* GIPSY LEE and MITT READER.

Mitt reader: A carnival fortune-teller of either sex, although they have tended to be mostly aged females too old for other carnival work. The practice is of gypsy origin. Gypsy fortune-tellers can still be found carrying on their work largely at roadside camps, much as they did in Europe in earlier times. The names mitt reader or duke reader, however, are native to the United States and were coined at the St. Louis Pan-American Exposition. Both terms, of course, refer to one's hands.

(To) mix in the tip: Carnival phrase describing the practice of having one pitchman remain in the crowd (tip*) while another is giving a spiel.* Often the one acting as the shill will ask questions of the other pitchman so as to bring out the merits of his product or to start the crowd by making a purchase. *see* BOOSTER, COME-ON, SHILL, SPIEL, and TIP.

Mixed group: Circus term for a wild animal act of several different species.

Mixing: Common practice in today's smaller clubs where strippers and other girls circulate and induce customers to buy them expensive, watered-down drinks; the girls receive a commission on the drinks they "sell."

Mnemonics: A memory system used by magicians for learning and retaining large amounts of often unrelated knowledge and isolated facts.

Mob: The group of men employed by one carnival joint.* *see* JOINT.

Moduc: One of the several small dummies set up to be knocked over by balls at a carnival concession. *see* CAT RACK and SIX-CAT.

Moll: Carnival slang for a girl. In the carnival, a moll does not carry the unsavory connotation that it does in the underworld.

Moll-buzzer: In various forms of outdoor amusement, this is a thief, frequently a youthful one, who specializes in snatching women's purses from baby carriages. By working in pairs, one can distract the woman's attention while the other grabs the purse and runs. The first thief will block, while pretending to assist in the second's capture.

Monday man or worker: A thief who, at one time, had the exclusive right in a circus to steal from village clotheslines while the residents were out front watching the circus parade or at the show.

Money guy: The owner of a burlesque house.

Money store: Any carnival game that pays off in cash rather than in merchandise.

Money wagon: *see* RED WAGON.

Moniker, monicker, monniker, monacer, or monica: A name of a person or his nickname or alias. Used in the carnival world, although originally a hobo word passed on to the underworld.

Monkey: In the carnival, this is a rube,* chump,* or victim who has been taken in or fleeced. *see also* CHUMP, LUKEN, MARK, MOOCH, RUBE, RUM OR RUMMY, and SUCKER.

Monkey jump: An acrobatic leap in a circus act. *see* LION'S LEAP.

Monologist: A performer offering a monologue in vaudeville, usually without songs or dances. After vaudeville died, a number of performers continued this tradition in concert performances. *see* ONE-MAN TROUPES and TALKING SINGLE.

Monte: A variation of the three-shell game, which is, in turn, a descendant of thimble-rig,* played with three thimbles weighted in the top. The three-shell game requires that the player guess under which of the shells the pea will be found; three-card monte* requires that the sucker* guess which of the three rapidly shuffled cards is the selected one. In addition to nimble fingers, the operator depends on misdirection* in beating the sucker, which he invariably does. *see also* BROAD TOSSER, MISDIRECTION, MONTE, SUCKER, THIMBLE-RING, and THREE-CARD MONTE.

Mooch: Carnival slang for a sucker* or a mark.* Sometimes it is used in the sense of a person who watches a pitchman but does not buy or play. *see also* CHUMP, LUKEN, MARK, RUM OR RUMMY, and SUCKER.

Mop fair: An English fair that became associated with the hiring of domestic servants, although the term is also found in a number of sources to mean a country fair in general terms. *see* CHARTER FAIR, HIRING FAIR, and STATUTE FAIR.

Mope or mope away: In circus slang, to walk away from a show.

Moral lecture: A term sometimes used in the United States to describe a dramatic reading or performance in order to avoid possible censorship, especially during the eighteenth and early-nineteenth centuries. *see* EXHIBITION ROOM and MUSEUM.

Morgue: A theatre showing an unsuccessful production, or a dead town where a carnival or circus is playing.

Motordrome: *see* DROME.

Mother, Home, and Heaven lectures: Inspirational talks given at traveling chautauquas.* The most famous lecture of this type was Russell H. Conwell's "Acres of Diamonds," delivered over 6,000 times. *see also* CHAUTAUQUAS.

Motto singer: A variety singer in vaudeville who specialized during the 1880s and 1890s in singing songs based on one-line sayings, such as "You'll never miss the water till the well runs dry."

Mountain goats: Expression used by older comics for the influx of comedians trained on the Borscht belt* who crowded a lot of the older comics out since they would work for less. *see also* BORSCHT CIRCUIT and MOUNTAINEER.

Mountaineer: A graduate of the Borscht belt* circuit. The location of the Borscht belt in the Catskill Mountains explains the use of "mountain" in this and the preceding entry. *see also* BORSCHT CIRCUIT and MOUNTAIN GOATS.

Mouse game: A carnival wheel* with a live mouse. This is one of the most fascinating carnival games to watch, although it is easily gaffed.* A large, revolving, horizontal wheel is divided into sections, each numbered. At the outer rim there is a small hole in each numbered section. A mouse is placed in the center of the horizontal wheel and covered with a can, and the wheel is then spun vigorously. When the wheel stops, the can is removed and the mouse then moves around the wheel until it ducks into one of the numbered holes for safety. This is the winning number. There are, of course, many variations of this game: colored rather than numbered sections, a "live" ball instead of a mouse, and so forth. *see also* CARNIVAL WHEEL and GAFFED.

Mousetown: An exhibition of performing mice; a more common name in England than in the United States.

Mouthpiece: A local legal representative used by a circus or carnival; the term comes from the criminal world.

Move: 1. The jump* between towns on an outdoor show's route.* *see also* JUMP and ROUTE. 2. Manipulation required for a magician to perform a trick.

Mud: Cheap merchandise, souvenirs, trinkets, and the like given as prizes at carnival concessions. *see* PLASTER, RINKY-DINK, and SLUM.

Mud op'ry: *see* MUD SHOW.

Mud show: Originally, a circus mud show traveled overland by a horse-drawn wagon, the wheels of which were frequently mired in mud. Prior to 1872, in fact, all circuses were mud shows, and some continued to travel that way until the early 1920s. Later, the term was applied to any circus that traveled overland by wagon, truck, or automobile. Such a show, sometimes called an overland trick or a mud op'ry,* usually played small towns or the suburbs of large cities. Today, it is a derogatory term used by the large circuses who move by private train to refer to any show not using the luxury of steel rails. *see* BICYCLE OPERAS.

Mug joint: A carnival and circus slang expression for a tent, booth, or gallery in which one's photograph is taken and printed "while-you-wait." *see* MUGMAN OR MUGSNAPPER.

Mugg or Variety mugg: The name given to a reporter working for *Variety*.

Mugging: As used in vaudeville and applicable to the theatre as well, a contortion of the facial features to gain laughter, irrespective of its consistency with the lines or action.

Mugman or mugsnapper: Carnival and circus name for an itinerant photographer. *see* MUG JOINT.

Mule: A rubber-tired tractor used at one time by circuses to move empty wagons and load the show train. *see* MULE SKINNER.

Mule skinner: A tractor driver. *see* MULE.

Multi: English circus term for bad. *see* MULTI KATIVA.

Multi kativa: Term meaning no good. From the Lingua Franca (also the Italian *molto cattivo*). *see* MULTI.

Mumbo jumbo: A circus expression for the mesmerizing spiel* of a show talker.* *see also* SPIEL and TALKER.

Murder: Heavy demand for theatre tickets.

Muscatel: Circus term (principally of the English circus) for coffee.

Muscle grind: A series of revolutions on the aerial rings in a circus act.

Muscle reading: Named after the artistry of Axel Hellstrom, one of the greatest of muscle readers, this means, in its simplest terms, an ability to interpret the unconscious, muscular telltale movements of a spectator in order to find some hidden object. A useful ability in a magician.

Museum: Many places of entertainment in the nineteenth century were called museums in the United States in order to give the aura of respectability. Invariably, this meant a place of amusement with a theatre (or lecture halls), some exhibits, human oddities, pictures or statuary, and a few live animals or snakes. Some of these establishments, such as the Boston Museum and, to a lesser extent, Barnum's American Museum, became the home of excellent stock companies, and their live entertainment became the major attraction. see also EXHIBITION ROOM and LECTURE ROOM OR HALL.

Mush: Circus slang for an umbrella or a mouth. see KISSER.

Music exploitation man: see SONG PLUGGER.

Music hall: The most precise meaning refers to the British form of entertainment in which a series of turns* by individual performers were presented before an audience (usually given as music-hall). Similar to, but in many ways different, from American vaudeville, its nearest American kin. The name was used, however, in this country in another way, that is, to refer to a motion-picture theatre in which variety entertainment was provided between film showings. The greatest of these is Radio City Music Hall in New York. see also TURN.

Musical comedy: A genre of theatre which would require a lengthy book of its own to cover all its facets and, in many ways, not strictly a form of popular entertainment in all its mutations. In general, this describes a form of play with interpolated songs and dances. The name is sometimes a misnomer, since many are not necessarily comic. The American form evolved from the light opera* and operetta of the 1890s and 1900s. After World War I, the genre became, in general, lighter, slighter, and faster-moving, with more dancing and less accent on romance but with more comedy. In the past fifteen years, musical comedy has become extremely variegated, so much so that a simple definition is now impossible to encompass such disparate musicals as *Sweeney Todd, A Chorus Line,* and *Hair,* for example. see also LIGHT OPERA.

Musical mokes: A black-face musical minstrel act, specializing in the playing of various instruments. Outstanding examples in vaudeville included Bryant and Hoey, and Wood and Beasley.

Mutual wheel: An offshoot of the Columbia burlesque wheel* or circuit, which in the 1920s added greater permissiveness in their shows. Like the Columbia wheel,* this group of theatres from coast to coast booked burlesque shows and revues. It lasted until some time in the early 1930s. *see also* COLUMBIA WHEEL and MINSKY BURLESQUE.

Muzzler: Circus and carnival slang word for a low-principled person.

N

Nail nick: In magic, to mark an object secretly by pressing with the fingernail or thumb.

Nail writer: A device used by mentalists and magicians for writing predictions and other information without the audience knowing that any writing is being done. Most of the various kinds of nail writers attach to the thumbnail and are so minute as to escape detection. Known also as the swami gimmick.

Name-gatherer: *see* PAPER BOY OR MAN.

Nanty: English circus term for no, not, or nothing. *see* NUNTI OR NANTE.

Nark: Carnival slang for a plainclothes policeman or informer paid by the police for detecting illegal games of chance or offenses against local moral codes. When spoken on the lot, accompanied with a nudge and nod of the head, it meant to get rid of the illegal operation quickly.

(The) National Vaudeville Association (N.V.A.): An organization financed by Edward F. Albee in 1916 in order to counteract the White Rats.* In order to play in an Albee-dominated theatre, a performer had to be an N.V.A member, which meant not being a White Rat. *see also* (THE) WHITE RATS.

Natives: In circus lingo, local townspeople.

Natural: 1. A successful circus act. 2. A listener of a pitchman who buys. *see* CHUMP, MARK, MONKEY, and MOOCH.

Nautical drama: *see* AQUATIC DRAMA.

Neat: Word in vaudeville to describe a dancing act that avoided buffoonery or acrobatics.

Needle test: Magician's trick of thrusting needles through the arm and other parts of the body without apparent pain or bleeding.

New faces: New talent in show business.

Next to closing or next to shut: The next-to-last position in a vaudeville bill. This was invariably reserved for the chief star of the show.

Next week, "East Lynne": A phrase that entered the vocabulary before the turn of the century, in the days of traveling companies. With each actor carrying a stock of costumes and standard roles in his or her repertoire, it was possible for the manager to announce the next week's performance with little notice. *East Lynne*, like *Uncle Tom's Cabin*, usually was guaranteed box-office success. Any time a troupe was in trouble the manager would call out backstage, "Next week, East Lynne." In time, the phrase came to mean trouble, trouble of any kind, and the possible solution to the problem. *see* LINE OF BUSINESS.

Nice people: Vaudeville agents' name for performers who gave them more than their 10% commissions.

Nicked: Term used by pitchmen in medicine shows for injured.

Nickelodeon: *see* KINODROMES.

Nigger boards: Derogatory term for the platform sections spread on the ground in many nineteenth-century circuses as a floor for concert acts, dancers, and the like, before stages became common in the circus tent.

Nigger heaven: The topmost gallery in a theatre or place of entertainment; common at the end of the nineteenth century, since Negroes were segregated in most theatres. *see* GALLERY GODS, PARADISE, PEANUT GALLERY, and TOP SHELF.

Nigger rich: Derisive term once used in the circus for spending money foolishly.

Nigger minstrel or show: A derogatory term for a minstrel show of the nineteenth century.

Nigger wild: Med-show term for unerringly.

Night lunch: A meal or snack eaten by performers after a vaudeville or burlesque evening show.

Night riders: Opposition billposters for two or more circuses who, working at night, tore down paper* and covered the opposition's advertisements with their own. *see also* PAPER.

Night stand: Short for one-night stand.* *see also* ONE-NIGHT STAND.

Nikola system: A memory system originated by Louis Nikola, the famous magician and magical inventor, based upon association of ideas.

Nitery or nightery: A nightclub.

Nix: Popularized by the show-business paper *Variety* ("Stix nix hix pix"); means no, to veto, to reject, to cancel, to avoid, thumbs down, a ban, unfavorable, or any of a number of negatives.

Nobbings: In an English circus, the take or receipts.

Not with it: A circus outsider. *see* WITH IT.

Notch house or notcherie: Circus name for a brothel.

Novelty act: A skit, acrobatic feat, or the like, which is unusual and perhaps has a new wrinkle. Used in vaudeville.

Nudie: A show or performance in which a female nude or nudes appear; also used as a name for a performer in such a show. *see* LEG PIECE OR SHOW.

Nudnick: Theatrical use from the Yiddish for a bore or an obnoxious person.

Number: A distinct portion of a production, such as a song or dance act or a comedy team in vaudeville or musical comedy.

Number two act: The second act on a vaudeville bill, usually an insignificant one.

Nunti or nante: Means no or don't in the English circus and the nineteenth-century British theatre; from the Lingua Franca. *see* NANTY.

Nut or burr: Term used in most forms of entertainment for the total cost or expense of a show. In the theatre, it is the actual or estimated cost of operating a show, usually figured on a weekly basis. If the production has begun to make a profit, it is off the nut. If overhead reserves have to be used, it is operating on the nut. "Cracked the nut" means the same as off the nut but is a distortion of the circus meaning of the word, which is a bolt off a wheel axle and not a nut that grows on a tree. There are several apocryphal stories of this word's origin. The most common is that, when wagon shows, in the 1820s, moved overland, the lead wagon was an elaborately decorated wagon with huge wheels. To make sure the show paid its bills in each town, the sheriff would take a nut off the axle of the wagon. The estimated cost of expenses would determine the number of nuts taken. If bills were settled, the nuts would be returned. Since there were no standard-made wagons then and nuts were expensive, few shows had spare nuts. Those that did needed no credit anyway. *see* (TO) CRACK THE NUT.

Nut sharps: Med-show slang for alienists or those who treated mental disorders.

Nuts: Carnival slang for having the drop on someone, as in being covered with a gun. Also, synonymous for the infamous shell game, with the three half-walnut shells and the little pea.

Nuts and peas: Necessary accessories at one time on the midway; used in the shell game. *see* MONTE.

O

Oakum: Old-time minstrel jokes. *see* GRAVY.

OBs or obies: *see* ASTRAL PROJECTION.

Oday: Circus use of pig-Latin for dough or money.

Off to Buffalo: Vaudeville expression for a traveling step in dancing used to exit from the stage.

Off the nut: *see* NUT OR BURR.

Office: A circus's business headquarters. Also complaint room or sign of understanding. *see* (TO) OFFICE OR GIVE THE OFFICE.

(To) office or give the office: To tip someone off; a subtle warning in the carnival and some circuses given by clearing the throat or with a look or wink.

Office show or ride: A carnival or amusement-park ride or show that is owned by the midway owner and is not an independent attraction.

Oil: In pitchmen's slang, any kind of petroleum product, such as liniments, salves, machine oil, or hair preparation.

Oil of Milk (OOM): *see* MILK SUBSTITUTE.

Okito box: A box used in coin magic invented by Theo. Bamberg, the famous American magician known as Okito.

Old bean: Med-man's word for an Indian chieftain or a sachem.

Old folks: Circus slang for monkeys.

Old man: Owner or director of a circus.

Old rag: Another circus word for the big top.

Old stager: Once used to denote a veteran actor. *see* STAGER.

Old star bucks: Circus term for reserve seats, so-called because of stars painted on the backs. Also called starbacks. *see* BLUES and HARD TICKETS.

Olio or oleo: 1. A curtain, drop, or backing hung several feet behind the front curtain in a theatre, vaudeville house, burlesque theatre, and the like, in front of which a vaudeville act or specialty act was performed while another scene was being set farther back. In vaudeville, an olio was used often to close-in* on acts playing in two,* three,* or four.* *see also* CLOSE-IN, FOUR, THREE, and TWO. 2. The act played in one* before an olio backing. *see also* IN ONE. 3. The traditional second part of a minstrel show and adapted by burlesque. Invariably, this type of olio comprised a medley of songs, dances, comic sketches or bits,* and the like. *see* BIT.

Oliver or Ollie: Oliver is traditionally a slang word for moon but has been used in the circus world to mean an officer of the law. *see* COOKIE-CUTTER.

O. M.: Abbreviation for a pitchman who sold products of his own manufacture. Such products usually did not require a license in order to be sold, although it was frequently necessary to mollify the legal authorities in order to sell them in a town.

Omney: Used by the British circus and theatre to mean a man; extracted from the Italian *"uomo"* via Linqua Franca. *see* HOMY.

On: 1. Short for on stage; the phrase "you're on" was common in vaudeville. 2. More frequently used now to mean that a performer carries his theatrical behavior into his personal life.

On and off: Vaudevillian's way of indicating when he or she was working and when not working.

On the burr or on the nut: To owe a circus money. *see* NUT.

On the circus or on the show: Performers and all others connected with a circus—rarely "with the show or circus." *see* WITH IT.

On the send: An unhappy victim of a carnival or circus game who is after more money.

On the straw or strawing them: Seating circus patrons on straw on the ground in front of other seats when all regular places have been taken.

On the walk: Selling tickets to a show on the sidewalk near the theatre. *see* WALK MEN.

On with others: From the turn of the century, theatrical expression referring to those in a company without speaking parts. *see* PAINTED ON THE DROP.

One: The part of the vaudeville stage nearest the audience, directly behind the footlights. *see* IN ONE.

One ahead: A system used in mind-reading magic in which the performer discovers the written thoughts of audience members before the audience realizes the magician is doing so.

One-ball game: A carnival and amusement park percentage game* in which a player throws a softball against a wooden backboard from which the ball rebounds and falls down into the game layout, divided into numbered squares. The one on which the ball stops determines whether or not the player wins or loses. *see also* PERCENTAGE OR P.C. STORE.

One-liner: A joke that, theoretically, contains its punch in one sentence or can be written in one line on a sheet of paper.

One-lunger: A theatrical presentation that takes place in one set of scenery; also stagehand term for a one-set show.

One-man troupes: Name used to describe monologues delivered by a single performer, frequently portraying or representing several characters. Popular in circuit chautauquas. *see also* CHAUTAUQUA, MONOLOGIST, and TALKING SINGLE.

One-night stand: A production or presentation given in a particular theatre or hall for a single evening, or the town or theatre in which such a performance takes place. Touring or traveling companies played one-night stands and such a practice was among the most grueling of theatrical activity. Generally, when traveling companies were common, a circuit included full-week stands, but it was necessary to play in isolated areas between these stops to meet the operating expenses. Most traveling companies specialized in popular fare, either dramatic, musical, or variety. Burlesque companies regularly presented two shows a night on one-night stands. *see* ONE-NIGHTER and (TO) WEEK-STAND.

One-nighter: *see* ONE-NIGHT STAND.

One-sheet: In vaudeville and burlesque, in particular, this meant to give an act minor billing, so named for the smallest size theatrical advertising poster used on billboards. *see* SHEET.

One-step: Style of dancing popular early in this century in which a step accompanied each beat in the music.

One-way pack or deck: A deck of cards with an asymmetrical design on the backs.

One-week house: A term, now rare, for a theatre usually booked for one week by a traveling company on the road.

Onion ballad: Show-business slang for a tearjerker.

OOM: *see* MILK SUBSTITUTE.

Ooser: Theatrical use, from the Yiddish, meaning hardly.

Open or open spot: A town or area receptive to pitchmen. *see* HOT SPOT.

Open cold: To be the first to try one's talents and charms on an audience; most common use in vaudeville.

Open set: Vaudeville term for a stage setting composed of a rear drop and matching side wings and not "boxed" or completely closed.

Open the show: The first act on a vaudeville program. *see* CLOSE THE SHOW and FOLLOW THE ANIMATED.

Open town: A town in which pitchmen may work after payment of a license fee. *see* OPEN OR OPEN SPOT.

Opener: The talker* who encourages patrons to buy tickets for a circus or carnival show. *see also* OPENING, SPIELER, and TALKER.

Opening: The initial lecture or ballyhoo* made outside a carnival or circus show to attract customers. Openings are sometimes repeated for shows that are grind shows* but more frequently those that repeat themselves only a limited number of times. Openings are divided into two parts: the first opening consists of the material calculated to draw the crowd near the front,* and the second opening is needed for those potential customers who begin to drift away after the ballyhoo or lecture. *see also* BALLYHOO, FRONT, and GRIND SHOW.

Opera house: *see* CONCERT HALL.

Operating on the nut: *see* NUT OR BURR.

Operator: Technical term used by some magicians for a hypnotist.

Opery: Word sometimes used synonymously for circus.

Opera House: Synonym for a theatre, especially used during the late nineteenth and early twentieth centuries. *see* CONCERT HALL.

Opposition paper: Advertising papers that were put up by a competing circus.

Opry: *see* RAG SHOW OR RAG OPERA OR OPRY.

Opry-house: A disparaging theatrical term once used for an old, dirty, rundown, or poorly equipped theatre, the type so frequently encountered by traveling companies.

Orange Juice Gulch: Theatrical name once given to Times Square in New York City because of the large number of fruit-juice stands that were there.

Orchestra: A general term for any sort of musical group carried by a tent show, such as a Toby show.* *see also* TOBY SHOW.

Oriental dancer: Exotic name given a striptease belly dancer or cooch* dancer. *see also* COOCH OR COOTCH DANCING.

Oracle worker: Nineteenth-century English term for a press agent. *see also* PRESS AGENT.

Ork, orc, or orch: Abbreviation for an orchestra or a dance band, as popularized by *Variety*.

Oscar: *see* HAVE YOU SEEN OSCAR?

(An) Oscar Hammerstein: Name applied to a minstrel high hat on parade. Named after the impresario/manager Oscar Hammerstein I (1847-1919) who was noted for wearing high hats. *see* ELEVEN FORTY-FIVE and HI HENRY.

(To go) out under canvas: A term once used when Ringling Bros. went out on the road with a tent show after its spring indoor engagements.

Out-jog: The action of a card magician replacing a card on the deck so that its edge projects away from the performer. *see* JOG.

Outlaw: The name given to an unreliable circus laborer or boss.

Outriders: Circus advance men* responsible for checking to see that other advance crews had done their jobs and that posters and lithographs were prominently displayed. *see also* ADVANCE AGENT and ADVERTISING CARS.

Outside flash: The series of banners,* also called valentines, in front of which a talker* makes a spiel* for a sideshow attraction. *see also* BANNERS, SPIEL, and TALKER.

Outside man: A carnival game employee who pretends to be a player and assists in the build up;* frequently he has been an older man who is a glib talker. *see also* BOOSTER, BUILD UP, CAPPER, COME-ON, FRONTWORKER, SHILL, and STICK.

Outside talker: On a circus or carnival midway, the person who sells the show from in front of the tent on a bally stand* or stage. *see also* BALLY STAND and TALKER.

Overact: Although this once meant to excel in acting, it now denotes an exaggerated, out-of-proportion type of acting. *see* HAM.

Overland trick: *see* MUD SHOW.

P

P. A.: Abbreviation for press agent, personal appearance, or public-address system.

Pacer: A stripteaser who strips double-time to slow music. *see* STRIP WOMAN.

Pacific water dog: Circus name for a seal.

Pack: 1. Circus and some carnival use to mean depart. 2. A deck of cards; in Great Britain, called more frequently a pack of cards.

Packed to the ring curb: Circus expression for a crowded performance. *see* RING CURB and RING FENCE.

Pact: Short form for a contract, or to sign a contract with a person or organization. Popularized by *Variety*.

Pad: 1. Pitchmen's term for a subscription blank for magazine orders. *see* PAPER BOY OR MAN and SHEET WRITER. 2. A flat platform strapped to a horse's back in the circus.

Pad room: Circus dressing room, so named because of the trappings and pads* (for horses) that were once kept there. *see also* PAD.

Paddle wheel: A carnival wheel,* the numbered sections of which contain one, two, or three numbers. Usually, such wheels have a counter lay-down raffle or chart on which bets are placed, and some operators sell paddles, or numbered paper slips, which correspond to the numbered spaces on the wheel. *see also* CARNIVAL WHEEL, LAY DOWN, and SLEEPER.

Painted on the drop: A performer who has no lines to speak, as used especially in burlesque. *see* ON WITH OTHERS.

Painted ponies: Circus slang for zebras. *see* QUAGGA.

Pale meat: A name given to an anemic hamburger sold at a carnival.

Paleface: A white-faced circus clown.* *see also* WHITE-FACE OR WHITE-FACE CLOWN.

Palm: Magician's term for secretly concealing a small article in the hand.

Palmy days: The so-called good old days of the stage, remembered most often by old actors who have forgotten that such times really never existed.

Palooka: In show-business slang, an oaf, from the expression for an athlete, especially one lacking ability, experience, or a competitive spirit.

Pan: Med-show term for talent.

Pan lifters: Pitchmen's expression for pot holders.

Panatrope: English fair term for a record player with a loudspeaker.

Panel dress or skirt: A piece of material that extends down from a stripper's waist, to either the floor or to her heel. Worn over the G-string,* it usually consists of a piece of string tied at the waist from which hang two or more strips of cloth, usually a narrow one in front drapped over the crotch and a large one in back covering the buttocks. The panel or panels give the stripper more to work with in disrobing after an actual dress is removed. Sometimes the panel is the last to come off, or, if they work stronger,* they remove the G-string last. Originally designed by Sherry Britton. *see also* G-STRING and WORK STRONG.

Panel girl: A female used in a badger game. As she distracts the attention of the mark,* her partner steals valuables from his clothing through the panel of a wall to an adjoining room. *see also* MARK.

Panic 'em or panicked the house: A vaudeville or legitimate theatre expression for a big hit. *see* LAY 'EM IN THE AISLES and TAKE THREE BENDS AND AN ENCORE.

Pan or pam: *see* PANORAMA.

Panorama: A form of optical entertainment which originally, in the mid-eighteenth century, meant the painting of a broad scene on a cylindrical canvas. The word, drawn from "pan" (all) and "-orama" (sight), soon gave birth to an enormous number of "-oramas," and the original panorama, by the time its popularity reached the United States, had come, in most cases, to mean a moving panorama, that is, a series of related scenes painted on a single cloth that rolled from one cylinder to another. Such panoramas were either used in concert with a production as a background or independently as a self-contained entertainment. The nineteenth century saw a series of popular panoramas, usually showing scenes depicted on a trip down the Mississippi or Ohio rivers, that were toured throughout the country. *see* DIORAMA.

Pantomime: As a form of popular entertainment, pantomime, from the Latin *"pantomimus"* (to mime all), has never experienced widespread acceptance in this country, although in an Americanized version of the British pantomime (a combination of dance, fairytales, or other fantastic popular tales, characters from the Italian commedia dell' arte, clowning, and, ultimately, dialogue and song), the work of George L. Fox (1825-1877) and that of the Ravels earlier in the century and the Kiralfys during the last quarter of the century brought forms of extravagant pantomime to American audiences.

Paper: 1. All paper circus advertising, including posters, lithographs, bill boards, and the like. *see* BILL-STICKER. 2. A pass or free ticket to a theatre or circus. 3. To paper is to distribute as many free tickets or passes as necessary to a theatre or circus in order to assure a large audience, thus a paper house* means that most of the patrons have received comps* or freebees.* *see also* COMP and FREEBEES.

Paper boy or man: 1. A pitchman who sold magazines or took subscriptions for magazines or papers (these were frequently farm papers). Also known as a leaf worker, name-gatherer, and sheet worker. *see* SHEET WRITER and WRITE SHEET. 2. A pitchman who sold books of tickets or coupons, each redeemable for certain kinds of merchandise. 3. Sometimes used for a kind of advance agent* or biller who set up posters and other advertisements in a town that was to be worked by a large pitch show. *see also* ADVANCE AGENT.

Paper house: A theatre or circus audience composed largely of people admitted on passes or free tickets. *see* PAPER.

Paper section: The section of seating in a circus in which spectators with passes are placed.

Parade: 1. Originally, this was a short farce or comic dialogue performed free in front of a theatre to attract an audience and induce them to pay to see the show inside; in other words, a kind of bally.* These were especially popular in France in the seventeenth and eighteenth centuries. *see also* BALLY. 2. In American terms, a parade can refer to a circus procession in the street or in the big top, or to the preliminary march across the stage in full costume in a burlesque show. 3. In England, a parade also can refer to the front of a fair booth or concession. *see* PARADER.

Parade girl: A burlesque term for a show girl.

Parade strip: In burlesque, a performer who walks around and does little real dancing or acting but sells herself primarily by her sexuality with few bumps* or grinds.* *see also* BUMPS and GRINDS.

Parader: The English equivalent of an outside talker.* *see also* OUTSIDE TALKER.

Paradise: The topmost seating area in a theatre. *see* NIGGER HEAVEN, PEANUT GALLERY, and TOP SHELF.

Pardner: The person responsible in a Punch and Judy show* for beating the drum in order to attract an audience and for carrying the portable stage from location to location and collecting donations. This term replaced the bottler* and the interpreter.* *see also* BOTTLER, INTERPRETER, and PUNCH AND JUDY SHOW.

Parlari or palarie: English circus term for talk; of Italian origin.

Parlor magic: Magic performed in intimate surroundings, such as a parlor, a popular place for gatherings and amateur magic shows in the nineteenth century. *see* CLOSE-UP MAGIC and DRAWING-ROOM MAGIC.

Parni or parnee: English circus term (Anglo-Indian) for water; also common among nineteenth-century strolling actors in England.

Parody: In popular theatre terms, a dramatic composition that imitates in order to burlesque or ridicule something else, such as fashion, other literary works, well-known personalities, and the like.

Part: In vaudeville, a part was the manuscript of one character's speeches and business and not just the character taken by an actor; as a verb, to take or play a character. *see* SIDE.

Pass: 1. In magic, either the gesture that accompanies a "magic" word, or the secret exchange of position of two halves of a deck of cards (also known as a shift). 2. In a circus aerial act, the flight from one trapeze to another.

Pass off: A magician's term to describe the process of secretly having some article carried offstage by an assistant or a mechanical device.

Pass out or passout: 1. An act that failed to get applause in vaudeville. *see* BRODIE and DIE. 2. Free merchandise given out by a pitchman to attract and hold a crowd; also a pitchman's sales.

Paste: Pitchmen's term for razor-strop dressing.

Pasteboard or paste-board: A ticket of admission to a game, prizefight, or circus.

Pasty or pastie: One of a pair of small circular nipple caps, required by law in many states, affixed with adhesive, maline,* or toupee tape, and worn by a burlesque performer, exotic dancer, or stripteaser. *see* G-STRING and MALINE.

Patch: A circus or carnival legal adjuster* or fixer* for complaints and accidents. The role of the patch, especially in carnivals, involves patching up in a public relations sense (but more often in a financial sense) any carnival-related complaints or misgivings held by local officials. Also, the patch intercedes when a mark* complains about a game or when the local constabulary discovers that one or more of the strippers are actually female impersonators. *see also* ADJUSTER, FIXER, and MARK.

Patch or in the patch: A small piece of material covering the front pubic area of a stripper in burlesque. A small piece is sometimes used underneath a G-string* so that when a stripper works strong,* she can remove the G-string and then be "in the patch."

Patter: The lines spoken rapidly and fluently by a hoofer,* acrobat, magician, animal trainer, or other similar performer. In some vaudeville billings, the word was used synonymously with jokes. For the magician, patter can often serve as a means of misdirection.* *see also* HOOFER and MISDIRECTION.

Payoff or pay off: In circus terms, either payday or the climax of an act.

Pay off in the dark: Circus phrase meaning a failure to pay.

Peaks: The uppermost part of a tent in a circus or tent show.

Peanut gallery: The top gallery or the highest row of seats in a theatre. *see* GALLERY GODS, NIGGER HEAVEN, PARADISE, and TOP SHELF.

Pearl diver: Common slang expression used in the circus for a dishwasher.

Peasants: Show-business term for unknowledgeable or unreceptive audience members..

Pedestal: The stool or "tub" on which an animal sits in a circus act.

Peek: 1. In carnival terminology, this is the same as miscount, that is, the use of a gaff* that does not depend on mechanical means to cheat a customer. *see also* ALIBI STORE and GAFF. 2. In magic, to sight a card or other object quickly and secretly.

Peek store: A flat joint* in which part of the gaff* consists in the operator's peeking at a number and then miscalling it, or resorting to a sleight-of-hand* move to cheat the customer. *see also* FLAT JOINT, GAFF, PEEK, and SLEIGHT.

Peekaboo waist: A term from minstrelsy describing a woman's summer shirtwaist with eyelet embroidery.

Peel: To undress or do a striptease act on stage.

Peel his rind off: A med-show term meaning to injure someone.

Peeler: A striptease dancer or stripper. Also called ecdysiast,* shucker,* and slinger.*

Peep show, peep-show, or peepshow: 1. A miniature theatre in a box designed for viewing through a single eyehole or peephole. This device was invented in the fifteenth century and reached its apogee in the eighteenth and early nineteenth centuries. Peep shows were frequently quite simple, revealing a simple scene at the back of the box, or they could be quite elaborate with moving scenery and movable wooden or cardboard figures. 2. A supposedly private or surreptitious view, usually through a hole in a wall or tent, of nude women, couples engaged in sexual intercourse, or other sexual acts. In U.S. versions, the prostitute, if not a professional performer, often finds a partner unaware that anyone is watching. Such shows were once traditionally part of small carnivals as well as brothels. In many cases, the show was a complete hoax and little was actually seen; complaints were few since most viewers were too embarrassed to say anything. 3. Infrequently used to refer to any burlesque show, nightclub act, or other similar entertainment that features chorus girls in scant attire, strippers, or the like.

Peep-show kinetoscope: An early form of optical entertainment fathered by Thomas A. Edison in 1889. The first kinetoscope parlor was opened by the Holland brothers in 1894 on Broadway with ten machines. The apparatus involved a film shown in a peep-show machine, activated by insertion of a penny and operated by turning a crank.

Peg-joint: A carnival gambling device operated with numbered pegs, the numbers being concealed until after the customer plays.

Pen or pencil: *see* INFO.

Penny arcade: *see* KINODROMES and PEEP-SHOW KINETOSCOPE.

Penny pitch: Pitchmen's term meaning to sell very cheap articles, most of which cost five cents or thereabouts, none exceeding ten.

Pepper's Ghost: A phantasmagoria (an optical illusion produced by a magic lantern* or the like in which figures increase or diminish in size, dissolve, and so on) invented by a civil engineer and scientific lecturer named Henry Dircks (first called the aetheroscope) and popularized in London by Prof. John Henry Pepper (1821-1900). The illusion was based on a new principle using mirrors in conjunction with living actors, creating "spectral optical illusions." *see also* MAGIC LANTERN.

Percentage or P. C. store: Any carnival game that earns its profits by paying off winners at less than the correct odds. As a gambling game, as many people can play as there is space at the game counter. Among the more popular versions are carnival wheels* and spindles, electrically operated flashers,* "One-Ball" group games, the "mouse game," "Chuck-a-Luck," "Beat the Shaker," "High Dice," "Under and Over Seven," and other games of chance in the guise of skill games. *see also* CARNIVAL WHEEL, FLASHERS, and SPINDLE.

Perch: A pole of steel, bamboo, or aluminum on which a performer climbs; often this is the pole balanced on an understander's* head, forehead, shoulder, stomach, hands, or feet, on which a person or animal does a trick. It can also refer to the small aerial platform of a trapeze act. *see also* PERCH ACT.

Perch act: A balancing circus act involving a perch* upon which one person is performing while being balanced by another. Also called the pole balancer's performance. *see also* PERCH.

Performance director: *see* RINGMASTER.

Personal proof or personality presentation: A description of the winning attitude that a magician attempts to establish from his audience.

Pete Jenkins or a Pete Jenkins act: This is an old circus act, generally performed by a riding clown, dressed in rags or civilian clothes, feigning intoxication, who appears to be a bungler for a time and then, discarding the rags, becomes a daring bareback rider, frequently the star equestrian of the circus. Often, the impostor is a plant in the audience.

Phantasmagoria: *see* PEPPER'S GHOST.

Philly: Show-business abbreviation for Philadelphia.

Phone in the act: *see* I THINK I'LL PHONE IN THE ACT.

Phony: Circus word for spurious.

Physic man: Circus name for a medicine pitchman or med man.

Physic show: Circus term for a medicine show.

Pick-out: An animal, usually a pony, horse, dog, or similar animal, who selects objects at the trainer's cue or command.

Pick up an audience: A nineteenth-century theatre phrase meaning that the performance is so convincing that members of the audience become so empathetic with the emotions displayed that they wish to intervene in the action. Thus actors would "pick up an audience into their arms."

Picking: Medicine-show term meaning an opportunity for gain.

Pickled bastards or punks: Human fetuses preserved in glass jars and exhibited in so-called embryo shows. Also called coughed-up-skeletons. Now rare in most carnivals, although frequently in the past the specimens on view were real.

Picture act or act-beautiful: A circus act primarily consisting of a series of tableaux featuring gracefully arranged combinations of animals.

Picture gallery: The tattooed man or woman with a circus.

Pie car: Circus and carnival term for the dining car of a railroad train.

Pie in the face: A blackout* routine especially popular in burlesque. Substituting for the ingredients of a real pie, which were seldom used, were soapsuds and ground meal arranged on a paper plate so that the appearance to the audience was that of a whipped-cream pie.

Pig: English circus term for an elephant. *see* BULL.

Pig iron: Outdoor amusement term for riding devices, especially the heavy, flat-type rides.

Pigeon hole: Theatrical term, now rarely used, for a box for spectators with a small arched opening, or the top gallery. *see* NIGGER HEAVEN, PARADISE, and PEANUT GALLERY.

Piggie bank: Slang used in the circus for a fat girl's stocking.

Pinch: Slang word for an arrest, used in the circus as well as in other contexts.

Pineapple: In the outdoor amusement world, this is a procurer or one who entices others into criminal deeds.

Pinhead or pin-head: A colloquial word since the 1890s for a stupid person and used in the circus for a microcephalic human, one with an extremely tiny or pointed head. This type of human deformity was a classic circus sideshow attraction. Among the most famous were "Zip, the What-Is-It?" and "Cuckoo, the Bird Girl." Though lacking in intelligence, these people were usually well liked and gentle human beings in the circus community.

Pink slip: In the circus, this was a dismissal notice given a work hand, indicating that this person could not be rehired by another department on the show but must leave the circus. A white slip meant he could be rehired by another boss for another type of work. To receive a pink slip was to be run away from the show, run down the track, or run off the lot.

Pip: Circus word for an exceptionally good thing or person.

Pipe: 1. In the circus, this is a holdover from an early nineteenth-century custom of leaving on an enemy's doorstep a mocking ballad rolled into a tight pipelike cylinder. It is used to mean, therefore, a letter, note, or other written message. 2. In the carnival, it is used to mean a business or leisurely conversation over business matters, or an exchange of personalities. 3. In pitchmen's terms, a news report from the field, describing business conditions and telling of the movement of pitchmen. This referred especially to the pitchmen's department in *Billboard** known as "Pipes for Pitchmen." It can also be used as a verb, meaning to write a letter, send a message, give information, or to talk or tell. *see also* BILLBOARD. 4. Less frequently, it has been used to mean a pitchman's selling talk.

Pipefest: A leisurely conversation held by several pitchmen when they gather in a hotel or rooming house. *see* PIPE.

Pirate: In the circus, to appropriate or take over another performer's routine, costume, or props without his consent. In the theatre, this once meant, before adequate copyright laws, to steal another's play, usually changing the title.

Pirouette: A dance term, meaning to whirl quickly and completely about, applied to several acts in the circus. In equestrian acts, it is performed on the toes or by an upward leap and spiral. In aerial acts, it is a quick turn or spin in space after the flyer* leaves the catcher* and just before he reaches his trapeze. *see also* CATCHER and FLYER.

Pit: An enclosure formed by fencing an area with a waist-high wall of canvas, plywood, or some similar material, in which carnival acts are performed or animals, human oddities, snakes, and such, are exhibited. The spectators would stand around the four sides of the pit and look down into it. *see* PIT SHOW.

Pit show: A carnival, and sometimes circus, show in which exhibits are shown in pits.* A show with one pit or attraction was sometimes called a Single-o, while one with ten pits or attractions was called a ten-in-one.* *see also* PIT and TEN-IN-ONE.

Pitch: 1. As a verb, to sell or vend articles, either on a show lot or on the street. At one time, pitchmen were frequently seen occupying the doorways of vacant stores in cities. 2. A pitchman's or street vendor's place of business or arrangement of wares. Also, the sales talk or spiel* given by a pitchman. *see also* HIGH PITCH, LOW PITCH, and SPIEL. 3. The above meanings are common among pitchmen, in carnivals and circuses. In the circus, it can also mean, in acrobatics, the controlled throwing of one acrobat by another. 4. *see* TOBER.

Pitch getter: The English equivalent of a pitchman.

Pitch show: Entertainment built around a pitchman and his pitch.* The prime function of the entertainment is to attract the patrons in order to sell them the pitchman's product. *see also* PITCH.

Pitch till you win: A circus phrase that refers to an eating place or boardinghouse where one could eat as much food as wanted.

Pitching: In the English fair and circus, to set up small shows and acts.

Pitchman: One who operates a pitch* concession, usually selling novelties, balloons, souvenirs, and the like, although it can apply to salesmen for a wide variety of concessions. A pitchman can work also on the street or in empty lots, as well as on a circus or carnival lot. Also called a racketeer. *see also* HIGH PITCH, LOW PITCH, KEISTER, and PITCH.

Pitmen: Musicians in the orchestra pit of a theatre.

Pitt: Show-business abbreviation for Pittsburgh.

Pivetta: *see* SWATCHEL OR SWAZZLE.

Plange: From the French *"planche,"* the circus aerialist's body swing-overs in which the body is fully extended with one hand and wrist placed in a padded rope loop equipped with a swivel. *see* SAFETY LOOP.

Plankman: *see* SEAT BOSS.

Plant: A type of shill* common in vaudeville and stage magic, in which a member of an act is placed in the audience or the orchestra pit and either performs his share of the act from that location or comes up on the stage from the audience or orchestra pit to take part in the performance as a supposed nonmember of the profession. In magic, the plant, a confederate or stooge in the audience, is put there either to hand in a prepared article (also known as a plant) when the performer asks to borrow an article, or to play some prearranged part in a trick. Most magicians feel that a plant takes unfair advantage of the audience and choose not to use them. *see also* SHILL.

Plant show: Short for a plantation show or Negro minstrel show once seen on early midways.

Plantation show: *see* PLANT SHOW.

Plaster: 1. Any cheap novelties, such as small plaster statues, given as prizes at the various carnival joints.* *see also* JOINT, MUD, RINKY-DINK, and SLUM. 2. The mortgage on a circus.

Platform show: A small carnival or circus attraction presented on an elevated stage or platform under a small canvas tent.

Platform tricks: Magic that must be performed on a platform or stage for full effectiveness because of the size of the apparatus and the necessity of keeping an audience at some distance and in front of the magician in order to prevent detection of the secret. Also known as stage magic. *see* CLOSE-UP MAGIC and PARLOR MAGIC.

Play a blank or play a bloomer: Outdoor amusement term meaning to do no business on a date. *see* BLOOMER.

Play on: In vaudeville and burlesque, a performer was "played on" with music.

(To) play them in: *see* SPOT.

Play to (or for) the gallery: In theatrical terms, to act with special attention given to the acceptance of the spectators in the gallery or upper balcony. This usually meant overacting, since spectators in this area were thought to be less sensitive to subtleties and nuance.

Play to the gas: To perform before an almost empty theatre.

Play the streets: An outdoor amusement phrase meaning to set up on the streets or sidewalks for an engagement. A number of smaller carnivals frequently (and still) played in city streets, blocking off intersections for this purpose. *see* BUSK.

(To) play up: In vaudeville, to pitch the key of a scene high or to play with speed and emphasis.

Playbill or play-bill: A program, bill,* or poster, usually restricted to theatrical use. *see also* BILL.

Playboard: The front extension at the bottom of a glove or hand puppet stage. *see* GLOVE OR HAND PUPPET.

Playing area: The portion of a room or stage in which a performance of any kind is to take place.

Playing the sticks: To perform in small towns of the country.

Playing time: The total weeks or days of employment of a vaudeville act.

Pling: Circus and carnival term meaning to ask for donations for help, or to beg or mooch.

Plot show: A tent-show company presenting plays, as opposed to vaudeville or musical entertainment; thus a show that played script bills.

Plot trick: A magic effect that utilizes a story in the patter.* *see also* PATTER and PROCESS TRICK.

Plugger: In vaudeville, one who boosted or sang new songs in order to aid their popularity. *see* SONG PLUGGER.

Plum: A good date for a carnival or pitchman. *see* RED and RED ONE.

Plush ulster of ideas: Medicine-show phrase meaning logically sound.

Plushery: In general show-business use, a first class establishment, such as a hotel or restaurant.

Pocket index: A magician's accessory that allows him to keep an entire deck of cards or a series of predictions in pockets which may be then obtained by feel. *see* INDEXING.

Point: 1. In vaudeville and burlesque, a point was the laugh-line or punch line* of a gag* or the funny observation of a monologue. *see also* GAG and PUNCH LINE. 2. Actors in the past, especially in the late eighteenth and early nineteenth centuries, often played for points, that is, gave special attention to scenes or soliloquys especially popular to audiences.

Point of focus or pointing: The place where a magician wishes an audience's attention, usually physically indicated by the performer. *See* MISDIRECTION.

Poke: Circus and carnival slang for a purse or pocketbook. In English circus slang, it means money. Also called denari and medzies.

Poke a tip: Originally used by pitchmen and later adopted by the circus and carnival to mean giving a free show or free gifts in order to attract a crowd. *see* TIP.

Pole: A circus wagon tongue, or circus tent poles. *see* CENTER POLE and QUARTER POLE.

(The) pole balancers' performance: *See* PERCH ACT.

Poler, pollar, or poller: Circus laboring man who steers wagons being loaded or unloaded at runs* on and off railway flatcars. *see also* RUN.

Pomato: An artificial or comedians' word (potato plus tomato).

Ponger: English term for somersaulting.

Pony and ponies: The smallest girl or girls in a chorus line. They usually stand above five feet tall, are hard-working dancers, but get the minimum salary. A left-legged pony is one who is not proficient in dancing.

Pooving: English circus term for free grazing.

Pop: 1. In the circus, the meaning is a single time, item, or package. 2. Short for popular prices. 3. The traditional nickname for the stage doorkeeper, with the initial letter capitalized.

Popper: 1. A cracker or snapper on the tip of a lash whip* made of plaited hemp or flax used in the American circus. *see also* LASH WHIP. 2. In the English circus, a gun.

Popular drama or theatre: In the context of this glossary, this refers to drama that succeeds with the general public, despite its lack of merit or the presence of merit. Generally, this type of drama is thought of as having little literary value, which, though often true, is not always the case. The deciding factor is its mass appeal. The classic American example is *Uncle Tom's Cabin*. *see* TOM SHOW.

Portable: English fair term for a light engine used to power lights.

Poser: A stripteaser who takes a few steps, turns, and poses while disrobing.

Possession of parts: Largely a nineteenth-century practice in the theatre in which actors, due largely to their lines of business,* played the same roles for most of their careers. *see also* LINE OF BUSINESS.

Possum belly: A compartment built underneath a circus railway car or an animal cage, between the front and rear axles, which, entered by a trapdoor in the floor of the car or cage, provided extra storage space. Apparently, some tent shows used this area on trains to stow away extra personnel. *see* BELVEDERE.

Post in the gallery: Someone stationed in the upper balcony to keep the gallery gods* orderly and quiet. *see also* GALLERY GODS.

Postcard: *see* INFO.

Posturer: A circus contortionist who specializes in front bending. *see* BENDER.

Pot boiler: In the context of this glossary, a play or performance devised for the sake of making money. *see* BOILING.

Pot boiling: This describes what an artist of considerable capabilities does when a work of mediocrity is produced. *see* POT BOILER.

Prad: In English circus use, a horse. Also called a grai.

Prairie comedian: Obsolete slang for an inferior actor. *see* BARN-STORMER.

Prat in: A pickpocket's term used in the outdoor amusement world which means to jostle a mark* into a favorable position by backing into him. *see also* MARK and (THE) SHOVE.

Prat or pratt cooler: A fan or blower in a funhouse. These are normally placed so that they blow from below, under the skirts of female customers.

Pratfall or prattfall: A comic fall on the buttocks (prat).

Pratt out: Carnival term meaning to push a knocker* out of a crowd (or tip)* or play by shoving him with one's prat or buttocks. It can also mean to beat with a short-con game.* *see also* KNOCKER, SHORT-CON GAME, and TIP.

Prattman: A member of a pickpocket gang, but one with little ability. The function of this person is to bustle or jostle a mark in a crowd in such a way as to expose his rear trouser pocket so that the claw* can easily pick the pocket. *see also* CLAW, DIP, GUN, PRAT IN, and (THE) SHOVE.

Preacher plays: Plays presented by traveling tent shows in which the leading man was a minister, or a play with a strong moral and religious message. They were used in an attempt to divert church criticism from the shows.

Prearrangement: The process in magic of arranging, before a performance, articles (such as a deck of cards) in some recognized order.

Prediction: In magic, the revelation of some fact by the performer before it happens; also, the printed message itself.

Prediction knife: A standard piece of mental apparatus used by magicians to slip open a letter with a prediction inside. The knife looks ordinary but secretly holds a piece of paper which is loaded* into the envelope in the act of opening it. There are other devices that work in the same way (prediction pens, letter openers, and such). *see also* LOAD.

Premature conclusion or consummation: A magician's technique of fooling the audience by making it think a trick is over before it really is. *see* MISDIRECTION.

Press agent: General show business term for a person employed to promote the interest of an entertainment or entertainer by gaining favorable publicity through whatever means possible.

Prestidigitation: Literally, "rapid finger work," but has come to mean magic of all kinds.

Prestidigitator: A fancy word for one who performs magic.

Pretty boys: Circus bouncers who help keep order.

Prima donna or wench role: A name given female impersonators in white black-face minstrelsy. *see also* FEMALE IMPERSONATOR.

Principle girl: In vaudeville and burlesque a female performer who plays major roles in skits or bits.

Principle: Method by which a particular kind of trick or series of tricks is performed by a magician.

Privilege: The consideration paid for the rights to operate a concession on a midway.

Privilege car: This usually was an empty baggage car or a club car on a circus or carnival train which, in addition to serving as a dining car, was equipped to serve show people in other ways on long jumps* or after night performances. It often served as a lounge where gambling was promoted (show people were even known to have been fleeced by someone representing the circus or carnival owner). *see also* JUMP.

Privileges: Refreshments or souvenirs, trinkets, and other articles sold around a circus or carnival. *see* PRIVILEGE.

Pro ams: Short for professional amateurs,* such as those who appeared in so-called amateur vaudeville. *see also* PROFESSIONAL AMATEURS.

Process trick: A magic effect involving a process complicated enough to be interesting to an audience in its own right. *see* PLOT TRICK.

(To) produce: In vaudeville, to mount or stage a scripted scene or play on the stage. It did not mean what produce in the legitimate theatre means today.

Producer: In vaudeville, roughly equivalent to today's director, that is, one who stages plays, playlets, and other acts.

Producing clown: A circus clown who designs and stars in gags* and is responsible for building all props needed. *see also* GAG.

Production: 1. In vaudeville, an act with elaborate scenery and requiring a company of some size. 2. In magic, a magic trick in which an object or person appears in either a container or enclosure that has previously been empty, or from nowhere.

Production clown: *see* CARPET CLOWN.

Production gag: *see* GAG.

Production number or routine: A spectacular ensemble number in revue, musical comedy, vaudeville, or burlesque.

Professional amateurs: Vaudevillians who made a career out of playing amateur nights at small vaudeville houses or entertainment saloons. *see* PRO AMS.

Professor: 1. The leader of a vaudeville house orchestra; called in England the conductor. 2. Operator of a Punch and Judy puppet show* especially in England, where the art has been handed down from father to son. There are few "Professors" left today, even in England. *see also* PUNCH AND JUDY SHOW.

Program: In magic, the order of tricks, illusions, or effects in a magic presentation, the structuring of which is vital.

Programming: The making up of a season of plays in repertory or stock.

Prohandle: A professional name, usually "Doc,"* appropriated by some pitchmen who dealt with medical supplies. This gave a certain prestige to themselves and their product. Such med men were ultimately prohibited in many states and in 1924 were excepted from the proposed pitchmen's organization. *see also* DOC.

Promote: In the circus, the process of getting something needed that is difficult to obtain, often by resorting to stealing.

Promoter: Circus term for one who is always working for his own interests.

Prop gag: A comic routine depending on a property. *see* PROPS.

Properties: Stage accessories or objects handled by a performer on-stage in vaudeville, scenery excepted, as in legitimate theatre. *see* PROPS.

Property man: The man who takes care of the properties.

Props: 1. Short for properties. *see also* PROPERTIES. 2. Short for the property man. *see also* PROPERTY MAN. 3. In a circus, props include elephant tubs, jugglers' paraphernalia, aerialists' apparatus, and the like. 4. In magic, the apparatus, both seen and unseen, needed for the performance of a trick, as well as general objects handled by the magician in the course of a performance, including tables, stands, and the like.

Pros: Circus abbreviation for a prosecuting attorney. *see* KEYSTONE.

Prostie: *Variety*'s method of identifying female characters comparable to those in early Mae West plays.

Protein, protean actor, or protean artist: A performer who plays several roles in a dramatic scene, usually by making quick changes in appearance while performing alone. Such an act was especially appropriate in vaudeville. *see* QUICK-CHANGE ARTIST.

Provinces: Originally, any area outside of London and the immediate area; in the United States it came to mean the hinterland or the sticks, that is, any place or theatre outside of New York City. *see* (THE) ROAD.

Psychometry: The so-called science of discovering the nature of the writer of a message or owner of an object by handling some possession of the spectator's. Popular technique used by mentalists and magicians. *see* MENTALISM.

Pudding wagon: Circus or carnival frozen custard truck.

Puffs: Publicity that praises extravagantly a performer's ability or experience, a dramatic piece, or a show. Used in the jargon of most entertainment forms. Puffs once were common in reviews of performances, and some reviewers (puffers) were actually paid by the theatre or show they were reviewing.

Pull: A magician's device of mechanical construction for the vanishing of an object by making it go from one place to another. Although some of these devices are quite sophisticated, the simplest might be a piece of elastic used to make an object vanish up the sleeve or under a coat. The more elaborate versions, utilizing drums, clock-barrels, cog-wheels, catches, and the like, can move a heavy object completely off a stage.

Pull down: English term for the dismantling of a circus or the packing up of rides, shows, and concessions of a fair.

Pull up or pull over teams: *see* HOOK-UP TEAMS.

Pull the sticks: To take the stick* out of a game of chance so that the live ones may be taken. *see also* LIVE ONE and STICK.

Pulled into the groove: In pitchmen's slang, this means to have set up a stand and started to work.

Pulse control: *see* BLOODSTOPPING.

Pumpkin fairs: Circus and pitchmen's term for small-time country fairs full of pumpkins and bumpkins, profitable for pitchmen.

Punch and Judy show: A popular type of comic puppet show with stock characters, featuring Punch, a hook-nosed hunchback in Italian costume (although primarily an English character), who, amidst much rough-and-tumble and slapstick, slays his wife Judy,* and sometimes others as well, beats up his child, and, though brought to trial, escapes the gallows. His pattern evolved over a long period of time, with Italian, French, and English influences, until the well-known English pattern evolved. By the nineteenth century such glove or hand puppet* shows were seen throughout England at fairs and on the street and soon emigrated to the United States where such shows experienced considerable popularity, though never as great as in Great Britain. *see also* GLOVE OR HAND PUPPET and JUDY.

Punch line: The closing line or finish of a scene or joke. Writers for burlesque tried to get a bucklebuster* at the end of a scene or bit* and thus conclude with a strong finish. *see also* BIT, BUCKLEBUSTER, GAG, and POINT.

Punks: Circus and carnival slang for young animals or a person of immature age, usually those in the show. *see* GAZOONIE and GUNSEL.

Punk mark: Carnival slang for a town boy or girl.

Punk pusher or rouster: In a circus or carnival, a worker who supervises the work of young town boys. In carnivals, this can also refer to one who chases underage children away from gambling concessions while games are going on.

Punk rides: Carnival rides that cater to small children, such as boat rides, miniature trains, and the like.

Punter: English term for a gambler, used in fairground terms to mean one who participates in the various games.

Pup tents: Circus slang for overshoes.

Puppet: A doll, simulating a person, animal, or other animated object, usually appearing on a miniature stage and operated by a manipulator or puppeteer inside the stage enclosure. *see* GLOVE OR HAND PUPPET and MARIONETTE.

Push: Outdoor amusement-world term for a crowd of people. To gather a push is to attract a crowd by the spiel* or bally.* In carnival lingo, a push is also the process by which a customer or chump* is bustled up close to a game or pitch.* *see also* BALLY, CHUMP, PITCH, SPIEL and TIP.

Pusher: An assistant to a circus boss or head of a department.

Pushpole tent: A type of tent used for smaller shows and assemblies as opposed to the bale-ring tent* used by circuses. Its area was adequate for a width of fifty feet or less, thus it was useful for various kinds of sideshows or tent-repertoire companies. *see also* BALE-RING TENT, DRAMATIC END TENT, and ROUNDTOP.

Put it up: Toby-show* phrase meaning a decision to schedule a bill. Thus, managers of such shows said, "We'll put it up" rather than "We'll present it." *see also* TOBY SHOW.

Put on the Bee or B: A carnival and less frequently circus expression, meaning to ask for a loan. In the summer, when the show is playing, it is considered a loan; in the winter, when the show is not on the road, it is thought of as a donation.

Put on the hype: Carnival phrase meaning to increase prices over and above normal, as is often done by hotels during fair week when a carnival is playing a midway. *see* HYPE.

(To) put out: Carnival lingo meaning either to give a prize to a customer at a gambling joint or for a woman to prostitute herself. The context would make it clear which was meant.

Putting up paper for yourself: Bragging; although, without the last two words, it can mean, in circus lingo and in other entertainment forms, getting or giving publicity for a show or a performer. *see* BUTTON-BUSTER, HANGING HIS OWN, and THREE-SHEET OR THREE-SHEETING.

Putty nose: A nickname for a low comedian, because of the fake putty nose often worn by such comics.

Q

Quad rat: Circus slang for one lower than another.

Quack: Circus slang for a pretender, as in a quack doctor.

Quagga: Used in the circus as a synonym for a zebra, although this is an extinct, equine mammal of southern Africa that resembled the zebra in that the foreparts of the body and the head were striped. Also called ponies.

Quarter pole: Poles that support a circus tent midway between the center poles* and the side walls.* *see also* CENTER POLE and SIDE WALL.

Quarters: The winter quarters* where outdoor shows rest and refit for the coming season. *see also* WINTER QUARTERS.

Queer: In carnival lingo, a person with so-called abnormal sex notions.

Question and answer act: A kind of mental magic performance in which the performer seems to divine questions, written or unwritten, of audience members. Also called question answering. *see* MENTALISM.

Quick-change artist: The rapid substitution of one costume for another during a performance. A vaudeville specialty act. *see* PROTEIN.

Quick show: *see* JOHN ROBINSON.

Quince: Med-show word for a sap.

Quiver: In the striptease, a rotating or oscillating of the breasts and/or torso, sometimes accompanied by peristaltic movements of the abdomen.

R

Rabbit hider: A magician who produces rabbits mysteriously.

Racket or trick: Any kind of concession at a carnival or circus; also, the way an outdoor showman speaks of the show with which he is connected. *see* JOINT and STORE.

Racketeer: *see* PITCHMAN.

Rad show: A pitch show* that sells spot eradicators. *see also* PITCH SHOW.

Raffle wheel: *see* PADDLE WHEEL.

Rag: 1. Theatrical slang for the front curtain. *see* HISTE THE RAG. 2. Circus slang for a tent, in particular the main tent of a circus. Conveys roustabouts' attitude toward the canvas. *see* BIG RAG.

Rag bag: In Carnival lingo, a show that is run-down or in some way suspect. *see* GILLY SHOW.

Rag front: A tent show circus, or carnival, or, more strictly, the canvas banners and signs erected in front of the show as advertisements. The word originated to describe small shows whose show fronts were canvas instead of heavy carved and elaborately gilded wooden fronts used by larger operations.

Rag-heads: A derogatory term for gypsies, who, though involved with the carnie* world, are generally considered outsiders. *see also* CARNY and GYP, GIP, OR JIP.

Rag house: A tent. *see* RAG.

Rag show or rag opera or opry: A dramatic stock company under canvas or under a rag,* such as chautauqua* presentations, traveling tent shows doing melodramas, musical presentations under canvas, and the like. Their heyday ended during the late 1920s. *see also* CHAUTAUQUA and RAG.

Ragging: The process of making the circus tent taut by tightening the guy lines of the side poles.* *see also* SIDE POLE.

Rail-the-route: A practice of old-time overland circus wagon shows when rail fences were common. At a "Y" or intersection in the road, the telegraph wagon crew would lay a "borrowed" fence rail part way across the wrong turn as a signal to the following caravan of wagons not to turn that way. More recently, it has come to mean any method of marking a route from town to town. *see* ARROW THE ROUTE and TELEGRAPH WAGON.

Railroad show: An outdoor show that travels by railroad on its own train, consisting of flatcars and sleeping cars.

Railway contractor: A circus advance agent* or advance man who was responsible for arriving at a given stop as much as three months before the show was to visit, arrange transportation, and book the excursion trains that would bring people to the site. *see also* ADVANCE AGENT OR ADVANCE MAN and ADVERTISING CARS.

Rain or shine: A phrase, dating from the 1820s and the first use of circus tents, meaning that the show would play no matter what the weather.

Raincoat Charlie: Stripteaser's slang for an overly enthusiastic spectator who masturbates underneath his raincoat.

The Ranch: The 101 Ranch Wild West show, which, by 1908, had become a permanent institution, a by-product of an Oklahoma ranch empire founded by George W. Miller in 1892. 101 was their brand.

Raree show or rarity show: A cheap street show, usually exhibiting or advertising unusual items. Often nothing more than a peep show.

Raspberry: In medicine-show lingo, this implied ridicule without mercy. It is commonly used to mean a vulgar, derisive noise made by placing the tongue between the lips and blowing.

Rat: A sidewalk ticket speculator. *see* DIGGER.

Rat sheet: A handbill* or poster especially printed with negative comments about a competitor's circus. *see also* HANDBILL.

Rats on my rafters: Medicine-show slang phrase meaning that one's power of deductive reasoning has been seriously impaired.

Rattler: Carnival and circus lingo for a railroad train.

Rave: Originally, an unfavorable criticism, but circa 1925 its meaning was reversed and today means a most favorable review.

Razorback or razor-back: A circus train hand or laborer who loads and unloads the show's rolling stock and handles other heavy work connected with a road show. Not to be confused with roustabout.* The term razorback came from the command of the boss to "raise your backs," given in earlier circus days when a group of workers lifted, by the power of their backs, and turned short cage wagons so that they loaded crossways on a flatcar instead of lengthwise, thus saving space. *see also* ROUSTABOUTS.

Razzle-dazzle: In some carnival circles, this means a prostitute.

Reaching rods: Apparatus used by ghost-show* operators to float luminous "ghosts" over the heads of the audience. *see also* GHOST SHOW.

Read the lot: To inspect a circus or carnival lot,* after the show has packed, for tent stakes, lost articles, money, or equipment left behind. *see also* LOT and LOT READER.

Reader: A license to exhibit a circus or carnival, or a pitchman's license to peddle. Most shows must have state, county, and city readers before a show can operate. Less frequently, a reader can refer to a sign, advertisement, poster, or announcement.

Readers: Playing cards marked on the backs so that a magician can "read" the faces without seeing them.

Reading a shirt: Carnival slang for hunting for lice. Also called seam squirrels. *see* CIRCUS BEES.

Real estate: A midway concession space. *see* JOINT and STORE.

Rebound acrobatics: A modern term describing a circus vaulting genre* using some form of catapult or spring device to produce elevation, such as a teeterboard, Russian swing, minitramp, and the like. Vaulting is one of the oldest acrobatic genres. *see also* GENRE and TEETERBOARD ACT.

Recovery: Technical term in magic meaning the resumption of control of an article used by the magician, such as a ball secretly placed under the arm and hidden.

Red: Carnival and circus lingo for a place where business is excellent. *see* COLD, HOT SPOT, PLUM, RED ONE, and SOFT SPOT.

Red-hot mamma: A type of large, lively, and earthy female singer very popular during the 1920s.

Red lighted: Carnival and circus use for being forcibly ejected from a train, and to kill by so doing, or leaving one behind. By extension, to be fired.

Red-nosed comedian or comic: A performer who appears in a comic role with a red nose, indicating inebriation. Most common among burlesque comics.

Red one: In circus and carnival lingo, a place where or day when business is unusually good, or, good business in general. The term probably came from red numbers or letters, winners on a gambling chart. *see* RED.

Red wagon: The circus box-office wagon and main office of the circus, also known as the money wagon. So called because it was formerly painted red, although the name stuck no matter what color was used. *see* SILVER WAGON, (THE) WAGON, and WHITE WAGON.

Red wagon music: Circus music, usually marches or fast gallops.

Refined vaudeville: *see* ADVANCED OR REFINED VAUDEVILLE.

Regular dancer: A burlesque term for a dancer of average size.

Rehashing tickets: Circus and carnival practice of selling used tickets, the proceeds of which are kept by the ticket seller and split with the ticket taker. *see* RERIDES.

Releases: One method used by magicians to perform an escape,* but also used to conceal the performer's part in some trick. Releases are devised so that the performer can fasten himself up again. *see also* ESCAPE.

Rep: Abbreviation for repertory. *see* REP SHOW.

Rep show: 1. Abbreviation for a theatrical repertory (or repertoire) company. 2. Carnival or circus term for a snake show.

Repeat trick or repeater: A magic trick whose dramatic effect is enhanced by repetition.

Repeater: A tent-show term for a script bill, or plot show,* that is so popular that the company could use it twice during a week stand. *see also* PLOT SHOW and (TO) WEEK-STAND.

Repetition: A magician's method of repeating an innocent action often enough so that no attention is given the action when it is changed into a secret move. *see* MISDIRECTION.

Repertoire or repertory: Playing a series of plays during one engagement. *see* REPERTOIRE OR REPERTORY COMPANY.

Repertoire or repertory company: In tent-repertoire shows (and, in particular, Toby shows*) the play was usually changed each night during an engagement, with the same actors in every show. Most of these small companies employed five men and three women, and plays were chosen (or written) to fit this size cast. Such companies toured "opera houses" and other performance spaces (often makeshift) in rural America from about 1850 until about 1910. Beginning around 1910, many toured with tent theatres in summer, and some were tent shows exclusively. Nearly all presented vaudeville entertainment between the acts. Repertoire companies were never referred to as repertory companies, a term reserved for the sophisticated cousins in the cities. *see also* TOBY SHOW.

Reprise: Clown gags* done between circus acts to entertain the audience during equipment and rigging changes. Reprises also serve the function of periodically releasing tension created by dangerous acts. *see also* GAG.

Repster: In Toby shows,* a trade-paper term applying to anyone connected with a repertoire show, be it an actor, musician, or canvas men. *see also* CANVAS MEN, REPERTOIRE OR REPERTORY COMPANY, and TOBY SHOWS.

Rerides or re-riders: Selling tickets to persons already on rides for another ride. *see* REHASHING TICKETS.

Reset: In magic, to prepare a piece of apparatus that requires attention each time it is used.

Resin-back: English circus term for the horse of a bareback rider. *see also* ROSIN-BACK.

Resting: *see* AT LIBERTY.

Reuben: A rustic, rube,* or hick. Originating in the circus and carnival, it was soon shortened to rube. *see also* RUBE.

Reversed card: A playing card that is returned to the deck either back to front or upside-down, so as to help a card magician locate it.

Revue: To some, the revue form was nothing more than glorified burlesque. When fully realized, the revue became a unique, dazzling, and universally appealing form, combining a musical revue with songs, skits, and blackouts, talented comedians, singers, and a showcase of beautiful girls, scantily clad but with the extreme elegance of costume and decor, giving dignity to the nakedness and raising the whole far above the level of burlesque. The life span of the revue was approximately forty-five years, from 1894 to 1939. Although related to vaudeville, it differed from that form in its topicality and because it was more than a string of specialty* acts. Instead, it used a single cast presenting dialogue, sketches, songs, and dance numbers written especially for the show. The first revue in the United States was *The Passing Show* in 1894, presented by George Lederer at the Casino Theatre. Early revues, until about 1915, usually had some story line, no matter how tenuous. After 1915, plots became more incidental. The best known of the revues were *Ziegfeld's Follies* (1907-1931), *George White's Scandals* (1919-1939), *Greenwich Village Follies* (1919-1928), and *Earl Carroll's Vanities* (1923-1932). To this list might be added the Shuberts' *The Passing Show* (no connection with the 1894 revue) and the *Hitchy-Koo* series created by Raymond Hitchcock in 1917. The revue was also called, by its various creators, extravaganza, spectacular drama, spectacular musical production, jumble of jollification, and so on. *see also* SPECIALTY.

Rib: used in the circus and carnival to mean to taunt or tease.

Ribbon: Silk ribbon over which a circus ballerina* jumps from a galloping horse. The term is most commonly used in the English Circus. *see also* BALLERINA ACT and BANNERS.

Ribbon spread: Magician's term for laying out playing cards in a long line by a single sweep of the hand.

Ride: An amusement-park or midway mechanically driven, passenger-carrying amusement machine or device.

Ride foreman: The person in a carnival or at an amusement park used for upping and downing the ride he or she is assigned to. A second man serves as an assistant and is less experienced and paid less. After the ride is assembled, both the foreman and the second man operate the ride during the stand of the carnival, or, if a permanent ride, they simply operate the ride and are not involved with upping and downing, although a foreman may be responsible for maintenance. This job would most likely fall to the ride superintendent. *see also* RIDE SUPERINTENDENT.

Ride superintendent: A kind of grand mechanic who knows how to assemble, disassemble, and repair all of the major riding devices in a carnival or at an amusement park. He is also responsible for keeping rolling stock, such as tractor-trailers, in good working order.

(To) ride the white horse: A carnival expression meaning to be featured as the glorified star of a publicity story or broadcast.

Ridge pole: A horizontal pole at the top of a circus tent from which much of the rigging hangs. *see* RIDGE ROPE.

Ridge rope: A strong rope or cable stretched the length of a circus tent at the tops of the center poles,* thus forming the top ridge of the structure. *see also* CENTER POLE and RIDGE POLE.

Riding act: An equestrian circus act featuring a group of performers, sometimes members of the same family (or advertised as such), demonstrating various leaps, jumps, and other tricks off and on the backs of galloping horses.

Riding master: In the English fair, the owner of one or more rides, who leases ground to other showmen.

Riding rubber: An expression used in the circus, meaning to go in an automobile.

Riffle: Card magician's method of thumbing the ends of the playing cards so that one card falls rapidly after another. *see* DOVETAIL.

Riffle shuffle: *see* RIFFLE.

Rig: To put up circus aerial rigging.* *see also* RIGGING.

Riggers: Those who put up circus aerial rigging.* *see also* RIGGING.

Rigging: The tackle, gear, ropes, wires, cables, and pulleys used to adjust and secure gymnastic apparatus used in various aerial circus acts, such as trapezes, tight and slack wires, webs, high-wires, and so forth.

Right-hand side: Preferred midway location for early opening shows catering to children and the family trade. *see* LEFT-HAND SIDE.

Right racket: Slang expression for a success in entertainments.

Ring: 1. In the circus, the performing arena, derived from the horse ring used for equestrian shows of the eighteenth century and earlier training schools. The European circus has retained the one ring, while the American circus quickly moved toward multiple rings, finally settling on three. It is generally agreed that the ideal size for a circus ring is one whose inner circumference will accommodate a horse at full stride. The only true connection between ancient forms of circus and the modern circus is the meaning of the word circus, which comes from the Latin word for circle. There is not, however, any rule that requires that a circus performance be presented in a ring. Simon suggests that in psychological terms, however, the circus is a universal symbol for totality, wholeness, and healing, and the circus ring tends to enhance such an association. 2. In conjuring, ring is a very old word for making a secret substitution, perhaps shortened from "ring the changes." Today, the word switch* is more common. *see also* SWITCH.

Ring barn: a round or octagonal, barnlike building housing a regulation-sized circus ring (forty-two feet) where riders and other acts learn and practice their acts while at their winter quarters.* *see also* WINTER QUARTERS.

Ring carpet: *see* CARPET.

Ring crew: Circus workers responsible for setting up and removing equipment, rigging, and props for each act that occurs in a circus ring.* In smaller circuses, ring crew members are stationed in a formal line just outside the ring during the show in case of emergencies. *see also* RING.

Ring curb: The low wooden barrier defining the circus ring and serving as a boundary between audience and performers. The ring may be crossed by a performer during a show but may not be crossed by a member of the audience unless invited. *see also* RING and RING FENCE.

Ring fence: English equivalent of the ring curb.* Small English circuses sometimes use canvas fences, while larger circuses use limewashed wood with a flat red top. *see also* RING CURB.

Ring horse: A horse that performs in the circus ring* and is trained to maintain timing despite distractions. *see also* RING.

Ring No. 1: The circus ring nearest the main entrance.

Ring No. 2: The center circus ring.

Ring No. 3: The circus ring nearest the back entrance. *see* BACK DOOR.

Ring the bell or hit the ball: Phrase which means to succeed or meet with approval, from the carnival device in which a bell rings when a player is successful. *see* HIGH STRIKER.

(To) ring up: 1. Tent-show term meaning to begin the show, usually with a curtain speech by one of the performers. In legitimate theatre, cues for changing scenery or drawing the curtain were at one time given by ringing a bell or blowing a whistle. 2. Circus slang meaning to disguise partially.

Ringbank: In the early days of the American circus, banks of dirt literally were created in forming the rings. *see* RING CURB.

Ringmaster: Originally, the ringmaster was the master of the ring,* with as many ringmasters as there were rings. His main job was to keep horses under control during an equestrian act, but he was subordinate to the equestrian director.* Today, the ringmaster has become a combination show announcer and stage manager, responsible for all activities in the ring, although in very large circuses, such as Ringling

Bros. and Barnum & Bailey, the position has become a singing ring-master with virtually no control over the rings (a job handled by the performance director*). As he has evolved, the true ringmaster, none-theless, should have authority over performers, ring crew,* and roust-abouts* before, during, and after the performance. In many circuses today, the ringmaster and equestrian director are separate identities, with the former serving as the announcer* and the latter as director of performing personnel. see also ANNOUNCER, EQUESTRIAN DIRECTOR, PERFORMANCE DIRECTOR, RING, RING CREW, ROUSTABOUT, and WHISTLE TOOTER.

Ringstock or ring stock: Performing circus animals including horses, llamas, camels, and ponies, as opposed to baggage or work horses. Since they do no heavy work and are led to and from the cars by attendants, they are sometimes called lead stock.* In the American circus, ringstock frequently is limited to horses or ponies. see also HEAD STOCK..

Rinky-dink or rinkydink: 1. From carnival lingo meaning cheap, gaudy merchandise or junk. see MUD, PLATTER, and SLUM. 2. A cheap place of amusement or a honky-tonk.* see also HONKY-TONK.

Riot panic: Circus slang for great applause.

(A) Rip Van Winkle: see (DO A) JOE JEFFERSON.

Risley act: A foot-juggling act in which one person lies flat on his back and balances and juggles with his feet, usually another human. In some acts, more than one acrobat does the foot juggling. Although this is one of the circus's oldest acts, its name comes from the name of a famous nineteenth-century acrobatic juggler, said to be the first man to perform this act in the modern circus. see ANTIPODIST and TRINKA.

(The) road: The territory of the United States outside the New York metropolitan area traveled by shows, especially theatrical companies. The term has been applied to the area and the time spent wandering or traveling. Also called the sticks. see PROVINCES, ROAD COMPANY, and ROAD SHOW.

Road apple: A performer on tour, that is, on the road.* see also (THE) ROAD.

Road combination: Turn-of-the-century term for a group of variety perfomers moving from town to town.

Road company: A group of actors touring a production. *see* (THE) ROAD and ROAD SHOW.

Road show: When rural America was hungering for release from a rather humdrum existence, the road show became one important outlet. Although the conditions, the salaries (which often left actors stranded in the middle of nowhere), and the one-night stands* were taxing and generally despised by actors, audiences loved the entertainment. In 1911, there were more than 175 companies touring to small American towns. The increasing competition with the movies and their wider and cheaper offering of entertainment signaled the end of the road show. *see also* KEROSENE CIRCUIT, ONE-NIGHT STAND, and REPERTOIRE.

Road smart: Carnival slang for one who has learned through experience.

Robbing boxes: A carnival office agent in the act of gathering up and taking money from ticket boxes to the office.

(The) Robe: Carnival slang for a judge who pronounces sentence on grifters.* *see also* GRIFTER.

Rock'n'Roll: *see* CAKEWALK.

Rocking chair: The unemployment compensation on which some circus show people live in the winter off-season.

Rocks: Circus slang for salt.

Rod: Used by carnies* to mean a pistol or revolver. *see also* CARNEY and RUSTY-DUSTY.

Rodeo clown: Because of the rodeo context, this talented and daring type of comic performer is virtually forgotten in the entertainment world. Nevertheless, a rodeo clown frequently wears makeup and costumes similar to a circus clown and participates in comic byplay with the announcer and performs gags.* In the rodeo, the status of the clown, in fact, is as high as the star cowboys since it is his job to ensure the safety of the rodeo contestants by diverting the attention of bulls and wild broncos after a cowboy has been thrown. Like a bull fighter, the clown provokes the animal, allows a chase to ensue, and at the last moment dives into a barrel for safety. Many of the better clowns began as expert rodeo competitors. *see also* GAG.

Rola-bola: A circus act (and the performer) in which a rolling cylinder is used, upon which is balanced a short board. One or a team of gymnasts perform a balancing and acrobatics act on the board.

Roll down: A carnival concession in which numbered or colored marbles roll down a runway filled with numbered depressions. A type of flat joint or store.* A similar joint,* more common at English fairs, is called a roll up, in which balls are rolled up an incline board and fall into circular holes, each with a numerical value. *see also* FLAT JOINT or STORE.

Roll up: *see* ROLL DOWN.

Roll-ups: *see* PLANGE.

Roman riding: Circus term for a rider standing on the backs of two horses, usually bareback.

Roman rings: Large rings used in aerial gymnastics.

Romeo: Now in general use, this term probably originated in the theatre late in the nineteenth century to indicate an actor inclined to be quite fond of the ladies. Its source is obvious.

Rope caller: The boss of a circus tent guying-out crew* who chants rhythmic directions to the workmen as they proceed systematically around the big top pulling and shaking, taking up the slack in the canvas, and so forth. Ballantine, in *Wild Tigers*, says that the call varied from show to show, but went something like: "Take it, shake it, make it, break it, walk along." On occasion, the boss would command to speak Latin and the rope caller would sing a much older song: "Ah, heebie, hebby, hobby, hole, golong." *see* GUY.

Rope cement: A substance sometimes used by magicians to join two pieces of rope.

Roper: Circus lingo for a cowboy.

Rosinback or rosin back: A circus horse broken for bareback riding, so called because its broad back is sprinkled with fine rosin before entering the ring in order to make the footing surer. Also called a resin-back.

(To) Rotten apple: Theatrical slang meaning to hiss.

Rough soubrette: In Toby shows,* an actress who played hillbilly or rural girl parts. *see also* SOUBRETTE and TOBY SHOW.

Roughing fluid: A chemical substance which, when applied to playing cards, caused them to adhere slightly to one another, thus allowing a magician to show two cards as one.

Roughneck: Carnival and circus term for a laborer or working man. *see* ROUSTABOUTS and WORKING MEN.

Roughneck's delight: Carnival lingo for a girl who keeps company only with working men.

Round: Circus term meaning to turn without attracting attention. Also called round natural.

Round actors: A live actor on stage, in contrast to one seen in motion pictures or television. *see* FLESH.

Round heels: Show-business slang for a pushover.

Round natural: *see* ROUND.

Round off: A complicated and important move, fundamental to the performance of tumbling acrobatics, created centuries ago in the Arab countries. When an acrobat, running forward, must move in the same direction to execute a tumbling pass, beginning with a trick (such as a back flip) that requires his body to be reversed, he does a round off. This action repositions his body 180° without affecting momentum.

Round on or round 'un: A circular stall (joint) or booth in an English fair. *see also* JOINT.

Roundabout: 1. A conventional-type tent with both front end and back end the same. This type tent was used for dramatic entertainment prior to the invention of the dramatic end tent* but had the problem of the last center pole in front of the stage area, obscuring the view of the audience. Also called a round top. *see also* BALE-RING TENT, DRAMATIC END TENT, and PUSHPOLE TENT. 2. The most common English term for a carousel.

Roundtop: A conventional type of tent which is symmetrical in shape with both front end and back end the same.

Roust: Carnival and circus term meaning to chase or run away.

Roustabouts: Circus workers used for comon labor around a circus. Sometimes called roughneck.* *see also* CANVAS MAN, ROUGHNECK, and WORKING MEN.

Route: Traveling show term for a series of playing dates or list of towns and events played each season. In vaudeville, to route meant to book acts.

Route card: Card listing an outdoor show's play dates for about ten days in advance. *see* DATE BOOK.

Route the show: To lay out a season's play dates. *see* ROUTE.

Routine: 1. In vaudeville and to a lesser extent in burlesque, the text or arrangement of the parts of a stage offering; the material used in an act, which often belonged to a specific vaudevillian. 2. A magician uses the term to mean a well-rehearsed arrangement of a trick or series of tricks so that they blend easily and naturally. "To routine" is to arrange a sequence of tricks into a complete, unified show.

Routining a show: In vaudeville, the planning of the running order of a vaudeville bill. The typical vaudeville bill had eight acts and each act was carefully placed.

Row of chicken feed: In a med show the placement of small change on the platform so that customers could make their own change. Also known as fractional kale. *see* KALE.

Rub joint: A cheap dance hall or nightclub that provides women with whom lonely men can dance (usually for a price).

Rubber cows: Circus name for elephants. *see* BULL and PIG.

Rubber man: Circus slang for a balloon vendor.

Rubber vags: Carnival slang for those who live in house trailers.

Rube: The classic word used in most forms of traveling entertainment for a rustic, hayseed, outsider, newcomer, chump* or sucker.* A rube in the theatre was a farmer character. *see also* CHUMP, HEY RUBE!, REUBEN, and SUCKER.

Rum Col or Cul: English term for the boss or circus proprietor. In the nineteenth century it also meant the manager of a poor theatrical troupe, especially a travelling one.

Rum or rummy: An easy victim. *see* CHUMP, LUKEN, MARK, MOOCH, MONKEY, and SUCKER.

Rumdum or rum-dum: Principally, a carnival word and some circus use for no-account, shiftless, or intoxicated.

Rumble: Circus word meaning to spoil or, as a noun, a complaint. It is sometimes used with the meaning "discovered."

Run: 1. The distance between circus or carnival dates, or the move between show dates. 2. In magic, to draw off one card at a time when shuffling a deck of cards. 3. English fair term for a number of successive fairs. 4. Theatrical use for a series of performances.

Run away from the show: *see* PINK SLIP.

Run down the track: *see* PINK SLIP.

Run-in: In the English circus, the wide passage from the stables into the circus ring.

Run-in clown: English term for a carpet clown. *see also* CARPET CLOWN.

Run off the lot: *see* PINK SLIP.

Run-out working: In the English fair, the selling by market men of their wares.

Running a high striker: Pitchman's expression meaning playing in towns where business is consistently good.

Running ground mount: A run across the ring by an equestrian acrobat followed by a flying leap onto the back of a cantering horse. *see* FORK JUMP, LIFT, and VOLTIGE.

Running strong: A carnival game played with the gaff* in, that is, a concealed control. *see also* STRONG GAFF and STRONG.

Runs: Circus term for the place where trains are located and are loaded and unloaded. Sometimes used for the steel flanges over which the wagons are loaded/unloaded from the flatcars. *see also* CHUTES, CROSS-ING, and GO TO THE RUNS.

Runts: Circus and carnival slang for dwarfs* and midgets. *see also* DWARF.

Runway: A long, narrow extension of a stage into the audience on which a performer can walk. There are two classic types: one is a "T"-shaped runway that extends into the audience from the stage directly forward and can be of any size; the second is the horseshoe runway, which goes around the orchestra pit. Runways have been used in vaudeville and revues and, especially, for stripper parades in burlesque. Also called a catwalk. *see* VARICOSE ALLEY.

Ruse: In magician's lingo, a way of fooling the audience by doing something openly, which simultaneously covers up a secret move or action. *see* MISDIRECTION.

Rusty-dusty: Once theatrical slang for a prop or toy gun: originally slang for an old, rusty gun. *see* ROD.

S

S. and D. : Vaudeville abbreviation for song and dance.* *see also* SONG and DANCE.

Sachem: *see* OLD BEAN.

Safety Loop: The loop part of a web rope into which a circus performer puts the wrist in aerial ballet numbers. *see* PLANGE.

Saint Louis: *see* ST. LOUIS.

Salamander: Traveling theatrical tent-show term for drumlike stoves once used for heating.

Salamandering: An English show term for the act of eating indigestible substances such as glass, metal and the like. *see* GEEK.

Sales barn: One large store in which several pitchmen have concessions. A platform was placed in the center of the store on which each pitchman had an opportunity to speak.

Salome dancer: An early term for cooch* dancer or belly dancer. *see also* COOCH or COOCH DANCING.

Salon juggling: A nineteenth-century type of juggling in which the juggler usually worked in formal dress and juggled such objects as canes, gloves, top hat or derby, and articles to be found in the drawing room, such as flower bouquets, billiard balls, and cues.

Saltee: *see* SAULTI or SALTEE.

Salting: Magician's term for the process of hiding small objects in unlikely places about a room where the audience supposes the performer has never been before.

Sand: English circus word for sugar.

Sandwich man: Signs on double-faced boards worn on the front and back of a walker who advertises some product or entertainment. This means of advertising was used in vaudeville as early as 1906; often the acts themselves carried the signs in front of vaudeville houses.

Sap: 1. A rube* that has been taken in. *see also* RUBE. 2. In circus slang, a cane. 3. As a verb, to sap means to strike with a cane, club, or fists, and is sometimes used specifically in the circus in reference to the striking of a blow by an elephant's trunk. 4. Circus and especially carnival argot for a heavy blow.

Saulti or saltee: English circus word for a penny.

Sauskee: Carnival slang for fifteen dollars.

Sawbuck: Carnival and circus slang for a ten-dollar bill.

Sawdust or saw-dust eater: *see* KICKING SAWDUST and TENT-SQUIRRELS.

Scare wig: *see* FRIGHT WIG OR HAIR.

Scarper: English circus term for depart or run away.

Scarpering letty: *see* LETTY OR LETTIE.

Scenario: In magician's terms, this is the plot of a trick or routine.*

Schill: *see* SHILL.

Schlar: Yiddish and German for a blow. *see* BRUTAL.

Schnorrer: This word was sometimes used by show people to mean a chiseler or someone who got something for nothing.

School: Short for high school. *see* HIGH-SCHOOL HORSE.

Science game: *see* SKILL OR SCIENCE GAME.

(To) scissor fingers: In burlesque, to cut the bit. *see also* BIT.

Scissorbill: *see* GILLY-GALOO.

Scissors: A movement in voltige;* the term is more common in the English circus. *see also* VOLTIGE.

Scoff: Carnival term meaning to eat. Sometimes used with the connotation of having breakfast in bed. *see* SCOFFINS.

Scoffins: Circus and carnival argot for food in the cookhouse. Also known as gorge* and chuck.* *see also* CHUCK, COOKHOUSE, and GORGE.

Scope worker: Carnival slang for a pitchman who sells astrology books and charts; one who deals in horoscopes.

Scout for a location: To look for a town to replace one dropped from a circus route.

Scram: Carnival and circus word meaning to beat it or get away, often as a command. Possibly for scramble but more likely from the German slang, *"schrammen"* (beat it). *see also* BEAT IT and DUCK.

Scram-bag: Circus use for a suitcase packed in readiness for any sudden but necessary departure. *see* SCRAM.

Scratch: Money. Also called geedus, gelt, and kale. *see* TAKE.

Scratch wig: A rough-textured wig worn by comic performers. *see* FRIGHT WIG OR HAIR.

Screechie: The name given to the sound man in a circus. Like a number of such jobs, the name reflects the work done.

Screw: English circus term for see or look.

Scribe: A card writer. *see* INFO.

Scrip: A book of penny mileage used in lieu of cash for railroad fares; also good for Pullman occupancy. Railroad companies used to sell scrip books to the general public, although they were (and in some cases still are) used primarily by show people. Some carnivals still use them, though not circuses. It would be purchased by the general agent* when he made the railroad contracts for moving a show and then be used by the show's advance agent.* *see also* ADVANCE AGENT OR ADVANCE MAN and GENERAL AGENT.

Script bill: *see* PLOT SHOW.

Scruff: A term that originated in the carnival world meaning to barely make a living or to live from hand to mouth. *see* SCUFF.

Scuff: Outdoor show-business term for having a hard time securing enough food for regular meals for any sea lion, especially one trained to perform; also used for a high diver or fancy swimmer, in particular one in the outdoor show world.

Seam Squirrel: *see* CIRCUS BEE.

Seat block: Circus term for a solid, heavy cube of wood used in the preliminary training of large cats in order to provide them with a secure home base. When they are at ease, lighter-weight tubes or pedestals of metal and wood are substituted.

Seat boss or plankman: The superintendent in charge of putting up and taking down all seats in a circus.

Seat man: Circus slang for a shill.* *see also* SHILL.

Seated riding: *see* HIGH RIDING.

Second banana: *see* BANANA and TOP BANANA.

Second business: A Toby show* term for actresses who could play either soubrettes* or heavies. *see also* SOUBRETTE and TOBY SHOW.

Second count: Circus term for a short-changer's* method. *see also* SHORT-CHANGE ARTIST.

Second deal: In card magic, to deal the second card from the top of the deck instead of the first card.

Second lead: Traveling tent-show term for the second most important actor in a play.

Second man: *see* RIDE FOREMAN.

Second opening: *see* OPENING.

Secretary: Any accountant or bookkeeper with a carnival or circus.

Seed worker: A pitchman who sold laxative seeds.

Segue: Music bridge used in making a transition from one tune or piece of music to another without making a full stop. Used in virtually all entertainment forms that utilize music, such as the circus, musical theatre, revue, burlesque, and vaudeville.

Sell-out: A completely successful show or a hit.

Sell out a hod: *see* SLOUGH.

Sender: From the jazz world, one who shouts encouragement from the audience or the dance floor and, by extension, anything or anyone that is very good or creates enthusiasm.

(To) separate the palms: Burlesque term that means to stretch the bit,* an instruction that would come from the wings backstage. *see also* BIT and STRETCH.

Seriocomic: Used in vaudeville and early variety, once a term for an old-time soubrette* who was capable of singing straight tearjerkers and comic songs equally well. *see also* SOUBRETTE.

Servante: A technical term in magic for a hidden shelf or receptacle concealed from the audience and used for loads* and steals.* *see also* LOAD *and* STEAL.

(To) serve up the gonk: *see* GONK.

Set (to): To prepare a piece of apparatus for a magician's performance. *see* RESET.

Set: Short for scenery, usually in the theatrical sense.

Set-joint: A carnival gambling device operated with a numbered wheel and arrow-spindle.* Equipped with a gaff,* which prevents a customer from winning too often, the set-joint may be played without the gimmick in use in order to lead the player or until a large bet is placed. At the right strategic moment, the operator applies the gimmick and the customer loses. *see also* CARNIVAL WHEEL, GAFF, and SPINDLE.

Set-up: 1. In burlesque, the female performer's figure. *see* SWELL SET-UP. 2. In magic, the prearrangement of apparatus, usually a deck of cards, in order to accomplish a specific trick or series of tricks. *see* SYSTEM.

Sex appeal: A 1940s show-girl slang expression for falsies.

Shack: In carnival and circus slang, a brakeman of a freight train.

Shadow show: An entertainment, usually a pantomime, featuring actors, puppets, or flat cutout figures that move between a light and a translucent screen. The audience sees them on the other side of the screen as shadows. Called also shadow play, shadow pantomime, shadow theatre, and shadowgraph. Never a major form of American entertainment and rarely performed or manipulated by professional showmen.

Shake: A carnival term for a frame-up between police, lawyers, and their alleged clients, designed to force showmen to pay them money. It sometimes means a raid after a fix* has been expedited. *see also* FIX, SHAKE DOWN, and SQUARE THE SHAKE.

Shake down: In addition to the above meaning for shake,* this means a bribe or payment for a show or its concession men to local authorities for the privilege of working without fear of imprisonment. As a verb, it means to collect a shake down. *see also* SHAKE.

Shakes: Carnival and circus slang for an earthquake.

Shaky: Pitchmen's term for risky to work, or, by implication, a location where the pitchmen would have to pay a shake down* in order to work freely. *see also* SHAKE DOWN.

Shamus: Carnival word (and some circus use) for the police. Also known as fuzz.* *see also* COOKIE-CUTTER, COP, DICK, FUZZ, and TINS.

Shandy, shanty, chandelier, or chandy: An electrician or the man or men who operate or superintend the lights for a circus. The term was more prevalent in the days of torches, gasoline lamps, and gas lights.

Shapes: Carnival and circus word for crooked dice made to order.

Shark: In most forms of outdoor amusement, this is a professional card player or dice thrower who is extremely competent, as well as shrewd.

Shaving bandit: A carnival worker who collects money for giving shaves.

Sheckles or shekels: Circus word for money in any form.

Sheet: 1. A circus poster. They are identified by the number of standard sheets of advertising paper required for a full poster (each sheet is approximately 28 inches by 42 inches); thus, one-sheet, three-sheet, and so on. 2. A journal handled by a sheet writer.* *see also* SHEET WRITER.

Sheet up: Circus term meaning to post bills or posters.

Sheet worker: *see also* PAPER BOY OR MAN.

Sheet writer: A solicitor for journals giving prizes with subscriptions. *see* PAPER BOY OR MAN.

Sheetie: Short form for sheet writer.* *see also* SHEET WRITER.

Sheeting or sheeting 'em up: *see* SHEET UP.

Sheets: Carnival slang for newspapers.

Shekels: *see* SHECKELS OR SHEKEL.

Shelf: Circus and carnival word for an upper berth in a sleeping car or truck.

Shell: A hollow or half-dummy fake* used by magicians to simulate an object, such as a ball or wand, that is actually somewhere else. A shell coin, for example, is a simulated coin hollowed out on one side so that a second can fit within the first. The two then look like one coin. *see also* FAKE.

Shell game: *see* NUTS.

Shelve: To take a circus off the road and stop using its name.

Shift: 1. In magic, another name for the pass* with cards. *see also* PASS. 2. An obsolete term for a dressing room.

Shill: A confederate of a pitchman or an employee of a carnival, circus, or the like, who entices customers to buy tickets, play a game, or the like by pretending to be a real customer or player. "To shill in" means to walk by the doorkeeper with a nod or to pass in free. As a verb, "to shill" is to act or work as a shill. Also called shillaber.

Shimmy or shimmy shaking: Originally performed according to tradition by Little Egypt at the Chicago World's Fair in 1893. Perfected by stripteasers as a frenetic dance in which the entire torso oscillates in a rapid flurry of controlled, vibrant quivers. Strippers use it to mean simply to quake or shake the body all over. *see* STRIPTEASE.

Shine: 1. A clown who has not flattened his makeup with powder. *see* GREASEBALL. 2. An actor who is not up to the accepted standard.

Shiner: Circus slang for a diamond.

Shiny back: An orchestra musician, so called for the shine on the backside from sitting so much.

Shipping close: Circus lingo for sending too much money home.

Shit kicker: Show-busines slang for one who pretends false modesty, or, on occasion, a phony or fraud.

Shiv: Pitchmen's term for a knife or razor, usually of the pocket variety.

Shivaree: *see* CHARIVARI, CHIVAREE, OR SHIVAREE.

Shoestringer: An inexpensive or cheap theatrical operation.

Shoot: To say or write something pertaining to pitchmen. *see* PIPE.

Shooter: English fair term for a shooting gallery or range.

Shooting quarter poles: The process of inserting and pushing up the intermediate poles of a circus tent. *see* QUARTER POLE.

Short: Circus term for a pass without a reserved seat coupon.

Short card: A magician's playing card which is shorter than the rest of the deck. *see* LONG CARD.

Short-change artist: The operator of a carnival concession or circus sideshow who is adept in cheating customers by returning to them less than their proper change. *see* CAKE CUTTER, GRAFTER, HYPE GUYS OR HYPERS, and WALK AWAYS OR WALKS.

Short-con game: 1. A confidence game in which little preparation and small stakes are involved. 2. A brief but aggressive pitchman's spiel.* *see also* SPIEL.

Short life and a merry one: An old-time phrase for an actor with a brief career.

Short side: Circus term for the section of the cookhouse* in which the staff and performers eat. *see also* COOKHOUSE.

Shorting: Circus term for short-change, stealing, or holding out money. *see* GRIFTER.

Shot: Circus word and some carnival use for a photograph, or, as used more commonly today, ruined or destroyed.

(The) Shove: With the frequence of pickpockets on carnival lots, it was natural that specific terms for the professionals of the vocation evolved. To do the job well, three persons are necessary: the shove pushed the victim and diverted his attention; the dip* goes for the pocket, hip, or otherwise; and the loot is then handed to the wire so that if one of the other two are caught, they would not be caught with the evidence. *see also* DIP, PRAT IN, PRATT OUT, and PRATTMAN.

Show biz: Abbreviation for show business.* *see also* BIZ, BUS, and SHOW BUSINESS.

Show box: *see* MARIONETTE SHOW.

Show business: Professional performance in all its branches.

Show girl: In burlesque, a more pretentious performer than a chorus girl.* She wore more expensive costumes, sometimes had a few lines, did the nude or seminude tableaux, and got the bigger salary. She was not considered a dancer and did little more than parade.* According to Sergel, she was rarely under five-feet eight-inches tall and frequently over six feet. The so-called medium show girl, on the other hand, was around five-feet six-inches tall, danced several numbers, sometimes sang and, on occasion, replaced a show girl. Like the regular show girl, she was better paid than a chorus girl and sometimes was included in the near-nude tableaux. The show girl was sometimes called a clothes-horse. *see also* CHORUS GIRL, PARADE, and SWING GIRL.

Show-letter: The weekly report of an outdoor show, often published in *Billboard*. *see also* BILLBOARD.

Show lot: *see* LOT.

Show print: Advertising for a traveling theatrical tent show; also the printing company doing the printing.

Show-shop: Slang for a theatre.

Showboat or show-boat: A term used exclusively in the United States for a river steamboat on which entertainment was presented, often of a dramatic type. Most showboats were equipped with a playhouse, a company of actors, a calliope,* and musicians, although doubling in brass* was not unusual. Showboats once provided the major entertainment for towns on the Mississippi and Ohio Rivers and, to a lesser extent, on the Great Lakes. The first showboat to move from one stop to another, "The Floating Theatre," was built in 1831 for William Chapman. During the Civil War, their number diminished greatly, but they were revived in more elaborate form during the 1870s with sidewheelers and steamer tows. Originally, most showboats presented legitimate, classical theatre fare, but after the Civil War melodrama and vaudeville became more common. Among the more famous of the showboats were "The Goldenrod," "The Cotton Blossom," and French's "Sensation." Also called a floating stage* or theatre. *see also* CALLIOPE, DOUBLING IN BRASS, and FLOATING STAGE.

Showboater: One who worked on a showboat.

Shower: In juggling, a pattern in which all objects flow in the same direction along the same path, in the same rhythm, thus creating a fluid, pure, circular image. *see* CASCADE.

Showing: The amount of circus advertising visible in a town.

Showman: Anyone connected with professional performance, especially a stage presentation. It is normally used to denote a producer, actor, performer, or an author with a flair for success. In its broadest sense, it can be applied to one in any form of popular entertainment, including a carnie* with panache. *see also* CARNY.

Shrimp: Medicine-show term for a business association.

Shrine circus: A circus performance put on by a Shrine Temple; Shriners are great circus fans and are responsible for a growing number of circuses.

Shtik: A small piece of business* that is put into a scene, bit,* or routine* that will supposedly enhance the moment. *see also* BIT, BUSINESS, and ROUTINE.

Shucker: A stripper. *see* ECDYSIAST, PEELER, POSER, and SLINGER.

Shuffle off: To conclude a false shuffle of playing cards by genuinely shuffling the balance of the deck.

Shut out of town: A circus that is not allowed a permit to play a town.

Shylock: Circus and carnival term for the office secretary.

Side: An actor's lines on a sheet of paper with only the necessary stage directions and cues. Despised by virtually all actors, their use has diminished considerably, although some publishers of musicals still rent these in lieu of full scripts. *see* PART.

Side-grip: Magician's term meaning to hold a deck of cards by the long edges.

Side pole: Short supports along a circus or show tent's outer canvas wall. Also called a wall pole. *see* CENTER POLE.

Sideshow or side show: An auxiliary show, usually under canvas, attached to a circus, or an exhibition or show of some sort with a carnival. The most common sideshow exhibits freaks or human oddities, although the term includes girlie shows, revues, or any other type of exhibition or entertainment. The first sideshow dates from circa 1904. By the 1930s and 1940s there were several hundred of the

freak-show type of sideshow. Today, because of the difficulty involved in populating them, there are less than a dozen traveling with
carnivals and circuses. *see* PIT SHOW and TEN-IN-ONE.

Side stuff: A colloquial English fair term meaning a linear arrangement of sideshows. Also can be used to mean booths with one side
open to the public.

Side wall: The vertically hung canvas curtains forming the outside
walls of a circus tent. To sneak into a circus tent during a performance
is "to side wall." *see* WALLING.

Sidewalk conversation: A term for a pair of wisecracking comedians
during the days of variety and vaudeville who did their act in a street
scene in one.* Prime examples were Harry and John Kernell, and Nat
Haines and Pettingill. *see also* IN ONE.

Sight: *see* GLIMPSE and PEEK.

Sight act: *see* DUMB ACT OR SIGHT ACT.

Sight comedian: A comic performer whose appearance and movement
comprise the thrust of the act's humor.

Sight gag: A comic bit requiring no dialogue and usually derived from
situation, business, or properties.

Sign of understanding: *see* OFFICE.

(To) sign on: In tent-show terms, to agree to terms with a manager or
to accept employment with a show for a season.

Signal: *see* INFO.

Silent act: A magician's dumb act* in which the performer eliminates
patter* for pantomime, although music or sound effects often underscore the performance. *see also* DUMB ACT OR SIGHT ACT and PATTER.

Silk hat: Circus and some carnival use word for an egotist.

Silo circuit: Summer stock company circuit of dates in small, country
towns.

Silver-mounted toppings: Circus pastry with frosting on the top.

Silver wagon: The name once used for the circus owner's or manager's administrative wagon because it was often painted with silver gilt.*see* RED WAGON.

Simoleon: Circus slang for a dollar.

Simp: Pitchmen's term for a sucker.* *see also* SUCKER.

Simp twister: Carnival slang for a merry-go-round or carousel.* *see also* CAROUSEL.

Simulation: Magician's method of fooling an audience by pretending something is so, which is not. *see* MISDIRECTION.

Sing: Pitchmen's term for giving a sales talk or making a spiel.* *see also* SPIEL.

Singer: 1. In pitchmen's lingo, a squealer or stool pigeon. 2. A solo act in a nightclub or cabaret.

Single man or woman: In vaudeville, a man or woman who played alone; sometimes used for a monologist* or even a solo singer. *see also* MONOLOGIST and TALKING SINGLE.

Single-o: A carnival grifter* who works alone, although this is not common because of the great aid of the outside man.* *see also* GRIFTER, OUTSIDE MAN, and PIT SHOW.

Sinker joint: Circus and carnival slang for a doughnut stand.

Sis Hopkins or Susie: The female counterpart of Toby* in a Toby show.* *see also* TOBY and TOBY SHOW.

Sister act: Two women working together in vaudeville, revue, or burlesque, usually billed as sisters, whether they are or not.

Sit on one's hands: To give little or no applause to a performer, act, or the like.

Site: *see* LOT.

Six-cat: A flat joint or store* in a carnival in which the object is to toss three baseballs and knock over two large catlike objects. *see also* BIG TOM, CAT RACK, FLAT JOINT OR STORE, and MODUC.

Six-sheet: A large-sized theatrical or circus poster used on bill boards. Figuratively, used to mean one who exaggerates or boasts. In vaudeville, to six-sheet was to advertise an act prominently. *see* THREE-SHEET OR THREE-SHEETING.

Sketch: In vaudeville and revues, a comedy scene, normally with a slight plot line but all elements designed to elicit laughs. *see* BIT and SKIT.

Skill or science game: Any carnival game requiring skill to play and win. Some carnival games of chance are called a skill or science game in order to mislead the authorities who disallow games of chance.

Skin: Outdoor amusement-business slang for a shirt.

Skin joint: *see* TWO-WAY JOINT.

Skin oddity: Sideshow freaks with skin that looks like that of alligators or snakes.

Skin show: A name sometimes applied to burlesque or striptease shows during the post-1920 period.

Skinned: Pitchmen's and med-show term for impoverished.

Skinner: A circus teamster.

Skinny: Circus and carnival slang sometimes used for a ten-cent piece or a dime.

Skirmishing car: *see* ADVERTISING CARS.

Skit: A short comic act or sketch. *see* BIT, SKETCH and TURN.

Skookum: Med-show slang for authentic speech. *see* GAZUKUS.

Skull: 1. A free ticket or pass, especially in the circus. 2. A take* or a funny face. *see also* GIVE HIM THE SKULL and TAKE.

Sky boards: The decorated section along the top of circus cage wagons once used in parades. *see* PARADE, SPLASH BOARD, and TABLEAU WAGONS.

Slang: 1. In American outdoor show business, argot for a watch chain. *see* BLOCK AND TACKLE. 2. In the English circus, slang means the performance or the show. *see* SLANGER.

Slanger: English circus argot for a showman or, more specifically, a trainer of cats. *see* SLANG.

Slanging buffers:*see* BUFFER.

Slapstick: Literally, a comic weapon, originally called a batte, comprised of a pair of lath paddles or long, flat pieces of wood fastened together at one end and used by comics (especially in the commedia dell'arte and English pantomime) to create a great deal of noise with minimum danger when another person is struck. According to one story, told by Buster Keaton, Harry Houdini used this word during the time of the Keaton-Houdini circus in which Keaton's father worked with the escape artist. Keaton points to the Evans and Hoey's rough-and-tumble act that played the Columbia wheel* toward the end of the nineteenth century as the first knockabout act. It is obvious that the literal slapstick was translated into a term to describe physical or broad comedy. In vaudeville, the slapstick (the physical object) was often placed in the orchestra pit in the hands of the drummer who cracked it to make the sound of a slap in synchronization with some stage business. *see also* COLUMBIA WHEEL.

Slapstick business: Stage business* that elicits laughter through physical methods. *see* BUSINESS.

Sledge: A sixteen-pound hammer used in driving circus tent stakes.

Sledge gang: Circus term, especially common in England, for the crew of men who pound in circus tent stakes.

Sleeper: Circus and carnival term for money overlooked by a customer.*see* LAY DOWN.

Sleeper jump: In its most specific use, this meant in burlesque a dressing room (frequently a top-floor room) some distance from the stage. In more general show-business terms, it can refer to any great distance, such as a hotel room remote from the theatre, a lengthy railroad platform, and the like. It is also used as a theatrical gauge of distance, that is, the distance requiring an overnight railroad jump, usually in a Pullman sleeper.

(To) sleeve: Magician's term meaning to insert secretly an article in the sleeve.

Sleight or sleight-of-hand: A term used among magicians to refer to magic dependent on pure manual dexterity, or tricks produced by means of digital dexterity, a good sense of balance, and careful timing. Such magic works only with small objects, such as cards or coins, and does not rely on apparatus, preparation, or prearrangement; thus, such forms of magic as illusions are not covered by this term.

Slew: Outdoor amusement-business term for plenty.

Slice: Circus term meaning to reduce size, in particular, to reduce the width of a circus parade.

Slick card: Magician's term for a highly polished playing card that slides more easily than the rest of the deck.

Slicker: *see* GRAFTER and LUCKY BOY.

Sligh: Carnival term meaning to dismantle, as a tent.

Sling in: Obsolete term meaning to do or to perform, especially to dance.

Slinger: A stripteaser. *see* ECDYSIAST, PEELER, SHUCKER, STRIP WOMAN, and STRIPPER.

Slip: In card magic, a sleight* in which the top card of the deck is secretly placed on the lower half of the deck when the cards are cut. *see also* SLEIGHT OR SLEIGHT-OF-HAND.

Slobberswing: Primarily an English term for a complete circle on the circus horizontal bar.

Slough: Circus and carnival word meaning to close or tear down a show or concession, to be closed by the law, or, on occasion, to stop work for the day. Billposters once used the word for side-street areas where they could sell-out a hod or hang all the paper posters he had been given. *see* SLOUGH THE JOINT.

Slough the joint: Primarily a carnival phrase meaning to close up business for the day or at the conclusion of a stand, or to have a show or gambling concession closed by the law. *see* SLOUGH.

Slough the tip: Pitchmen's term meaning to disperse an audience. *see* SLOUGH and TIP.

Slow burn: Theatrical term for a facial expression that gradually becomes one of intense anger. Popularized by the late 1930s comedian Leon Carroll, famous for his slow burn. *see* TAKE.

Slow take: *see* TAKE.

Slug: Slang word for a dollar; transferred from hobo use to carnival and circus slang and thence to the theatre and general use.

Slum: On circus and especially carnival midways, the cheap merchandise or junk given as prizes at concessions. In gaffed* games the public only receives slum, although they are more frequently than not attracted by flash,* which they never win. *see also* FLASH, GAFF, GRIND STORE, MUD, PLASTER, RINKY-DINK, and SWAG.

Slum layout: A carnival joint* in which small, worthless prizes are given in the game of chance. Although attracted by flash,* the customers never win these large prizes. *see also* FLASH, JOINT, and SLUM.

Sly-grog shop: *see* BLIND PIG OR TIGER.

Smack stand: A carnival concession run by local people but one that takes advantage of the crowds.

Small-time: A circuit of vaudeville theatres that played three or more shows daily, sometimes with movies (especially during the latter days of vaudeville) and usually with general admission. Generally, small-time vaudeville depended on low-salaried acts, hence small-time acts or performers.

Smash: General show-business term for a successful act, performance, or production.

Smesh: Carnival term for a coin or, by extension, money.

Smoke: Outdoor amusement slang meaning to look.

(To) smoke up: Show-girl jargon meaning to smarten up; fairly recent derivation.

Smoke wagon: A long wagon, usually with two small, strong wheels mounted on an axle like an auto trailer, that circles the main circus tent and moves the heaviest poles to and from place to place. Originally, such a wagon would have been pulled by elephants.

Smooch: Carnival argot for borrow.

Smut: Synonym for minstrel's burnt cork.* *see also* BURNT CORK.

Snake eye: Mid-nineteenth-century circus term for a loose railroad rail that penetrated the floor of a car.

Snake type: A provocative stripteaser.

Snatch team: Circus term for an especially strong and energetic team of horses used to supplement other teams on rough or muddy ground.

Snatched: Carnival term for closed by the law.

Sneaky pete or Pete: Circus slang for cheap wine. Originally it meant any of various illegal alcoholic beverages.

Sneezed: Carnival slang meaning to be arrested.

Sniffer: Pitchmen's slang for a handkerchief.

Snipe: Outdoor show-business term for a built-up bill board that belongs to a local concern. *see* SNIPE PLANT.

Snipe plant: A company that owns and services the bill boards in any given area. *see* SNIPE.

Snipe the town: To put bills around a town. *see* SNIPE.

Sniper: A billposter who puts up his paper surreptitiously at night.

Sniping: The pasting of paper or bills on an available wall, fence, or other available space without permission from the owner of these spaces. *see* SNIPE and SNIPER.

Snorting pole: A pole from the top of a tent to the center of a platform on which a carnival stripper works. The carnival stripper pretends the pole is a phallus and presses against it, first with bumps and grinds, and then a climax.

Snow: Theatrical term for free admission passes and, by extension, used as a name for the deadheads in the house.

Snow balls: Pitchmen's term for cold weather.

Society circus: Term used between 1900 and 1935 for an indoor circus or a one-ring show.

Sock vaudeville: A fast-moving, hilarious variety show.

Socko: Theatrical term for a great or quick success.

Socks: Outdoor show-business term for punches or physical hits.

Soft: Easy money in carnival slang.

Soft lot: A wet or spongy circus ground.

Soft paper: Circus advertising poster or handbill* on which are printed dates and other current information. *see also* HANDBILL.

Soft spot: An unusually good or favorable circus show town. *see* RED, RED ONE, and SPOT.

Soft ticket: A reserved-seat circus ticket.

Soldier-reader: A pitchmen's license given to an ex-serviceman free. *see* READER.

Solid takes: Consistent good earnings of a pitchman.

Solo spot: A circus or variety act of such quality and expertise that it plays by itself.

Somersault: In circus parlance, the word somersault is used only for a complete revolution of the body, forward or backward, in the air.

Song and dance: An entertainment combining singing and dancing, especially in vaudeville, revue, and musical comedy. *see* S. AND D.

Song-and-dance man: Originally, a vaudeville term for a performer whose act normally consisted of singing a few songs, telling a few jokes, doing a dance routine (tap or soft shoe), and completing the act with a flourish of more complex dance tricks. By the 1920s, the term had been transferred to leading men in musical comedy.

Song plugger: A singer hired by a music publisher to help popularize and sell sheet music of specific songs; frequently a vaudeville performer who sang these songs in an act. Also known as a music exploitation man. *see* PLUGGER.

Songbird: Show-business term for a female vocalist.

Soubrette: 1. In burlesque, the head chorus girl and thus the lead in all the girl numbers. Sometimes used in a limited way in bits.* *see also* BIT. 2. In the Toby show,* this was an actress who specialized in teenaged-girl parts. *see also* ROUGH SOUBRETTE and TOBY SHOW.

Sounder: *see* LEATHER-LUNGED.

Soup and fish: A turn-of-the-century theatrical slang expression for male evening attire.

Soup dealer: Circus and carnival argot for a knife rack operator.

Soured: A Toby show* term describing a town that failed to yield expenses and, by extension, a company that failed or a marriage that breaks up. *see also* TOBY SHOW.

Spangles: *see* KINKER.

Spanish web: A soft rope made of canvas and filled with cotton, used by circus aerialists for climbing and for aerial ballet and gymnastics. *see* WEB.

Spec or spectacle: A circus pageant or parade,* usually based on some imaginative or historical theme, which is a featured part of the show.

The parade includes all the performers, human and animal, and occurs around the hippodrome track.* Formerly this was the grand-opening number but now is often presented just before the intermission. It should not be confused with the obsolete free circus street parade. Tournament is an archaic word for the spec. *see also* HIPPODROME TRACK and PARADE.

Spec girls: Attractive show girls who appear in the spec.* *see also* SPEC OR SPECTACLE.

Special agent: *see* ADVANCE AGENT OR ADVANCE MAN.

Specialty: Vaudeville term pertaining to the performance of specialized acts, such as songs, comic sketches, and dance (thus specialty act, specialty artist, and so on).

Specialty number: In musical comedy, a song that is not fully integrated into the show.

Spectacular extravaganza: A type of early American musical theatre most often set in exotic lands and lavish in its productional values. *see* MUSICAL COMEDY.

Spider: In magic, a mechanical device used to facilitate back palming. *see* BACK PALM and PALM.

Spiel: From the German "*spielen*" (to play), this word has a number of applications in popular entertainment: 1. Its most common meaning is a circus or carnival talker's bally* or pitch.* In other words, the glib talk that gets the customers in to see shows. *see also* BALLY OR BALLYHOO and PITCH. 2. The pitchman's sales talk. 3. A fast, boisterous dance. In this context, the word especially refers to the wild dances in which one's partner is swung clear off the floor, formerly a feat attempted only by the strong and experienced dancer at low resorts, in a time before adagio dancing became popular.

Spieler: 1. A circus or carnival talker.* Incorrectly called a barker.* *see also* BALLY OR BALLYHOO, BARKER, GRINDER, OPENER, SPIEL, and TALKER. 2. A fast, able dancer.

Spin: Carnival and circus term for the ability to speak a language or dialect fluently.

Spindle: 1. Synonym for a novelty gambling wheel. *see* SPINDLE MAN. 2. A metal or wooden arrow mounted on a horizontal base; a variation of the carnival wheel.* A paper, celluloid, rubber, or leather indicator protrudes from the arrow's point and brushes against the surrounding circle of posts or nails separating the sections. Here the indicator spins while the numbered sections and posts are stationary, just the reverse of the wheels. *see also* CARNIVAL WHEEL. 3. A metal tripod topped with a horizontally revolving disc on which a paw or hoof may be placed in a circus animal act.

Spindle man: One who operates a novelty gambling wheel on a circus midway. *see* SPINDLE.

Spinning one's wheels: *see* BEAT MY CHOPS.

Spinning wheel: English fairground name for a carnival wheel.* *see also* CARNIVAL WHEEL.

Spirit slates: Standard piece of mental magic or spiritualist's equipment in the form of one or more small portable blackboards on which messages may be written in chalk. Most of these operate with a secret rectangular piece that resembles the slate surfaces and fits over them, thus making the slates seem blank even though they might bear writing.

Spiritualism: Related to performance magic in that physical spiritualists or mediums who produce visible specters or signs are well versed in magical techniques. Mental mediums, those who only seem to contact the minds of spirits, are far more subtle in their professional abilities.

Splash boards: The decorated bottom edge of circus wagons used in parades. *see* PARADE, SKY BOARDS, and TABLEAU WAGONS.

Split deck: A deck of magical cards cut diagonally in half and consisting of twenty-six different cards alternating with twenty-six force* cards. These cards are covered with roughing fluid* so that when they are fanned only the backs of the force cards can be selected. Two spectators picking cards from different halves can then locate the two halves of a single card. *see also* FORCE and ROUGHING FLUID.

Split out: Outdoor show business term meaning to separate.

Split time: A week in which a production, especially a vaudeville act or bill, visited more than one location. *see* ACE and DEUCE.

Split week: A week in which a performer or traveling company worked several consecutive days in one theatre or town and the rest in another. *see* ACE, DEUCE, and SPLIT TIME.

Splits: Acrobatic term used in the circus. There are two basic versions, stride and center (or straddle), determined by whether the legs are stretched to back and front or sideways.

Spool or spool wagon: Circus term for a giant reel mounted on wheels on which canvas is rolled. A spool wagon was sometimes used to help raise and lower center poles. *see also* CENTER POLE.

Spot: 1. In vaudeville, the place of an act* or turn* on the bill.* To play the first spot is to open the show,* which, in England, was called (to) play them in. *see also* ACT, BILL, OPEN THE SHOW, and TURN. 2. In the circus, a location on the lot* or the placing of circus wagons in their proper places before a show begins. *see also* LOT. 3. Location of a pitchman's stand* or store.* *see also* STAND.

Spot in the scratch: A good pitchman's location. *see* SPOT.

Spots and stripes: Circus slang for leopards and tigers. Spots alone can refer to spotted horses.

Spotted: A circus or carnival that is scheduled to play on a future date.

Spotter: In the American circus, usually a person who stands by during an acrobatic act in order to insure an acrobat's safety should something go wrong. In the English circus, the name of a somersault* in which the performer's feet land on the exact place from where he took off. *see also* SOMERSAULT.

Spread: A circus, carnival, or amusement park newspaper notice that is completely across the page.

Spring: 1. Carnival and pitchmen's term meaning to begin work or open for business. 2. Carnival and circus word for digging into the pockets for more money. Also called *Kick*.

Springboard: A seesawlike device used to give lift to an acrobat making a jump. *see* TEETERBOARD ACT.

Springfield: Carnival argot indicating a cry used by onlookers when one goes to the pocket for more money. *see* SPRING.

Spring flowers: Artificial flowers used by magicians which can be concealed in a small space with springs inside that open them up when released from their storage place.

Sprung: To be released by a circus or carnival show's mender,* patch,* or adjuster.* *see also* ADJUSTER, MENDER, and PATCH.

Squadron: The front section of a circus train.

Square: 1. In magic, to adjust the edges of playing cards. 2. Circus word meaning to settle a dispute.

Square a beef: In the circus, to adjust a complaint, refund money, or pay back an amount short-changed. In the eighteenth century, to set up a hue and cry was to cry beef or give hot beef (perhaps suggested by a bull's bellow). By 1810, beef meant "stop thief," possibly a corruption or perhaps an example of rhyming slang. Around 1880, it had evolved into theatrical slang for a shout or yell.

Square the shake: In pitchmen's slang, this refers to a payment made to a policeman, sheriff, or some other local authority, which, in turn, frees the pitchman from the threat of conviction or a jail sentence. *see* SHAKE.

Square the tip: In pitchmen's argot, to pacify a crowd that has become unruly or suspicious by offering a gift or changing the line of the sales talk. *see* TIP.

Squarer: *see* FIXER.

Squash: Circus slang for a kiss.

Squawk or squeak: Circus and carnival argot for a complaint, usually one registered over losses incurred while gambling.

Squawker: A complaining customer. *see* SQUAWK.

Squeak: *see* SQUAWK.

Squeaker: *see* SWATCHEL OR SWAZZLE.

Squeeze: *see* JAM OR JAMB.

Squeezings: The sterno squeezed through sponges from "canned heat" and then drunk by some old-time circus personnel.

Squirt: Circus slang for twenty-five cents or a quarter.

St. Louis: Circus term for doubles or seconds of food, so called because a St. Louis engagement was played in two sections.

Stack: In magician's lingo, a prearranged deck of playing cards.

Stage-door Johnny: *see* JOHNNY .

Stage magic: *see* CLOSE-UP MAGIC and PLATFORM TRICKS.

Stage money: Imitation money, usually in bank notes, used for stage purposes, including stage magic.

Stage wait: In burlesque, a bit* lacking humor. *see also* BIT.

Stager: An obsolete term for an actor. *see* OLD STAGER.

Stake and chain: A circus wagon used solely to transport riggings, stakes, chains, bale-rings, hammers, and so forth. This was the wagon where canvas men* hung around while the show was going on. *see also* CANVAS MEN.

Stake-driver: *see* HAMMER GANG.

Stakers: Circus and carnival workers who handled the stakes that secured the tents and guy lines to the ground. Before motorized machinery, the stakes were driven with heavy mauls or mallets and most stakers were, of necessity, husky fellows.

Stall: 1. In circus parlance, this can mean to wait, kill time, survey, hold off or divert, or to approach carefully. 2. In the English fair, a concession.

Stall act: A circus act extended by superfluous business* in order ro retain an audience for some reason, or to pad an inadequate routine. *see also* BUSINESS.

Stall the push: Circus and carnival phrase meaning to gather a crowd around a show and attempt to coerce them in.

Stalling: Circus term, especially in England, meaning missing or fumbling a trick.

Stand: Outdoor show-business and traveling-entertainment term for a town or city where a show stops to play. In the circus, the show date is referred to as a stand, such as a one-day stand. In billposting, it refers to a location where advertising has been posted. The term seems to have originated from the minstrel show.

Stand him on his ear: Carnival and some circus use for the procurement of credit at a store or from an individual.

Stand-up joint: *see* GRAB JOINT.

Standard act: A vaudeville act well known to managers and bookers.

Standard rep: A term used by Toby show* managers to describe larger and more reliable companies, those with more elaborate scenery and equipment. The term was used primarily to distinguish such companies from the smaller Toby shows, even though the larger company might offer little else than Toby plays. *see also* REPERTOIRE OR REPERTORY and TOBY SHOW.

Star backs: The reserved or more expensive circus seats, so named because they originally had a star painted on each. *see* BLUES, HARD TICKETS, and OLD STAR BACKS.

Stash: In circus lingo, to save or hide money. Began as underworld cant (about 1811) for stop or put an end to, possibly a combination of either stop or stow and squash.

Statute fair: An English fair for hiring labor or animals. *see* CHARTER FAIR, HIRING FAIR, and MOP FAIR.

Staubs: Circus tent stakes driven into the ground to which are secured ropes for holding down or "guying" out tents.

Steal: Magician's term for secreting an article or a parcel of small objects concealed on the body in such a way that they can be obtained during the performance.

Steal a bow: Primarily, a vaudeville phrase for forcing encores or bows upon an audience when there is not sufficient demand. *see* MILK.

Steam fair: An English fair at which the rides are powered by steam.

Steam fiddle: *see* CALLIOPE.

Steamboats: A type of playing card with a plaid design on the back, favored by card magicians because of its flexibility and smoothness. Also used to describe cards with no white border on the back.

Steer: Circus term meaning to direct.

Steerer: A ticket speculator's representative who directs persons turned away from the box office to the speculator.

Stem: Circus term for any street. *see* GUT and MAIN DRAG.

Step dance: A type of dance, such as a clog or tap dance, especially popular in vaudeville. .

Step on a line: *see* CUE BITER.

Stick: 1. A kind of carnival shill* or confederate, especially one who pretends to be a player in order to attract and stimulate business and who later secretly returns prizes "won." When the live one* or ones begin to play, the stick is removed and delivers the prizes or winnings to one outside who has no apparent connection with the joint.* This is known as cleaning the sticks; the man is a cleaner.* *see also* BOOSTER, CLEANER, JOINT, LIVE ONE, and SHILL. 2. In pitchmen's slang, a fountain pen. 3. In theatrical jargon, a town outside of a large theatrical center, or a tank town.* *see also* TANK TOWN.

(The) Sticks: *see* (THE) ROAD.

Stiff: A legal attachment or writ in circus slang.

Still act: Circus term for a picture act.

Still date: 1. A carnival engagement not backed by a fair but which has usually been in existence for a long time and, weather permitting, guarantees good attendance. Such an engagement is normally sponsored by a local organization that furnishes the lot* and sometimes the electricity; in return, the organization receives a percentage of the gate. *see also* LOT. 2. In circus terms, the days on which the show is not advertised or billed.

Stinger gag: Circus slang for a press stunt.

Stitchy: Circus slang for a tailor, based on the work involved.

Stock: Either the portion of a deck of cards with certain cards placed in a specific order for dealing or at the top or bottom of the deck, or the main portion of the deck, that is, not those cards being dealt or used for playing or magical purposes. Also called the talon.

Stock burlesque: A nontraveling burlesque company performing out of a specific theatre.

Stock company: An acting company with its own theatre and a group of plays presented either in turn or in repertory.* Some traveling companies with a specific circuit of theatres were also called stock companies. *see also* REPERTOIRE or REPERTORY, ROAD SHOW, and STOCK THEATRE.

Stock joints: Carnival games that pay off in merchandise, such as dolls, lamps, blankets, groceries, silverware, fish, and so forth. They are specifically named for their merchandise, such as doll joints, lamp joints, fish joints, and so forth. Also called merchandise joints.

Stock man: A showman who produced his own show every week.

Stock stake: Pitchmen's term for a gift or loan of enough stock with which to work.

Stock theatre: A theatre with its own show and a change of show every week or so. A true stock theatre did not accommodate traveling shows. *see* STOCK COMPANY.

Stock whip: A lashless whip with a stock and braided leather end used by circus animal trainers.

Stomach timber: Outside carnival concessions demonstrators.

Stood 'em up: Theatrical slang for good business.

Stooge: 1. In vaudeville, a plant or foil in the audience who assisted the comedian. 2. In magic, a secret assistant* or confederate* who helps the magician; often pretends to be an audience volunteer.* *see also* ASSISTANT, CONFEDERATE, and VOLUNTEER. 4. In burlesque, a third banana. *see also* THIRD BANANA.

Stop: A clown number performed at various points around the hippodrome track.* The clown presents the routine in a fixed location, then moves on to a new location. *see also* HIPPODROME TRACK and WALK-AROUND.

Stop the show: Originally, a vaudeville expression indicating that an act or performer won so much applause that it caused a delay in the performance.

Store: A carnival or circus concession or game, honest or crooked. *see* JOINT and RACKET OR TRICK.

Store show: A cheap version of the dime museum* that set up for a few months or weeks or even a few days in most American cities prior to World War I. *see also* DIME MUSEUM.

Straddle: *see* SPLITS.

Straight back: An actor who does athletic feats and does not require a stand-in stuntman. Primarily, a term used during early motion pictures.

Straight man: 1. A medicine-show performer who worked without makeup, that is, straight. 2. A comedian's partner who acts as a foil or stooge.* 3. An actor who plays stright roles rather than character parts.

Straight man lectures on: Burlesque phrase for the talk of a straight man.

Strawhouse: Circus and carnival word for an overflowing house. The name came from the practice of placing straw in front of the regular seats when a circus was sold out so that additional patrons could be accommodated. The practice was supposedly discontinued after a horse, racing around the arena in a Ben Hur spectacle, threw a shoe and injured a small boy, resulting in a major lawsuit. *see* ON THE STRAW OR STRAWING THEM.

Strawing: *see* ON THE STRAW OR STRAWING THEM.

Stretch: A pantomimic gesture from the stage manager of a burlesque theatre meaning to prolong a scene. As burlesque eliminated variety acts and cut back on the number of chorus girls, the show depended more and more on the comics, straight men, and strippers. Comics were required to fill in more and more time, and the gesture of stretching from the wings became common. *see* (TO) SEPARATE THE PALMS.

Stride: *see* SPLITS.

Strides: Circus slang for trousers.

Strike: The process of taking down the circus tent and packing everything for a move to another location; also to take down theatrical scenery.

Strike night: A common term in stock theatres, meaning to take down the scenery, an occurrence that happened virtually every week. The actors were invariably expected to assist in the strike* and the set-up the following day of a new set. This is still true in small companies and amateur companies. *see also* STRIKE.

Striker: The English fair/carnival equivalent of the American high striker.* *see also* HIGH STRIKER.

String: Circus term for a long line of horses, animals, objects, and so forth.

String of talk: Turn-of-the-century phrase for a monologue. *see* JUNK and MONOLOGIST.

String show: Circus and carnival term for an open front show with a long line of canvas banners. *see* BANNER and BANNER LINE.

Stringers: *see* JACKS AND STRINGERS.

Strip: 1. The act of a burlesque or, more correctly, striptease dancer removing her clothes. *see* PEEL, STRIP WOMAN, and STRIPPING. 2. In the circus, this refers to a clown gag* ending with the sudden metamorphosis of the performer by the unexpected removal of clothing, usually the trousers. *see also* GAG.

Strip woman: A female performer in burlesque or the striptease who walks and "dances" to music and removes her clothes to the delight of a largely male audience. Today, most strip women or strippers are called exotic dancers* or sometimes topless dancers, though there are subtle distinctions between these appellations among the more artistic of the practitioners.

Stripes: Circus word for tigers. *see* SPOTS AND STRIPES.

Stripper: A striptease dancer. *see* ECDYSIAST, PEELER, SHUCKER, SLINGER, and STRIP WOMAN.

Stripper pack or deck: A deck of cards whose sides or ends have been tapered so that, if a card is reversed, it can be located by a card magician by touching the protruding edges. Also called a wizard deck.

Strippers: Playing cards that are wider at one end than the other. *see* BISEAUTÉ and STRIPPER PACK OR DECK.

Stripping: 1. The act of a striptease dancer removing her clothes. 2. The practice in the outdoor amusement business of removing and loading decorative portions of fronts,* rides, and equipment before an engagement ends. *see also* FRONT.

Striptease: An addition to traditional American burlesque beginning circa 1907, which not only gave it new life but, by shifting the emphasis away from the comic, also changed the form considerably and ultimately marked the death of burlesque. The strip is difficult to pinpoint in time but clearly began much earlier when females on stage undressed down to tights, often on high wires or stage runways. The art of the tease, involving audience response, developed from such a beginning. The secret, of course, was gradually to take off the clothes while sexually arousing the largely male audience. It was often unnecessary to actually appear nude at the conclusion of the striptease. *see* BUMP, G-STRING, GRIND, PASTY, SKIN SHOW, and STRIP WOMAN.

Stripteaser: A stripper.

Strolling players: A group of itinerant actors who took their repertory of plays from town to town, frequently on foot. An itinerant actor was once called a stroll or stroller.

Strong: 1. Carnival and circus term for providing dishonest profit. At one time it also referred to a price of twenty-five cents or more to play or bet at a concession. 2. Recent theatrical slang for something or someone that is well liked. *see* WORKING STRONG.

Strong City: Striptease term for a city where the obscenity laws are loose or less strictly enforced than elsewhere.

Strong joint: *see* TWO-WAY JOINT.

Strong performance: A striptease performance with a greater degree of nudity, flashing,* or obscene elements than normal. In carnival parlance, a girlie show* or a dirty show. *see also* FLASHING and GIRLIE SHOW.

Stuff: One's stock-in-trade, such as a comedian's jokes.

Stump speech: A comedy feature primarily in minstrel shows and vaudeville; a version of the traditional story-telling monologue. In minstrelsy* it was a major part of the olio,* the variety section, in which the minstrels concentrated on misuse of the language, making the stump speech more an exercise in the infinite possibilities for malapropisms and nonsequiturs than a commentary on the subject of the "lecture." Often, the stump speech in addition to making the speaker appear foolish, did voice serious social criticism. *see also* MINISTRELSY and OLIO OR OLEO.

Style or styling: In the circus, this is the grand flourish or graceful gesture inviting applause at the end of a trick or an act. It is also used for acknowledging and accepting the approval of the audience. Circus people never take bows but rather they style or "take a compliment" with a gesture frozen into a stylish pose.

Subscriptionist: *see* PAPER BOY OR MAN.

Subway circuit: Theatre on the outskirts of Manhattan, especially those in Brooklyn or the Bronx, available for engagements, especially by vaudevillians, on an alternating basis.

Sucker: Circus term for a townsperson. The inference is normally that these are gullible, unsophisticated circus patrons. *see also* TOWNER and TOWNIE OR TOWNEY.

Sucker gag or trick: A magic trick in which the audience members believe they have detected the secret or caught the performer in an error, but in the end are proved wrong, thus doubly confused.

Sugars: *see* HEAVY SUGAR.

Suggestion: A magician's way of misleading an audience by hinting that something is so, which is not, or just the opposite. *see* MISDIRECTION.

Suitcase outfit: A gilly show,* which is an ad hoc sort of affair, figuratively so small that it can be packed in a suitcase, or, as Easto and Truzzi explain it, "put together by an agent whose sole possession is a set of contracts for a series of engagements." *see also* GILLY SHOW.

Sunbursts: Highly decorated circus wagon wheels.

Sunday run: Circus slang for a long distance. *see* RUN.

Sunday school: A clean show or operation, especially in reference to an outdoor show, a carnival midway that doesn't allow crooked games or girlie shows, or a burlesque show that keeps its stripper from full disrobement (usually because the police are looking on).

Sunday school circuit: The name given to the vaudeville circuit of B. F. Keith, which aimed at a family audience and excluded all offensive material from its bills. Its strict censorship made performers call it the Sunday school circuit.

Sunday school show: *see* SUNDAY SCHOOL.

Sunshine trouper or sunshiner: A circus worker who disappears or lies down on the job when the work gets tough.

Super: 1. In pitchmen's slang and on carnival lots, either a stolen watch or a large and handsome watch displayed as a prize at a game of chance; frequently only a case without the works. It can also mean a superintendent or anyone in charge of a job or a piece of work, as it commonly does today. 2. In the circus, theatre, and most performance forms, an extra in an act* or a bit without lines. *see also* ACT.

Supper-turn: A vaudeville act* in continuous vaudeville* forced to go on at the dinner hour, about 6 P.M., when the audience was the smallest. *see also* ACT and CONTINUOUS OR CONTINUOUS VAUDEVILLE.

Sure-fire: An act in vaudeville that would get across under all circumstances.

Sure-thing man: *see* BOOSTER.

Susie: *see* SIS HOPKINS.

Suspension: A type of magic trick or illusion in which a person or object is placed in the air without apparent support and remains there. *see* LEVITATION.

Svengali deck: A trick card deck with every other card the same and cut short, making it easy to force* a card and perform other effects. *see also* FORCE.

Swag: An English fair and circus term for prizes won at concessions. *see* SLUM.

Swagman: A wholesaler of prizes for English circuses and fairs.

Swami gimmick: *see* NAIL WRITER.

Swatchel or swazzle: The apparatus used by a Punch and Judy puppeteer to give an inhuman timbre to the puppets' voices. Originally called a squeaker or pivetta.

Sweep the lot: To survey the circus lot* with a light after a teardown* to locate possible forgotten gear and equipment. *see also* LOT and TEARDOWN.

Sweep ropes: Ropes sewn into circus canvas tops to hold them together better or to make them stronger.

Sweet pitch: The sales talk or pitch* of the prize candy-seller before the performance or at intermission of a circus or burlesque show. *see also* PITCH.

Sweetened air: Circus and carnival argot for cotton candy. *see* FLOSS.

Swell kidder: Medicine-show slang for a fashionable hick or rustic.

Swell pipes: Circus slang for a good voice.

Swell set-up: Striptease/burlesque expression for a good or shapely figure. *see* SET-UP.

Swindle sheet: Circus slang for an expense account.

Swing: In the circus, to do as one pleases or wishes.

Swing girl: A chorus dancer or singer capable of doing each of the other chorus parts and can thus "swing" into each position on brief notice. In burlesque, a swing girl was one who relieved other girls on their nights off when shows played seven nights a week.

(To) swing with: Circus and carnival phrase meaning to take without the owner's permission or consent.

(The) Swinger: A flat joint or store* on a carnival lot* in which the customer swings a small bowling ball in such a fashion as to knock over a small bowling pin. *see also* FLAT JOINT OR STORE and LOT.

Switch: In magic, to secretly substitute one article for another. *see* RING.

Switchback: English fair circular ride with a number of cars driven around an undulating track. Similar to the American Caterpillar.

Symmetricals: Flexible forms that flesh out the calves, breasts, or upper arms of slender people and are concealed by clothing or costumes. Also, padded tights can be called symmetricals. Used by actors, young boys who played female roles, or young men who appeared as females in circus acrobatic and trapeze acts. *see* HEART.

System: Magician's term used in card magic to signify a secret method of arranging the deck so that various effects can be performed. *see* SET-UP.

T

T & K operator: Pitchmen's abbreviation for a tripod and keister operator, one who can work anywhere. *see* KEISTER and TRIPE.

Tab: Short for "tabloid," as in a burlesque tab, musical comedy tab, and so forth. A condensed version of a full-length show. *see* TAB COMPANY, TAB HOUSE, and TAB SHOW.

Tab company: A traveling dramatic show attempting to counteract and compete with vaudeville and the motion pictures by performing one-hour or ninety-minute condensed versions of successful musical comedies. In 1913, there were almost one hundred of these companies in operation, charging ten-, twenty-, and thirty-cent admissions. *see* TAB SHOW.

Tab house: A theatre specializing in presenting condensed versions of plays or musicals. *see* TAB and TAB SHOW.

Tab-lifter: A nightclub customer.

Tab show: An expurgated or condensed version of a longer show. Tab* comes from tabloid, as in a half-size newspaper. Musical comedies were usually cut down to an hour or ninety minutes so that they could be presented with movies three or four times a day, or in order to compete with vaudeville and motion pictures. *see also* TAB, TAB COMPANY and TAB HOUSE.

Tableau: A technique in nineteenth-century popular theatre whereby a dramatic pose was struck by members of the cast at the start or end of a play or scene in the hope of conveying the mood of the piece or to underscore a dramatic moment. These were commonly used to convey entire scenes, as if they were living pictures. *Uncle Tom's Cabin* always featured a number of such tableaux.

Tableau wagons: Ornamental circus parade wagons with costumed circus performers stationed on the tops. *see* SKY BOARDS and SPLASH BOARDS.

Tabled card: In card magic, the card on the table, in contrast to those in the hand.

Tack spitters: Circus employees who tacked advertising on brick walls. *see* BANNER TACKER.

Tackle the calfskin: Slang expression meaning to play the banjo; probably echoes back to the days of the minstrel show.

Tad comic: Term for an Irish comedian; most common usage was in vaudeville circles. Tad comes from Irish variants of "Thaddeus."

Tag: A banner* or streamer on the front of a circus tent. *see also* BANNER.

Tail up or trunk to tail: A circus command to an elephant to grab, with his trunk, the tail of the elephant in front of him in a parade* or march.* *see also* MARCH and PARADE.

Take: 1. In the circus and carnival, the gate receipts. *see* GEEDUS, GELT, KALE, and SCRATCH. 2. A comic reaction in order to heighten a comic effect, especially in vaudeville and burlesque. There are basically four types of takes. a. Skull:* The most sudden reaction, usually involving a snap of the head in the direction of the other performer. *see* GIVE HIM THE SKULL and SKULL. b. Double take:* A somewhat slower realization that things are not as they should be. The initial glance is followed by a more definite turn and focus on an object or situation. c. Body take:* Similar to the double take, but the entire body is used in the motion instead of just the head. d. Slow take:* a delayed reaction.

Take a compliment: *see* STYLE OR STYLING.

Take a powder: Carnival and circus phrase meaning to leave without giving notice or to slip away. Now in common usage.

Take down and put up: *see* COMIC UP IN ALL.

Take him for a walk: Carnival expression meaning to move a disgruntled gambler away from a gambling joint* and calm him down. *see also* JOINT.

Take the cake: *see* CAKEWALK.

Take three bends and an encore: Show-business expression implying that an act was well received. *see* KNOCK THEM IN THE AISLES, LAY 'EM IN THE AISLES, and PANIC 'EM OR PANICKED THE HOUSE.

Takes water: *see* JAKES OR TO BE JAKING.

Taking first count: *see* FIRST COUNT.

Talk: In magic, the telltale sound that some objects make and thus the risk taken in communicating to the audience some information that the magician wishes to be concealed. Palmed coins and cards, for example, talk unless manipulated extremely well.

Talker: The person who does outside talks and lectures in front of an attraction; never a barker.* Today, the talker most frequently uses electric amplification. *see also* BARKER AND SPIELER.

Talkers: Vaudeville name for sound films, rarely called "talkies" by vaudevillians.

Talking clowns: An early type of American clown before the development of multiple rings. America's first famous clown, Dan Rice, at his peak in the mid-1840s, was known for his combination of wisecracks, songs parodying popular topics, and jibes at the educated. An earlier talking clown, William R. Wallet, was a cultured man of wit, in the tradition of the court jester, as were most talking clowns.

Talking single: A one-person vaudeville act using for material stories, gags, and the like. A kind of early stand-up comic. *see* MONOLOGIST and SINGLE MAN OR WOMAN.

Talking woman: A female performer in burlesque who delivered lines in the bits.* This entertainer was a valuable asset to the comic and was normally a former stripper or one who continued to strip but doubled in bits and skits. During the heyday of burlesque, she had to be quite adept and know all the bits. Comics preferred to have the best talking woman possible and often used the same one for years. *see also* BIT.

Tall grass: Slang expression for especially remote one-night stands.*
see also ONE-NIGHT STAND.

Talon: *see* STOCK.

Tambo: One of the end men* in a black-face* minstrel show,* so called
because of the tamborine such an entertainer often played. *see also*
BLACK-FACE, BONES, END MAN, and MINSTREL SHOW.

Tamer: *see* TRAINER.

Tanbark: The shredded bark from trees from which tannin has been
extracted for leather tanning; used to cover circus arena ground
because of its excellence in guaranteeing good footing for animals and
performers.

Tank town: A small town considerably distant from major performance locations; sometimes simply tank.

Tank spectacle: *see* AQUATIC DRAMA.

Tap: Circus and carnival term for either the price of admission or
money collected from merchants in exchange for banner* advertising.
see also BANNER.

Tap city or tapped out: Circus term for bankrupt.

Taps: Minstrel-show slang for a drummer. *see* THUMPER.

Tapping: English fair equivalent for short-changing. *see* SHORT-
CHANGE ARTIST.*

Tassel: Bunches of thin strands of material, usually silver or gold,
attached to the bra or nipple covering of a stripper or showgirl. They
are sometimes attached to the back of the panties, one on each buttock.
see also PASTY and TASSEL TWIRLER.

Tassel twirler: A type of stripteaser who specializes in spinning tassels
attached to her bra cups or pasties,* and in some cases the haunches of
her buttocks. The trick is to twirl the tassels using nothing but pectoral
muscles, in the case of the breast twirling. Carrie Finnell is credited
with perfecting and popularizing this specialty. *see also* PASTY and
TASSEL.

Taylor trunk: A standard flat-top theatrical trunk, manufactured by the Taylor Trunk Company. Traveling repertoire actors regarded such a trunk as a sure sign of professionalism. see TOWEL TRUNK.

Tea reader: A fortune-teller who uses tea leaves. see MITT READER.

Teardown or tear-down: The nighttime process of taking apart a circus and packing it on its train, or the dismantling of a midway at the conclusion of an engagement.

Tearing a passion to tatters: see CHEWING THE SCENERY.

Teeterboard act: A circus specialty in which an acrobat stands on one end of a small seesawlike device while one or more additional acrobats jump from a platform on to the other end of the seesaw, hurtling the first acrobat into the air to land on a pyramid of people, in a chair, and so forth. Because of the topmost position of the first acrobat, this role is called the top mounter.* One of the more difficult of teeterboard feats is for the top mounter to land atop a three-man stand, called the four-man-high.* The bottom acrobat standing on the ground, usually the largest of the group, is the understander.* see also FOUR-MAN-HIGH, REBOUND ACROBATICS, SPRINGBOARD, TOP MOUNTER, and UNDER-STANDER.

Telegraph wagon: The lead wagon of the old overland horse-drawn circus caravan, the occupants of which had the job of directing the caravan over the correct roads to the next town. see ARROW THE ROUTE and RAIL-THE-ROUTE.

Ten-in-one, five-in-one, and so on: A circus or carnival sideshow or pit show* with ten, five, or fewer attractions or pits* under one top.* These were usually human freak attractions. see also PIT, PIT SHOW, and TOP.

Ten per and cakes: A ham* actor's salary. see also HAM.

Ten-twent'-thirt' or ten-twenty-thirty: Popular, sensational melodrama, so named originally because of the ticket prices of ten, twenty, and thirty cents. By the late-nineteenth century, it referred to companies performing popular melodrama of a stereotyped form in the smaller theatres throughout the country.

Tenant: An English showman who rents ground for his concession or entertainment from an English fairground lessee.

Tent rep: *see* REPERTOIRE OR REPERTORY.

Tent-squirrels: Slang for circus performers, also known as sawdust eaters. *see* KICKING SAWDUST.

Terp team: A ballroom dance team; from Terpsichore, the muse of dance.

Terper: A choreographer or a dancer.

Terpery: A dance hall.

Terps: Dancing.

Territory: During the heyday of the circus, the area of the country a major show considered its own.

Theme park: The modern equivalent of the amusement park, usually built around a unifying idea or "theme," such as "Disneyland" or "Six Flags over Texas."

Thief: *see* FLATTIE OR FLATTY.

Thimble rig: *see* MONTE.

Thimble rigger: A shell-game operator; played with a pea and three thimbles or acceptable substitutes. *see* MONTE.

Thin: Circus and carnival argot for short of money or close to broke.

Thin man: A term that might have originated with the circus and is still in general usage today. A nonexistent person on the circus payroll (the pay going into the pocket of the manager), who was said to be so thin nobody could see him.

Thinking part: A part in a popular drama in which the actor appears on stage but has no lines to speak, such as a butler, policeman, or other small part. *see* EXTRA MAN OR WOMAN.

Third banana: A stooge* burlesque comic who takes most of the falls and is generally mauled by his colleagues. *see also* BANANA, STOOGE, and TOP BANANA.

Third sex: Obsolete show-business term for a homosexual.

Thought-reading: *see* MENTALISM.

Thread-the-needle: A drill maneuver of horses used in the circus.

Three: In vaudeville, the stage space immediately above two* away from the audience. This was normally six or more feet beyond the boundary of two. *see also* IN ONE, ONE, TWO, and FOUR.

Three-a-day: A vaudeville house including three complete vaudeville bills daily. *see* CONTINUOUS OR CONTINUOUS VAUDEVILLE and TWO-A-DAY.

Three around: Three objects passed between two jugglers.

Three-card monte: *see* MONTE.

Three-card monte man: *see* BROAD-TOSSER and MONTE.

Three-card trick: Common English name for monte.* English variation is the concealing of money beneath one of three playing cards and having the public guess the correct card. *see also* MONTE.

Three-day stand: *see* (TO) WEEK-STAND.

Three high or three-men-high: A vertrical column made up of three acrobats. The three-men-high, or simply three high, is usually part of a series of circus tricks, such as a double back from a teeterboard to a three high. *see* MIDDLEMAN and TEETERBOARD ACT.

Three-marble tiv: *see* TIV.

Three-sheet or three-sheeting: Literally, this is a medium-sized advertising bill board (usually 42 inches by 84 inches) which sometimes comes in three separate sheets. These are associated especially with the theatre and the circus. By extension, it has come to mean boasting, bragging, or advertising one's unlikely accomplishments (typified by a performer accepting accolades in the lobby after a performance or wearing stage makeup away from the stage or arena). In a less derogatory context, it can also refer to the leading performer in an act,* in particular a vaudeville act. *see also* ACT, BUTTON-BUSTER, HANGING HIS OWN, and PUTTING UP PAPER FOR YOURSELF.

Three shell game: *see* MONTE.

Three-way joint: A carnival game that can be played from three sides. *see* FOUR-WAY JOINT.

They threw the babies out of the balcony: A vaudeville and burlesque expression that suggested how good a performer or act* had been. *see also* ACT.

Throw: 1. A term used by card magicians meaning to place the balance of cards on the rest after a shuffle. 2. Circus term meaning to give.

Throw a cop: In carnival jargon, to allow a stick,* and sometimes even a legitimate customer, to win a valuable prize at a gaming concession. Sometimes called throwing a prize or throwing out a prize. *see also* (TO) FAIRBANK, FLASH, STICK, and THROW-AWAY.

Throw-away or throwaway: 1. Allowing a member of the crowd to win a large prize at a gaming concession in order to stimulate business. *see* THROW A COP. 2. A ticket of admission sold at a reduced price. 3. An advertising circular or handbill.* *see also* HANDBILL. 4. A short, quickly delivered joke or witticism, incidental to a routine and usually sandwiched by a comedian between his major jokes. This meaning originated in vaudeville.

Throwing a prize or throwing out a prize: *see* THROW A COP and THROW-AWAY.

Thumb count: A sleight* used by card magic specialists in which cards are secretly counted by the thumb while held in the hand. *see also* SLEIGHT OR SLEIGHT-OF-HAND.

Thumb pushback: Magician's sleight* in which a chosen card is secretly moved to the bottom of the deck where it can be seen. *see also* SLEIGHT OR SLEIGHT-OF-HAND.

Thumper: Circus slang for a drummer. *see* TAPS.

Ticker: Pitchmen's slang for a watch. *see* SLANG.

Till-tapper: Outdoor show-business argot for a petty thief, in particular, one who works as part of a team and distracts a show owner so that a confederate may dip* his hand in the till and escape with loose cash. *see* (THE) DIP.

Tilt: English fair term for the canvas roof of a ride or show.

Time: Vaudeville engagement. *see* BIG TIME and SMALL-TIME.

Tin Pan Alley: The fabled music publisher's row, derived from the open-windowed brownstone house west of Broadway on New York's Twenty-eighth Street in the early 1900s, when show-business activities were focused between Union and Longacre (and later, Times Square). The theatrical reporter Monroe H. Rosenfeld is credited with having coined the term in an interview with songwriter-publisher Harry Von Tilzer. From that interview came the legend that Von Tilzer coined it. Currently, publishers and composers of popular music center their activities in the vicinity of Broadway and Fiftieth Street. Since similar areas in other cities are now known for their importance in the music business, the name, still in use, more correctly refers to the songwriting and selling business in general.

Tinhorn: Outdoor show-business term usually applied to a small-time gambler.

Tins: Carnival slang sometimes used for local police. *see* COOKIE CUTTER, COP, DICK, FUZZ, and SHAMUS.

Tinsel-molls: Carnival name for painted ladies found in areas of vice and corruption.

Tip: 1. A crowd of people or prospective customers gathered around a pitchman or before the bally stand* in front of carnival or circus attractions in response to the spiel* or ballyhoo.* *see also* BALLY or BALLYHOO, BALLY STAND OR BOX, PUSH, SPIEL, and TURN THE TIP. 2. Also, an old English circus term for a trick. *see* MISSING A TIP.

Tish note: Carnival slang for counterfeit or imitation money used to pay "strange broads for body rental," according to DeBelle.

Title: The name of a circus. After twenty-eight years of nonuse, the title passed into public domain.

Tiv: A carnival gambling device using red and black marbles, most frequently called three-marble tiv. *see* JACK-POT.

Tober: English term for a circus lot* or the total complex of a fairground, including the layout of the rides, concessions, and shows. Also known as the pitch. *see also* BLACK TOBER and LOT.

Toby: 1. The dog in a Punch and Judy show,* named after performing dogs of the eighteenth century but now usually dispensed with. His function was to sit on the playboard* of the puppet theatre with a ruff around his neck and, on cue, bite Punch's nose. *see also* PLAYBOARD and PUNCH AND JUDY SHOW. 2. The silly kid or light comedy role in a Toby show.* The stock character emerged from the traditional line of theatrical rustics inspired most directly from the Tobe Haxton part in the 1911 tent-repertoire play, *Clouds and Sunshine* (which is, in turn, a copy of *Out of the Fold* by Langdon McCormick with the part of Toby Tompkins). When he emerged as a stock-in-trade of most tent-repertoire companies after about 1915, he was invariably portrayed as a redheaded, freckle-faced, country boy, dressed in rural attire, and, at various times, brash, shy, shrewd, natively bright, stupid, industrious, and lazy. The actor playing the role would take on the manners of the region in which he appeared and could improvise his way into almost any play or style depending on the audience's wishes. There were scores of Toby* comedians, many known by their followers only as Toby. *see also* SIS HOPKINS OR SUSIE, and TOBY SHOW.

Toby boob and blackface—up in all and make them go: A phrase meaning an actor could play the usual comic roles in a Toby show,* the boob* or silly kid and blackface parts, knew all the sketches, and could make the audience laugh. *see also* BOOB and TOBY SHOW.

Toby clown: A circus clown who works as a come-in* worker in the seats among the audience. *see* COME-IN.

Toby play: Any play in which the principal comic character was called Toby. *see also* TOBY.

Toby show: An extremely popular form of rural theatre popular from around 1915 and reaching its peak of popularity just prior to the depression. Although not limited to the tent tradition, most companies were traveling tent companies presenting Toby plays* exclusively. Companies were relatively small, frequently a family show, and, by most standards, a tawdry outfit with poor acting. *see also* REPERTOIRE, TOBY, and TOBY PLAYS.

Tokus: Carnival term, from the Yiddish, for the posterior.

Tom: To travel as part of a theatrical troupe to a small town in order to give only one of a limited number of performances. Originally referred to performing *Uncle Tom's Cabin* exclusively. *see* TOM SHOW and TOMMERS.

Tom show: A production of *Uncle Tom's Cabin*, in its many forms and varieties, presented by a traveling company, or a theatrical troupe specializing in performing *Uncle Tom's Cabin* (and frequently other similar melodramas along with *U.T.C.*). Such companies toured for over fifty years and many actors made lifetime careers with Tom shows.

Tommers: Actors in a Tom show;* most specifically, actors in a traveling theatrical troupe specializing in performing *Uncle Tom's Cabin* or similar melodramas. Originally, Tommers played only in *U.T.C. see also* TOM SHOW.

Tonighter: A one-page circus flyer announcing an attraction that would appear that same day.

Took a bath: Show-business expression meaning to have gone into bankruptcy.

Took the fence: Circus and carnival phrase meaning to blow or leave with the receipts of a show, ride, or concession. *see* GO OUT WITH OR GO SOUTH.

Took the veil: Show-business expression meaning to have retired from public life.

Toomler: A comedian on the Borscht circuit* who provides a nonstop tumult for the entertainment of hotel guests. *see also* BORSCHT CIRCUIT OR BELT.

Toot up: Circus slang meaning to attract attention by means of a calliope.* *see also* CALLIOPE.

Tooth tinker: Circus slang for a dentist.

Top: In carnival and circus lingo, a top is any tent or canvas shelter, named more specifically in terms of its function, such as the cook top (dining tent), menagerie top,* kid top* (sideshow), dressing top, and so forth. Milburn claims that the only tent called a tent on a circus lot* was the horse tent, or stables, and it was sometimes called the horse top. Another exception was frequently the cook tent, which was more commonly known as the cookhouse.* *see also* COOKHOUSE, KID TOP, LOT, and MENAGERIE TOP.

Top banana: The number-one comic in a burlesque show or the comedian with the top billing* on the program. The top banana possibly received such an appellation because the top banana on the stalk is the ripest, therefore the number-one comic is the most experienced and the best. The second banana* usually did a bit* by himself, an opening scene, and then a double scene with the top banana. Second bananas aimed at becoming the top banana. *see also* BANANA, BIT, SECOND BANANA, and THIRD BANANA.

Top billing: A show-business act that headlined or was featured on a bill. *see* BILLING.

Top card: In card magic, the card lying face-down on top of the deck.

Top-line vaudeville: A high-class vaudeville house or theatre with two shows a day and a reserved-seat audience. *see* ADVANCED OR REFINED VAUDEVILLE and TWO-A-DAY.

Top liner: *see* HEADLINER.

Top mounter: In a circus acrobatic act, the performer at the top of a group of acrobats. *see* UNDERSTANDER.

Top shelf: A theatre's second balcony. *see* NIGGER HEAVEN, PARADISE, and PEANUT GALLERY.

Top stock: In card magic, the upper part of a deck of cards when the deck is held face-down.

Topper: Circus term for a featured act. *see* TOP BILLING.

Topping the bill: *see* HEADLINING.

Toppings: Circus pastry.

Torch singer: Show-business term for a singer of "blues songs" with a deep, passionate voice. Also called a torcher.

Torch swinging: A circus genre* in which burning torches are manipulated in patterns around the performer. Its roots are in the Swedish gymnastics of the nineteenth century, which used a system of body building based on swinging and twirling clubs around the body.

Torcher: *see* TORCH SINGER.

Torso-tosser: A cooch (or cootch) dancer. *see* COOCH OR COOTCH DANCING.

Torture stunts: A type of magical effect (used most by fakirs, mentalists, and hypnotists) in which physical pain is suppressed or apparently absent despite acts of physical torture, such as sticking pins through the arms, tongue, or hand, and chewing glass.

Tossing a bone: In the circus, to give money to someone destitute.

Tossing the broad: In carnival slang, this means shuffling cards in three-card monte.* The expression was supposedly coined by Slim Chambers when three queens were used instead of three aces, most common today. *see also* BROAD TOSSER, MONTE, and THREE-CARD MONTE.

Total blank or t.b.: Carnival argot for a town that is cold or a bloomer.* *see also* BLOOMER and COLD.

Touch: 1. Outdoor show-business word meaning to borrow (the lender being "touched" by a hard-luck story), to acquire, or to steal from. 2. In pitchmen's slang, a sale.

Tough: Pitchmen's term for hard to obtain.

Tourist: Anyone who joins a carnival or circus for the first time or simply in order to get away from somewhere or to see the country. It normally refers to a lazy workman.

Tournament: An archaic term for the circus spectacle.* *see* SPEC OR SPECTACLE.

Tourniquet: Technical magic term for the act of pretending to take an object in one hand while actually leaving it in the other. *see* FRENCH DROP.

Towel trunk: One of two trunks usually carried by performers who spent much of their time on the road and stayed in the better hotels. The towel trunk contained dozens of stolen hotel towels. *see* TAYLOR TRUNK.

Town hall: *see* CONCERT HALL.

Towners: Townspeople or, more specifically, those natives of a town where a circus or carnival is playing who are not connected with the show in any way. *see* TOWNIE OR TOWNEY.

Townie or towney: A resident of a town in which a carnival or circus is playing; a carnival or circus spectator. Usually used in a derisive way. *see* COWBOY, ELMER, and TOWNER.

Trail: Circus term meaning to follow.

Trailer: 1. A vagrant, beggar, or grafter* who follows a circus or carnival. This was frequently someone who capitalized on the show's patrons and sold some commodity but did not pay for the privilege.* *see also* GRAFTER, LOT LICE, and PRIVILEGE. 2. In the art of striptease, the introductory strut before the actual strip in order to kindle interest in the audience.

Train-poler: In the circus, the man who steered a wagon (by means of a pole) as it was being moved over the deck of the flatcars in the process of loading or unloading the show.

Trainer: A circus animal handler or trainer of animals. In the circus, never called a tamer.

Tramp clown: A circus clown who dresses like a tramp with an unshaven face and a reddened nose. More than most types of clowns, they are portrayed as figures of pathos. Also called a hobo clown. *see also* CHARLEY OR CHARLIE.

Trampoline: A piece of circus equipment which, in its simplest terms, is a canvas sheet stretched on springs.

Transposition: A magic trick in which objects or persons change positions.

Trap: Abbreviation for any trapeze.

Trapeze: A class of circus acts built around a bar suspended on flexible lines. There are two basic types: fixed or flying. The fixed type may swing, but the act is accomplished on the bar; the flying variety is left for a flight either to another trapeze or the hands of the catcher.* Other genres include high solo trapeze suited to the requirements of its performers. *see also* CATCHER and FLYER.

Traps: General term for drummer's equipment. In the circus, it can also be used for any paraphernalia.

Trapper: The circus groom who prepares horses for performances.

Traveling company: A touring company, usually theatrical in nature. Sometimes called a traveling theatre. *see* (THE) ROAD and ROAD COMPANY.

Traveling menagerie: A precursor of the circus in England and the circus and Wild West show* in America. An exhibit that showed strange creatures to people who had no other opportunity to view them. These were first seen in America just prior to the revolution. *see also* WILD WEST SHOW.

Traveling theatre: *see* TRAVELING COMPANY.

Travesty: A dramatic piece which burlesques or parodies another work. Such fare was especially popular during the latter half of the nineteenth century. *see* PARODY.

Trick: 1. In the circus and carnival, this refers to the entire show or organization. It can also allude to an act.* In the English circus, it most commonly means any feat performed by a circus artist or animal. *see also* ACT. 2. In the dramatic tent-show tradition, a trick was a small company performing, normally, a combination of movies, variety acts, and a tab* drama. *see also* TAB. 3. *see* RACKET OR TRICK.

Trick line: English circus term for any rope used to pull anything into or out of action.

Trinka: An upholstered cradle used by an antipodist* or Risley* performer in which the performer lies on his back when juggling with the feet. *see also* ANTIPODIST and RISLEY ACT.

Tripe: Short for tripod. Used by low pitchmen* to hold the keister* or case or suitcase from which small cheap articles (also known as tripe) are sold. *see also* KEISTER, KNIGHTS OF THE TRIPES AND KEISTER, and T & K OPERATOR.

Triple: A triple somersault* or three turns of a juggled object performed in the circus. The legendary triple is the standard of great flying and vaulting acts. *see also* SOMERSAULT.

Tripod and keister operator: *see* KEISTER, T & K OPERATOR, and TRIPE.

Tripod opinings: The opinions of a pitchman. *see* TRIPE.

Trot: *see* BREEZE.

Troupe: In the traveling-company tradition, the act of moving from town to town. It refers in more legitimate circles to a company of performers.

Trouper: 1. An actor, especially one who belongs to a company of traveling players. 2. In the circus, the word, which carries a connotation of great affection and approval, refers to any employee or member of the company. 3. In the broader amusement world, it usually means a person who has spent at least one full season with some type of traveling amusement organization.

Truck full of quits: A burlesque expression applied to some performers who were highly temperamental and were always quitting the show.

Trunk to tail: *see* TAIL UP OR TRUNK TO TAIL.

Trunk up: Command in the circus to an elephant to raise his trunk in a salute.

Try-out: In vaudeville, the first presentation of an act* before an audience with a view to booking. *see also* ACT.

Try it (out) on the dog: To test a theatrical piece, usually outside of the city where it would eventually be given its principal production.

Tubs: The name given the seats of many midway riding devices.

Tumbling pass: *see* CASCADE.

Tunnel of Love: Almost any amusement device incorporating a ride through a darkened tunnel. The name is used in England and the United States. *see* GHOST TRAIN.

Tunnel trade: Customers on a midway who patronize hood-covered rides, such as the Caterpillar.* *see also* CATERPILLAR.

Turkey: Virtually all forms of entertainment use this to indicate a bad or losing show. Its origin comes from actors (turkey actors) who opened poor shows on Thanksgiving Day in the hope of making money as part of the annual tradition. Possibly began in New England when a down-and-out producer found a nonroyalty play, some unemployed actors, a used set, and booked a date during turkey week, usually a period when healthy attendance might be expected. It is also said, however, that the phrase is attributed to the actor-writer-director Dion Boucicault, whose melodramas were the sensation of the 1890s. Boucicault once had a lousy show that opened on Thanksgiving and which he described as his turkey.

Turkey actors: *see* TURKEY.

Turkey shows: Traveling one-night-stand* shows; in particular, early dirty burlesque. *see* BEHIND-THE-TENT-SHOW and ONE-NIGHT STAND.

Turn: An act* in vaudeville or the circus. More commonly used in Great Britain than in the United States. *see also* ACT and UNIT.

Turn the duke: Carnival and circus phrase meaning to short-change a person. *see* DUKE.

Turn the push: To lead the crowd through a midway show so that there are no stragglers. *see* TIP and TURN THE TIP.

Turn the tip: In the circus, and especially the carnival, the accomplishment of the talker* or spieler* in turning or persuading a group of people to buy tickets for an attraction. The pitchman uses the phrase to signify that a crowd has been activated to buy. *see also* SPIELER, TALKER, and TIP.

Turnaway: In the circus, a sold-out show (literally, crowds turned away due to lack of room).

Turnaway biz: In pitchmen's lingo, a crowd so large that they cannot all be supplied, and some must be turned away.

Turned down: In theatrical usage, to be denied professional courtesies by a manager.

Turnip: *see* BLOCK.

Twenty-four-hour man (24-hour man): A circus agent or representative who travels one day ahead of the show to perfect arrangements for the circus and to meet and direct the show's arrival. Large circuses frequently use two men, alternating. *see* ADVANCE and ADVANCE AGENT OR ADVANCE MAN.

Twist: An acrobatic movement of a circus performer combining a somersault* and a pirouette.* *see also* PIROUETTE and SOMERSAULT.

Two: In vaudeville, the stage space between the olio* and the set of wings six or more feet behind the olio. *see also* OLIO OR OLEO.

Two-a-day: A vaudeville or theatre offering presented twice daily. This was known as big-time* since the more important houses in large cities utilized two-a-day. A group of such theatres would be part of the big-time circuit. *see also* BIG-TIME.

Two Bill show: The combined Buffalo Bill's Wild West and Pawnee Bill's Great Far East.

Two-bottle jump or two-quart jump: An indicator of the distance between engagements, especially in traveling burlesque. Since most burlesque shows traveled by coach, closing one stand and riding all night on a train in order to open in another town the next day, it was necessary for the cast, without sleepers, to sit, talk, and drink. The amount of drink that could be consumed would indicate the size of the jump.* For example, a 200-mile ride would be a two-bottle jump. *see also* JUMP and TWO DUKIE RUN.

Two dukie run: In the circus, a long trip or jump* between towns with two previously prepared meals served. The distance of the trip, therefore, would be indicated by the number of meals. *see also* DUKEY, DUCKIE, OR DUKIE RUN JUMP, and TWO-BOTTLE JUMP.

Two high: Similar to a three high* but with one less acrobat. *see also* THREE HIGH OR THREE-MEN-HIGH.

Two-line gag: A gag* that depends on two parts, a cue and a response. *see also* GAG.

Two-way joint: A carnival game that can be operated two ways, honest or crooked. Known also as a skin joint and a strong joint. *see* GAFFED JOINT OR G-JOINT.

Two-year rule: An English fair and carnival rule whereby a showman occupying the same site for two years has first option on the site the next year.

Typewrite: *see* INFO.

U and V

Uncle Friday: The paymaster in an English circus (Friday is payday).

Under canvas: Circuses or other types of entertainment performed in tents as opposed to the now-common practice of appearing in indoor arenas, ball parks, or stadiums.

Undercut: In card magic, a term that describes the process of placing the lower section of a deck of cards on the upper portion. *see* UPPERCUT.

Understander: The usually large and strong circus acrobat who supports on his shoulders or head other members of an acrobatic team; normally, he is stationed on the ground. *see* BEARER and BOTTOM MAN.

Union: The musicians of a vaudeville house orchestra. The term was used facetiously.

Unit: One act in a circus program. *see* TURN.

Unit show: A pitch show* or medicine show consisting of a few girls and a comedian presenting a small variety show, mainly musical, traveling as a unit and appearing in a series of brief engagements, usually in small towns. *see also* PITCH SHOW.

United Booking Office or U.B.O: An organization formed by B. F. Keith and E. F. Albee with other vaudeville theatre owners in 1906 in order to control the booking of all performers for the members' theatres. The U.B.O. exploited the performers rather ruthlessly, and they retaliated, unsuccessfully, by organizing their own union, The White Rats.* *see also* (THE) NATIONAL VAUDEVILLE ASSOCIATION (N.V.A.) and (THE) WHITE RATS.

Up: Outdoor showmen add this word to others without changing the meaning of the second word, but creating a special twist to their cant. For example, a four-horse team might have been referred to as a "four-up."

Up ahead or up front: Circus term meaning to be on the circus advance.

(To) up it: Carnival slang meaning to hand over whatever happens to be the subject of conversation.

Upstage or up-stage: In addition to its meaning in stage terminology (that is, the area of the stage moving away from the audience), it has come to mean stealing the attention of the audience from another actor or actors, by standing upstage or in front of the other actor or actors, or by distracting attention away from the major focus of the action in some manner.

Uppercut: In card magic, to take the upper section of a deck of cards and place it beneath the lower section. *see* UNDERCUT.

Upping: *see* RIDE FOREMAN.

Ush: Since the late-nineteenth century, this has been used from time to time to mean to work as an usher, usually in a theatre.

UTC or U.T.C. company: A common abbreviation for an *Uncle Tom's Cabin* troupe. *see* TOM SHOW.

V and X: Pitchmen's slang for any five- and-ten-cent chain store. Obviously obsolete.

Valentine: *see* OUTSIDE FLASH.

Vamp: A short, introductory piece of instrumental music, often repeated more than once, before a song or dance. Commonly used in vaudeville and burlesque, but also applicable to musical theatre.

Vanish: Magician's term for a trick in which an object or person disappears, or, as a verb, meaning to make such an object or person disappear.

Varda, vardi, or vardo: English circus term for a wagon. Apparently comes from the Romany *"vardo"* or *"wardo,"* meaning a cart.

Varicose alley: A burlesque runway. *see also* RUNWAY.

Variety: The name given an early form of American vaudeville, the name replacing it during the 1890s. The word continued to be used by some as synonymous with vaudeville, indicating a program composed of different kinds of acts. The English continue to use variety instead of vaudeville. It is also the name of the current actor's Bible. *see also* ACTOR'S BIBLE.

Vaude: Since about 1915, a common abbreviation for a vaudeville show, especially one attached to a circus as a sideshow.

Vaudery: Slang for a vaudeville theatre.

Vaudeville: A stage entertainment, extremely popular under this name from the 1890s (name was first used in the 1840s) to 1932, the symbolic date of its death (when movies took over the Palace Theatre in New York). It consisted of relatively brief but varied acts, usually unrelated, but carefully structured according to a tried-and-true formula. Acts included every possible form of amusement, such as magicians, acrobats, comedians, song-and-dance routines, unusual specialties, and the like. The word is French from nineteenth-century light pastoral plays with musical interludes, but the American form was completely indigenous. At its height, ten people attended a vaudeville show to everyone who patronized other forms of entertainment.

Vaudevillian: A performer in vaudeville. To be so called one normally had to be considered a seasoned trouper.* *see also* TROUPER.

Velvet: Pitchmen's term for money, or, more specifically, profit.

Ventro: Show-business abbreviation for a ventriloquist.

Vitascope: A device created by Thomas Armat in Washington, D.C., which projected moving pictures onto a screen and was little more than an extension of the peep-show kinetoscope,* which had been around since 1894, when the first such parlor opened on Broadway in New York City. The vitascope was added as a new entertainment novelty to vaudeville bills beginning in 1896. *see also* PEEP-SHOW KINETOSCOPE.

Voltige: English circus term for a rider or riders vaulting onto and off a horse. *see* FORK JUMP, LIFT, and RUNNING GROUND MOUNT.

Volunteer: An audience member chosen by a magician to help during a trick. *see* ASSISTANT, CONFEDERATE, and STOOGE.

Voting with your feet: *see* ANKLE A SHOW.

Vulcanizer: *see* FIXER.

W

(The) Wagon: The main circus office wagon, usually the main ticket or bookkeeping wagon where all accounts were kept. *see also* RED WAGON, SILVER WAGON, and WHITE WAGON.

Wait Brothers Show: In circus circles, this was a nickname for Ringling Bros. and Barnum & Bailey Combined Circuses, so named because "Wait for the Big Show!" appeared on their posters.

Walk across: In a burlesque show, when a person, usually a comic or the straight man, is talking and a girl walks by giving this person one or two lines and then a grind and a bump. *see also* BUMP and GRIND.

Walk-around: 1. In the minstrel show, this was a circular walk around the stage by the entire company—a kind of dance to lively music. Both the dance and the music were called walk-arounds. Though usually performed without words, this was an action-filled moment in the show with canes twirling, hands clapping, and give and take with the audience. This was frequently repeated at the end of the evening. This dance most likely antedated the buck and wing,* which became a popular dance in the minstrel shows. *see also* BUCK AND WING. 2. In the pit show,* the path or wooden walk from which customers viewed the attractions. *see also* PIT SHOW. 3. In the circus, clown routines performed at various points around the hippodrome track* while the clowns are parading completely around the arena. *see also* HIPPODROME TRACK, JOEY WALK-AROUND, and STOP.

Walk away or walks: Circus and carnival argot for the person, especially one purchasing a ticket, who leaves change behind absentmindedly, or the money acquired by a ticket seller by short-changing patrons. *see* CAKE CUTTER, GRIFTER, HYPE GUYS OR HYPERS, and SHORT-CHANGE ARTIST.

Walk men: Men on the sidewalk near a theatre who sell tickets to a show. *see* ON THE WALK.

Walk off the show: To quit a circus and leave without warning.

Walk-through: A pit show in which patrons move in and out without sitting down. Can be applied to any midway show or amusement, such as a fun house, in which the patron is self-ambulatory. *see also* GRIND SHOW and PIT SHOW.

Walk-up or walkup: Theatrical term for a patron who buys a ticket at the box office instead of getting a ticket in advance. In tent shows, this referred to a customer who bought at the gate instead of from a sponsoring organization in advance.

Walker: A stripper who disrobes while walking to music.

Walking gentleman or lady: An archaic theatrical term (common in the nineteenth century) for actors in minor parts. *see* BIT PART and SUPER.

Wall pole: *see* SIDE POLE.

Walling: The English circus equivalent of side wall.* The side canvases or walls of the circus tent. *see also* SIDE WALL.

Walter Plinge: The British equivalent of George Spelvin. In use since about 1900. *see also* GEORGE SPELVIN and JOE HEPP.

War-walk-through: An exhibition of war relics. *see* WALK-THROUGH.

Wardrobe: The dressing, costumes, and paraphernalia worn by circus performers, blankets on elephants for parades, and so forth. *see* FLASHING IT UP and HAMALAMA.

Washout: Circus slang for a failure, or, more literally, a railroad track that is washed out ahead of the show train.

Watch the tips: Carnival phrase meaning to observe a pitchman doing business or, by extension, to idle about. *see* TIP.

Wax opera: Carnival slang for a show featuring wax figures, usually a kind of walk-through.* *see also* WALK-THROUGH.

Waxie: A circus harnessmaker, from the waxed sewing thread used by the craftsman.

Way: *see* FOUR-WAY(S).

Web: The canvas-covered rope suspended from the top of the circus tent. The performer who uses the web in an aerial ballet sequence is a web girl, and the ground man who holds or manipulates the web for the aerialists is a web sitter. *see* CLOUD SWING, PLANGE, and SPANISH WEB.

Web girl: *see* WEB.

Web sitter: *see* WEB.

Wedged: Carnival and some circus use for being stuck or stranded in a hotel without adequate funds to pay the bill. It is sometimes used in a more general way for stranded with no funds.

Weed: Circus and carnival slang meaning to hand another person money or, as the word implies, to distribute (usually money) sparingly.

(To) week-stand: In traveling tent shows, this meant to play a community for a week at a time. Tent shows rarely played one-night stands,* so this term is rarely found in their argot. A three-day stand was fairly common. *see also* ONE-NIGHT STAND.

Weight juggling: *see* KRAFT-JUGGLERS.

Well: A secret cavity or compartment usually in the magician's table and concealed by the black-art principle.* *see also* BLACK-ART PRINCIPLE.

Wench role: *see* PRIMA DONNA OR WENCH ROLE.

Western pastimes: In the English circus, an act* including rope-spinning and tricks, whip-cracking, lassoing, knife-throwing, sometimes sharpshooting, and other skills which the English associate with the American West. *see also* ACT.

Western roarers: In the early minstrel show, the use of frontier folk stories and heroes to extol the West, put down the aristocracy, and promote jingoism and a nationalistic attitude.

Wham: A striptease in which the teaser removes all her clothes.

Wheel: 1. The name for a circuit of burlesque theatres controlled by a syndicate. The shows revolved around the circuits like spokes, and this system made burlesque into a big, centralized business, guaranteeing member theatres a regular supply of entertainment but uncontroversial shows, and providing performers forty-five weeks a year of steady work if they complied with the "cleaned up" performance code. Wheels date from the early twentieth century and presented shows that were usually less suggestive than burlesque without nudity. *see* MUTUAL WHEEL. 2. Any one of several gambling devices in the form of a wheel, used extensively at county fairs, amusement parks, and carnivals. Dishonest wheels are known as gaff* wheels. *see also* CARNIVAL WHEEL and GAFF.

Wheeze: An archaic word for a joke, gag,* or device, sometimes still applied to a clown's joke. *see also* GAG.

Whip ride: *see* KISS RIDE.

Whistle tooter: Circus slang for the equestrian director* or sometimes a ringmaster.* *see also* EQUESTRIAN DIRECTOR and RINGMASTER.

White elephant: A term originating in the nineteenth-century circus when rival operations conducted "white elephant wars," advertising white elephants which were sometimes hoaxes. The public began to believe that all so-called white elephants were hoaxes and thus the expression came to mean anything big, unwanted, and troublesome.

White-face or whiteface clown: The traditional circus clown with white makeup. In the European circus, the white face is the elegant partner of the more clumsy Auguste* and appears with a touch of red or black on an otherwise white face. *see also* AUGUSTE.

White meat: A white woman whose services or presence is for hire for legitimate purposes, normally as an actress or singer. Term dates from the 1930s but is rarely used today.

White money: Regular U.S. or Canadian coins and currency with which early carnivals paid their employees when they were doing good business.

(The) White Rats: Short-lived and relatively ineffective vaudeville performers' union formed in 1910 (chartered by the American Federation of Labor). The union was modeled on the British music-hall performers' Water Rats. When the vaudeville managers organized the National Vaudeville Association* to counteract the union formed by the artists (independent versus a "company" actors' union), the trust prevailed. *see also* (THE) NATIONAL VAUDEVILLE ASSOCIATION (N.V.A.).

White slip: *see* PINK SLIP.

White-stone worker: A pitchman who sold zircons or rhinestones.

White wagon: The main office on the circus lot.* *see also* LOT, RED WAGON, SILVER WAGON, and (THE) WAGON.

Wigwag: *see* INFO.

Wild cat: A circus that plays a territory* on short notice, due to unscheduled route changes. *see also* TERRITORY.

Wild West show: An exhibition illustrating scenes and events characteristic of the American Far West frontier, although not necessarily realistically. The upsurge of such outdoor entertainment dates from 1882 and reached its peak of popularity around 1893. Although Buffalo Bill Cody's show was the best known, in the course of its history there were over one hundred such shows. In form, such a show is distinctive from a circus, although after 1900 many merged with circuses.

Wildcatting a show: The process of investigating a town for potential business for an attraction and then booking it.

William Winter: An obsolete term for a drama critic, named after the New York critic William Winter (1836-1917).

Winch: Circus term for a portable derrick.

Windjammer: 1. Circus argot for a horn player in the band, sometimes used in a general way to mean a musician. 2. In minstrel shows, a trombonist.

Window card: Circus advertising on cardboard (14 inches by 22 inches) for placing in windows or tacking on poles.

Wing a part or wing it: Originally, the practice of attaching the sides* or dialogue of a script to a wing flat or other portion of the stage scenery for quick reference by an actor who was not secure in his or her lines during a performance. Today, it means to perform without having one's lines learned or one's act together but, rather, relying on brief glances at the script before coming on stage, or depending on one's innate ability to improvise. *see also* SIDE.

Wing-ding broad: In a circus or carnival, a girl or woman who faints in front of a geek* in order to arouse customers' curiosity and draw them into the tent. *see also* GEEK.

Wingy: Circus slang for a one-armed individual.

Winter quarters: The permanent home of the circus, occupied when the show is not on the road.

Wipes: Circus slang for handkerchiefs.

Wire: The rope or wire on which acrobats and aerialists perform in the circus.

(The) wire: *see* (THE) SHOVE.

Wire act: A balancing act, especially in vaudeville.

Wire walker: Other than its obvious circus meaning, this means in circus and carnival slang a telegraph delivery boy.

With it: Belonging to a circus or carnival troupe. This expression denotes great loyalty and attachment on the part of the trouper. It is also a way that insiders may know one another even though they have never seen one another before. In addition to the phrase, there is, apparently, a special way to deliver it in order to communicate its full meaning. *see* NOT WITH IT.

Wizard deck: *see* STRIPPER PACK OR DECK.

Woofle dust: An imaginary powder used by magicians when it is necessary to reach into a pocket (to extract the dust). Most magicians consider the need of such a ploy a sign of a magician's lack of imagination or skill.

Wop-jawed: Circus description of towners* on the midway staring with open mouths at the attractions of the freak sideshow. *see also* TOWNERS.

Work: 1. Circus term meaning to stage a performance with animals. 2. Pitchmen's word meaning to sell or deal in any commodity. 3. In the carnival, it has been used to suggest illegal action. 4. In a Toby show,* an actor never performed; he worked. *see also* TOBY SHOW.

Work a bag: A circus ticket seller who makes change from a bag or sack.

Work boy: Towner* boys who helped pitch the tent for a traveling tent show, such as a Toby show,* in return for a pass to the performance. *see also* TOBY SHOW and TOWNER.

Work lions: A lion trainer in the circus. *see also* TRAINER.

Work opposite another: In vaudeville, to play a character who appears with another actor with most of the lines.

Work strong: 1. In the circus, to give an exceptionally fine performance. 2. In burlesque, this indicated how far a stripper went in undressing on stage. The stronger she worked the less she wore at the end of the act.

(To) work the come-in: A circus clown who entertains the incoming audience. Also called clowning the come-in. *see* COME IN.

Worker: A carnival or circus pitchman or concessionaire.

Working in one: A vaudeville performer who appeared in front of the curtain or in the area nearest the audience. Most comics worked in one. *see* IN ONE and ONE.

Working men: 1. In the circus, one term for the canvas men, riggers, prop men, or other laboring workers essential toward keeping a traveling circus on the road. Not to be confused with a roughneck* or the roustabouts.* *see also* ROUGHNECK and ROUSTABOUTS. 2. Toby shows* and other traveling tent shows called those who assisted in putting up and tearing down the tent theatres working men. These workers were normally hired locally, although some companies had several full-time working men, in addition to a canvas boss.* *see also* CANVAS BOSS.

Wow: The sensational or striking success of a popular entertainment that makes an audience applaud loudly.

Write sheet: A pitchman who sold magazine subscriptions in small communities, usually for *The Progressive Farmer* or *The Hog World* or some other farm journal. *see* PAPER BOY OR MAN.

Write-up: In the circus, any mention in print of a circus performer or his act; never called a story, mention, or review.

X, Y, and Z

X: An exclusive concession or right of a pitchman or circus worker bought from the management of a carnival or circus to sell a product. The possession of an X conveys the knowledge that in the purchase of a concession privilege* there will be no competition from similar attractions or joints. Also known as an ex.* *see also* EX and PRIVILEGE.

Yaller gal: A beautiful, graceful female character who combined the refined features of whites with black women's fabled exoticism and availability. A popular attraction in black-face minstrel shows in the 1840s. This was possibly the first example of female impersonation in American show business. *see* PRIMA DONNA OR WENCH ROLE.

Yanced around: Once common on circus lots,* to herd, yell at, or cheat circus patrons. *see also* LOT.

Yankee: The first native character in popular American comedy, beginning most prominently with Jonathan, the shrewd yet uncultivated New England farmer, in Royall Tyler's *The Contrast* (1787). In many ways, Yankee Theatre was American comedy before 1850 and was not challenged until the introduction of "city plays" after mid-century. In addition to his place in American comedy, the Yankee became indispensible to native melodrama, such as *The Drunkard*. The Yankee created an American, sometimes localized but often generalized, who caught the imagination both in this country and abroad. Although most frequently a romantic exaggeration of the real thing, the role did introduce an identifiable and often native type and often a realistically developed character. Yankees appeared with various names, each suggesting that character's major traits (such as Solomon Swap, Jebediah Homebred, Deuteronomy Dutiful, Industrious Doolittle, Lot Sap Sago, and Jonathan Plowboy). Furthermore, numerous actors became Yankee specialists and performed little else during their career. Such a practice continued with Indian roles (though less pronounced), Western characters, city types and, the most obvious of the popular theatre roles, Toby,* the last of the line to survive the tradition. *see also* TOBY.

Yaps: Medicine-show slang for hicks or boobs. *see* RUBE.

Yard: Carnival and underworld argot for one hundred dollars. Around 1930 it changed its meaning in underground cant to one thousand dollars. *see* HALF-YARD.

Yard bull: Circus slang for a railroad detective.

Yea, bo: Medicine-show reply meaning "yes, sir."

Yid: Short for Yiddish and used around the turn of the century to mean a Hebrew or Jewish impersonator. *see* GOOSE and HEBE COMIC.

Yob: *see* JOSSER.

Yock: In vaudeville and burlesque, a word used to describe a loud laugh or a belly laugh.

You're on: *see* ON.

Z-Latin: In addition to the special words of the carnival, carnies use a unique form of pig-Latin to obscure even further from outsiders what is being said. In all of popular entertainment, this is perhaps the only true cant, that is, language designed to make this special group's conversation unintelligible to outsiders. The one qualification, however, is that cant is used, according to definition, by criminal groups. Some carnival use of Z-Latin would certainly fall into a criminal category, but often it is used for perfectly legitimate reasons. Consequently, as Easto and Truzzi point out, its use as cant is somewhat ambiguous. In the carnival, this special language is most commonly called Carny.* Like pig-Latin, Z-Latin involves a simple manipulation of normal English words. Easto and Truzzi offer the following rules for speaking this special language: 1. Separate any word on the basis of its natural syllables and then divide it on the basis of its vowels. The consonant or consonants preceding the vowel are modified by adding a long "e" sound to them. The vowel is replaced by the short "a" sound, and the consonants following the vowel have a "z" sound prefixed to them. For example, the monosyllabic word "fin" becomes "fee-a-zin." A polysyllabic word such as "assumed" becomes "eea-zuh-seea-zumed," which suggests one additional rule. 2. If the first syllable is only a vowel or consonant, then the long "e" and short "a" sounds are pronounced first. The "Z" sound then is prefixed to the sound of the single consonant or vowel and pronounced last. Easto and Truzzi also point out that Carny does not always conform to these rules but that idiomatic variation sometimes occurs whereby the syllables are not always separated in translation. For example, instead of "see-a-zep, a, ree-a-zated," for sucker (according to the rules above), the word might be rendered as "see-a-zuker." To further complicate the language, users often mix argot and Z-Latin, thus making the comprehension by an outsider virtually impossible. *see also* CARNY.

Zany: Originally a comic role, especially that of a servant, in Italian commedia dell'arte, or, even earlier, a clown who worked for Italian mountebanks. It is frequently used today to mean a clown or comic in more general terms.

Zekes: *see* CLOSS, GRAVEDIGGERS, OR ZEKES.

Zinc stearate: A chemical powder used by card manipulators to make cards smooth and easy to handle.

Zingaros: Carnival slang for gypsies.

Zulu tickets: Obsolete term for credit slips, worth a quarter, once given to Negro workmen in the spec.* *see also* SPEC OR SPECTACLE.

Zulus: Obsolete term for Negroes who participated in the spec.* *see also* SPEC OR SPECTACLE.

Select Bibliography

Of the hundreds of sources consulted for this glossary, this list represents only those sources that were most useful in the compilation of entries or are most highly recommended for further reading.

Adams, Ramon F. *Western Words: A Dictionary of the American West*. Rev. ed. Norman: University of Oklahoma Press, 1968.

Alexander, H. L. *Striptease,The Vanished Art of Burlesque*. New York: Knight Publishers, 1938.

Allen, Ralph G. "Our Native Theatre." In *The American Theatre: A Sum of Its Parts*, edited by Henry B. Williams, pp. 273-314. New York: Samuel French, 1971.

Altick, Richard D. *The Shows of London: A Panoramic History of Exhibitions, 1600-1862*. Cambridge and London: Belknap Press of Harvard University Press, 1978.

Ballantine, Bill. "Circus Talk." *American Mercury* 76 (June 1953):21-25.

———. *Wild Tigers and Tame Fleas*. New York and Toronto: Holt Rinehart and Winston, 1958.

Baral, Robert. *Revue: The Great Broadway Period*. New York: Fleet Press, 1962.

Birdoff, Harry. *The World's Greatest Hit—Uncle Tom's Cabin*. New York: S. F. Vanni, 1947.

Boles, Don. *The Midway Showman*. Atlanta: Pinchpenny Press, 1967.

Bowman, Walter P., and Ball, Robert H. *Theatre Language: A Dictionary of Terms in English from Medieval to Modern Times*. New York: Theatre Arts Books, 1961.

Braithwaite, David. *Fairground Architecture: The World of Amusement Parks, Carnivals, and Fairs*. New York: Frederick A. Praeger, 1968.

Burgess, Hovey. *Circus Techniques*. New York: Drama Book Specialists, 1976.

Chindahl, George L. *History of the Circus in America*. Caldwell, Idaho: Caxton Printers, 1959.

Chipman, Bert J. *Hey Rube*. Hollywood: Hollywood Print Shop, 1933.

Christopher, Milbourne. *The Illustrated History of Magic*. New York: Thomas Y. Crowell Co., 1973.

Clark, Larry D. "Toby Shows: A Form of American Popular Theatre." Ph.D. dissertation, University of Illinois, 1963.

Cook, Gladys Emerson. *Circus Clowns on Parade.* New York: Franklin Watts, 1956.

Corio, Ann, with Joe DiMona. *This Was Burlesque.* New York: Grosset and Dunlap, 1968.

Coxe, Antony Hippisley. *A Seat at the Circus.* London: Evans Brothers, 1951.

Croft-Cooke, Rupert, and Cotes, Peter. *Circus: A World History.* New York: Macmillan Co., 1976

Dadswell, Jack. *Hey There Sucker.* Boston: Bruce Humphries, 1946.

Dallas, Duncan. *The Travelling People.* London: Macmillan and Co., 1971.

DeBelle, Starr. *Webster Was a Sucker: Dictionary of Mid-Way Slang.* Cincinnati: Billboard Publications, 1946.

Dexter, Will. *Famous Magic Secrets.* London: Abbey Library, 1955.

DiMeglio, John E. *Vaudeville U.S.A.* Bowling Green, Ohio: Bowling Green University Popular Press, 1973.

Esslin, Martin, general ed. *The Encyclopedia of World Theatre.* New York: Charles Scribner's Sons, 1977.

Fox, C. P., and Parkinson, Tom. *Circus in America.* Waukesha, Wis.: Country Beautiful, 1969.

Fried, Frederick A. *Pictorial History of the Carousel.* New York: A. S. Barnes and Co., 1964.

Gibson, Walter. *The Freak Show Murders.* New York: Street & Smith, 1944.

Gilbert, Douglas. *American Vaudeville: Its Life and Times.* New York: Whittlesey House, 1940.

Graham, Philip. *Showboats: The History of an American Institution.* Austin: University of Texas Press, 1969.

Granville, Wilfred. *Theatre Dictionary.* New York: Philosophical Library, 1952.

Green, Abel, and Laurie, Jr., Joe. *Show Biz from Vaude to Video.* Garden City, N.Y.: Permabooks, 1953.

Green, William. "Strippers and Coochers—the Quintessence of American Burlesque." In *Western Popular Theatre,* edited by David Mayer and Kenneth Richards, pp. 157-68. London: Methuen and Co., 1977.

Gresham, William Lindsay. *Monster Midway.* New York: Rinehart and Co., 1953.

Griffin, Al. *"Step Right Up Folks!"* Chicago: Henry Regnery Co., 1974.

Hancock, Ralph, with Chafetz, Henry. *The Compleat Swindler.* New York: Macmillan Co., 1968.

Hartnoll, Phyllis, ed. *The Oxford Companion to the Theatre.* 3d ed. London: Oxford University Press, 1967.

Hay, Henry. *Cyclopedia of Magic.* London and New York: David McKay, 1949.

Hodge, Francis, *Yankee Theatre: The Image of America on Stage, 1825-1850.* Austin: University of Texas Press, 1964.

Hopkins, Albert A., ed. and comp. *Magic: Stage Illusions and Scientific Diversions Including Trick Photography.* New York, 1897. Reprint. New York: Arno Press, 1977.

Horton, Judge [William E.] *About Stage Folks.* Detroit: Free Printing Co., 1902.

Hoyt, Harlowe. *Town Hall Tonight.* New York: Bramhall House, 1955.

Inge, M. Thomas, ed. *Handbook of American Popular Culture.* Vol. 1. Westport, Conn., and London: Greenwood Press, 1978.

———. *Handbook of American Popular Culture.* Vol. 2. Westport, Conn., and London: Greenwood Press, 1980.

Irwin, Godfrey, ed. *American Tramp and Underworld Slang.* New York: Sears Publishing Co., [1933].

Jensen, Dean. *The Biggest, The Smallest, The Longest, The Shortest.* Madison: Wisconsin House Book Publishers, 1975.

Jessel, George. *So Help Me.* New York: Random House, 1943.

Kaye, Marvin. *The Stein & Day Handbook of Magic.* Edited by John Salisse. New York: Stein & Day, 1973.

Kirk, Rhina. *Circus Heroes and Heroines.* Maplewood, N.J.: Hammond, 1972.

Kusell, Maurice L., and Merritt, M. S. *Marquee Ballyhoo.* Los Angeles: Overland-Out West Publications, 1932.

Laurie, Joseph. *Vaudeville: From Honky-Tonks to the Palace.* New York: Holt, 1953.

Lee, Gretchen. "Trouper Talk." *American Speech* 1 (October 1925):36-37.

Lewis, Arthur H. *Carnival.* New York: Trident Press, 1970.

McArdle, John. *McArdle's International Dictionary of Magitain.* Newtown, Conn.: Published by the author, 1963.

McCullough, Edo. *Good Old Coney Island.* New York: Charles Scribner's Sons, 1957.

McDermott, John Francis. *The Lost Panoramas of the Mississippi.* Chicago: University of Chicago Press, 1958.

McKennon, Joe. *Horse Dung Trail: Saga of American Circus.* Sarasota, Florida: Carnival Publishers of Sarasota, 1975.

———. *A Pictorial History of the American Carnival.* Sarasota, Florida: Carnival Publishers of Sarasota, 1972.

McLean, Albert. *American Vaudeville as Ritual.* Lexington: University of Kentucky Press, 1965.

McNamara, Brooks. *Step Right Up: An Illustrated History of the American Medicine Show.* Garden City, N.Y.: Doubleday and Co., 1976.

McNeal, Violet. *Four White Horses and a Brass Band.* New York: Doubleday and Co., 1947.

McPharlin, Paul. *The Puppet Theatre in America.* Rev. ed. Boston: Plays, Inc., 1969.

Mangels, William F. *The Outdoor Entertainment Business.* New York: Vantage Press, 1952.

Mannix, Dan. *Step Right Up.* New York: Harper and Bros., 1950.

Marks, Edward Bennett. *They All Had Glamour: From the Swedish Nightingale to the Naked Lady.* New York: J. Messner, 1944.

Marsh, John L. *The Grandin Opera House, or Theatre on the Kerosene Circuit, 1872-1904.* Warren, Pa.: Warren County Historical Society, 1973.

Matlaw, Myron, ed. *American Popular Entertainment.* Westport, Conn., and London: Greenwood Press, 1979.

Maurer, David W. *The Big Con: The Story of the Confidence Man and the Confidence Game.* Indianapolis and New York: The Bobbs-Merrill Co., 1940.

———. "Carnival Cant: Glossary of Circus and Carnival Slang." *American Speech* 6 (June 1931):327-37.

May, Earl Chapin. *The Circus from Rome to Ringling.* New York: Duffield and Green, 1932.

Mencken, H. L. *The American Language.* New York: Alfred A. Knopf, 1919.

———. *The American Language: Supplement I.* New York: Alfred A Knopf, 1945.

———. *The American Language: Supplement II.* New York: Alfred A. Knopf, 1948.

Mickel, Jere C. *Footlights on the Prairie.* St. Cloud, Minn.: North Star Press, 1974.

Milburn, George. "Circus Words." *American Mercury* 24 (November 1931):351-54.

Morrison, Theodore. *Chautauqua.* Chicago: University of Chicago Press, 1974.

Moss, Arnold. "Jewels from a Box Office: The Language of Show Business." *American Speech* 11 (October 1936):219-22.

Mulvey, Ruth. "Pitchmen's Cant." *American Speech* 17 (April 1942):89-93.

Murray, Marian. *Circus! From Rome to Ringling.* New York: Appleton, Century, Crofts, 1956.

Nathan, George Jean. *Encyclopaedia of the Theatre.* New York: Alfred A. Knopf, 1940.

———. *The Popular Theatre.* New York: Alfred A. Knopf, 1918.

O'Brien, Esse F. *Circus: Cinders to Sawdust.* San Antonio: The Naylor Co., 1959.

Page, Brett. *Writing for Vaudeville.* Springfield, Mass.: Home Correspondence School, 1915.

Partridge, Eric. *Slang To-Day and Yesterday.* 4th ed. New York: Barnes & Noble, 1970.

———. *A Dictionary of Slang and Unconventional English.* 7th ed. New York: Macmillan Co., 1970.

Philpott, A. R. *Dictionary of Puppetry.* Boston: Plays, Inc., 1969.

Russell, Don. *The Wild West or A History of the Wild West Shows.* Fort Worth: Amon Carter Museum of Western Art, 1970.

Scarne, John. *Scarne's Complete Guide to Gambling.* Rev. ed. New York: Simon and Schuster, 1974.

Schaffner, Neil E., with Johnson, Vance. *The Fabulous Toby and Me.* Englewood Cliffs, N.J.: Prentice-Hall, 1968.

Seago, Edward. *Circus Company: Life on the Road with the Travelling Show.* London: Putnam, 1933.

Sell, Henry Blackman, and Weybright, Victor. *Buffalo Bill and the Wild West.* New York: Oxford University Press, 1955.

Senelick, Laurence. "George L. Fox and American Pantomime." *Nineteenth Century Theatre Research* 7 (Spring 1979):1-125.

Sergel, Sherman Louis, ed. *The Language of Show Biz.* Chicago: Dramatic Publishing Co., 1973.

Simon, Peter Angelo. *Big Apple Circus.* New York: Penguin Books, 1978.

Slout, William Lawrence. *Theatre in a Tent: The Development of a Provincial Entertainment.* Bowling Green, Ohio: Bowling Green University Popular Press, 1972.

Smith, Bill. *The Vaudevillians.* New York: Macmillan Co., 1976.

Sobel, Bernard. *Burleyque: An Underground History of Burlesque Days.* New York: Farrar and Rinehart, 1931.

———. *A Pictorial History of Burlesque.* New York: Putnam, 1956.

Speaight, George. *The History of the English Toy Theatre*. Rev. ed. Boston: Plays, Inc., 1969.

———. *Punch and Judy: A History*. Rev. ed. Boston: Plays, Inc., 1970.

Taylor, John Russell. *The Penguin Dictionary of Theatre*. New York: Penguin Books, 1970.

Thornton, R. H. *An American Glossary*. 2 vols. Philadelphia: J. B. Lippincott Co., 1912.

Toll, Robert C. *Blacking Up: The Minstrel Show in Nineteenth Century America*. New York: Oxford University Press, 1974.

———. *On With the Show: The First Century of Show Business in America*. New York: Oxford University Press, 1976.

Towsen, John H. *Clowns*. New York: Hawthorn Books, 1976.

Truzzi, Marcello, ed. "Circuses, Carnivals and Fairs in America." *Journal of Popular Culture* 6 (Winter 1972):531-619.

Truzzi, Marcello, with Truzzi, Massimiliano. "Notes Toward a History of Juggling." *Bandwagon* 18 (March-April 1974):4-7.

Wentworth, Harold and Flexner, Stuart Berg. *Dictionary of American Slang*. 2d supplemented ed. New York: Thomas Y. Crowell, 1975.

White, Percy W. "A Circus List." *American Speech* 1 (February 1926):282-83.

———. "More about the Language of the Lot." *American Speech* 3 (June 1928): 413-15.

———. "Stage Terms." *American Speech* 1 (May 1926):436-37.

Wilmeth, Don B., ed. *American and English Popular Entertainment: An Information Guide*. Detroit: Gale Research, 1980.

Wilson, Harry Leon. *Professor How Could You?* New York: Grosset and Dunlap, 1924.

Wittke, Carl. *Tambo and Bones: A History of the Minstrel Show*. Durham, N.C.: Duke University Press, 1930.

Zeidman, Irving. *The American Burlesque Show*. New York: Hawthorn Books, 1967.

About the Author

DON B. WILMETH is Professor of English and Theatre Arts and Chairman of the Theatre Arts Department at Brown University in Providence, Rhode Island. He was the former book review editor of *The Theatre Journal* and former editor and columnist for *Intellect* and *USA Today*. Currently he serves on the executive committees of the American Society for Theatre Research and the Theatre Library Association. His other publications include *The American Stage to World War I* (1978), *American and English Popular Entertainment* (1980), and *George Frederick Cooke: Machiavel of the Stage* (Greenwood Press, 1980). Currently he is co-editing the plays of William Gillette and Augustin Daly.